Audacity
of Leading Right

An Odyssey Towards Virtuous Leadership

Paul Omojo Omaji

National Library of Australia Cataloguing-in-Publication entry

Creator: Omaji, Paul, author.

Title: Audacity of leading right: an odyssey towards virtuous leadership / Paul Omojo Omaji.

ISBN: 9780994290809 (paperback)

Notes: Includes bibliographical references and index.

Subjects: Leadership.
    Social change.

Dewey Number: 303.34

Printed by Createspace, Amazon, USA

DEDICATION

All who are disciplined, dedicated and determined to <u>lead right</u> and, by so doing, lift humanity out of decadence. I salute your audacity, and trust that virtues - especially wisdom, courage, justice, temperance (self-control), and transcendence (nature-divine) - will help you to go higher and righter in your leadership journey.

"This a book that will last and bring forth impact in leadership"

Archbishop Sam Amaga, Chancellor/Founder

Salem University

CONTENTS

Dedication   i

Acknowledgments   iv

Prologue: This leadership thing…   viii

    Leadership discourse: state of play   ix

    Paradigms: branding leadership – an overview   xii

    Leading right   xiii

    Concluding remarks   xxii

1 Paradigms: branding leadership   25

    Defiant leadership   28

    Compliant leadership   30

    Authentic leadership   31

    Virtuous leadership   32

    Journey towards virtuous leadership   35

    Concluding remarks   46

2 Call: beginning well   48

    Role recollection - Nigeria   49

    Role recollection - Australia   50

Midnight call   51

Concluding remarks   55

3 Vision: clarifying the task   58

University business ideology   58

Interpreting the Task   64

The Imagined Future   84

Concluding remarks   87

4 Software: shifting values to principles   89

Core Values   90

Laying down some key principles   92

Concluding remarks   101

5 Travail: creating 'vision ownership'   105

The "Goliath" on our way   107

The change we must have   109

Called to be a change agent   116

Free the leader in you   120

Livewire: "My soul had a birthday"   128

The spirit of excellence   130

Time as resource   136

Performance Management   140

Journey to the high table: the pain and thrill of leading right   149

Concluding remarks   151

6 Edifice: turning vision into reality 153

    Decision at 'ground-zero' 154

    Corporate administration 155

    Infrastructural development and maintenance 163

    Academic management system 166

    Stakeholders Management 169

    Concluding remarks 175

7 Trophy: leaving footprints in hearts 178

    A place of importance! 179

    Trophies 180

    Futures in their wombs 190

Epilogue: freedom - ending well to aim higher and righter 193

    Reflections on paradigms 194

    Disengaging 199

    Beginning again 205

    Concluding remarks 209

Author's profile 226

ACKNOWLEDGMENTS

It is impossible for any book project to be accomplished solely by the effort of the author(s). This book is no exception. The reality, though, is that no full justice can be done to all the helpers in acknowledgements. I am mindful of that imperfection as I venture to list below a few of my helpers. So, I crave in advance the forbearance of those who may be left out. Nothing deliberate, only my shortcomings. Yet, you can be proud of your role in the book that you now hold in your hands.

Here is my imperfect list:

All those who fanned the embers of leadership in me with opportunities and acceptance from my younger years through to secondary and high schools, and throughout my adult years at universities, professional bodies and workplaces across several continents.

Salem University groups:

- The Proprietor, Board of Trustees, and Governing Council of Salem University who conceived of, birthed, funded, and/or guided the University on the platform of which I exercised and extended my cumulative experiences of leadership in general and higher educational administration in particular.

- All students and staff of the University – whom we fondly and aspirationally called Global leaders and Global staff respectively. Their loyalty and dedication made my passing through there more than merely 'taking a walk'.

- Global leaders who served in the Student Leaders Forum and became part of the avante-guard for the transformation agenda of the University.

- Staff in the administration, chaplaincy, academic, accounting, and physical development areas who genuinely patterned their contributions after our brand of leadership - in many cases, and within the prevailing wider societal context, at high personal costs to themselves. Mr. Daniel Itodo, Rev.& Mrs Osiri Wisdom, Professor Silas Dada, Mr. Alex Ocholi and Mr. Andrew Abutu deserve a special mention.

Reviewers who provided useful comments.

Friends (far and near) who lived a life of integrity, prayed for me, and in whose company I felt supported in the brand of leadership that we carried to the University.

My wife (Alice), our children (Ruth, Reuben, Timothy, & Tabitha) and their spouses, and our grandchildren (Cathrine, Joshua, Isaac, Elijah & Noah) who inspired and gave me zest for life. Alice read the manuscript and provided quite insightful comments. Iyei (my fond name for her), cherio!

My parents (Mr & Mrs Omaji Akwu – both now late) and siblings with whom I grew up securely to become a person embracing a worthy brand of leadership.

The Most High Triune God - my Creator, Deliverer and Sustainer, who models the ultimate (virtuous) leadership and makes me continually aspire higher and righter.

My thanks are not enough, but I offer them to you all nonetheless.

Prologue: This leadership thing…

"What is the scarcest resource in the world?… [Answer] Leadership. Its absence is the pandemic of our time. We don't need more smart people. We have plenty of those. It's a poverty of principle we face, a crisis of character… How tragic to leave a landfill when you can leave a legacy." (Clark, 2009).

Today, more than ever before in the history of humankind, the leadership question has become a matter of keeping a date with destiny. It is the difference maker between compromised destinies and fulfilled destinies. Individuals, organisations, communities or nations (hereinafter, human entities) that fail to grapple with it, do so at their own peril.

How do you convince cynical human entities which have spiraled down under unscrupulous leadership brands in a decadent world that redemption is possible? Don't tell them; show them! Using a live story, this book shows how essential factors come together to other redeeming leadership brands transform and indeed beautify their entities. The plot of the main narrative is in an educational (university) setting; however, the applicability of its insight is universal. The point of arrival is this: leadership is destiny.

Such is the destiny-changing power of leadership that a thousand lions following a lamb as their arrowhead would always be defeated by a hundred lambs <u>led</u> by one lion. There is something in the lion folk that protects, proclaims and propels any group they lead to victory. Of course, there is a precious place in life for the hallowed, harmless, and higher-than-heavens lamb. However, when it comes to *leading right* to post a flourishing destiny in a corrupt world, it is the audacity of a fearless, ferocious and fervent lion that can sustain.

We can attest to this proposition from, among various sources, our own leadership experiences over time. For instance, as pioneer Vice Chancellor at Salem University, Lokoja, Nigeria, it took upright discipline, dedication, and determination (basic hallmarks of *leading right*) for us to raise a University – conceived, birthed and funded by a private proprietor - from virtually ground zero to the status of an exemplar in academic and character transformation in Nigeria under challenging moral and resource circumstances.

There are several people in different fields in Nigeria and elsewhere, including other former Vice Chancellors such as Professor Oluwafemi O. Balogun[1] and Professor Francis S. Idachaba (of blessed memory)[2], whose experiences could profitably anchor stories of exemplary leadership. However, I have focused the narrative in this book on my own personal journey. The aim is not to produce an autobiography, as I have drawn on these other experiences – by study and by direct personal contacts - to crystalise a personal odyssey in leadership and to present an agenda about a brand of leadership that can radically change human entities for good. Along the way, we became more keenly aware that the leadership phenomenon generally remains enigmatic, even to the most engaged. How would you recognize leadership if you see it? What does it look like? What does it feel like? What sense would you make of it? What type of leadership produces what outcomes? These are key questions that continually confront those who put their minds to this area of human endeavours.

Already we know people who say leadership is confusing. Others say it is mysterious and scary. Still others say it is non-existent and, by that, conclude it is not deserving of any particular focus. Our own experience tells another story. For me, leadership is the pillar upon which everything hangs. So, it cannot be ignored. And yes, I am still on a journey of discovery (gaining a clearer view) of the leadership phenomenon day by day. On this journey, I have seen that **leading right** is even more challenging – both in discovery and in practice.

Thankfully, the experience behind the story I am about to narrate in this book has taken us a fair way on this journey. I am in a position to use real-life situations to make this phenomenon (leadership in general and *leading right* in particular) more accessible in a different and, perhaps, friendly light. Also, significantly, the experience has disposed me to be sympathetic to other people's reactions to leadership such as the ones mentioned above. This is not gratuitous sympathy. Rather, it comes out of an understanding of the basis for such reactions which I need to state upfront.

Leadership discourse: state of play

Barely two decades ago, Maxwell (1993, pxii) observed that there were very few leadership books and that "most [dealt] with management". The distinction between leadership and management in this observation is interesting; but it is the point about the paucity of materials on leadership even as lately as the early 1990s that shouted loudly to me, looking back from the vantage point of today. Google "leadership" now and you'll get over 150 million entries. Also, there are now about 400,000 books on this subject. Stack all of these books on each other, assuming each is about one inch thick, and you'll get a stack of over 33,000 feet high. That would be taller than Mt Everest! (Clark, 2009).

Confusing

If all these materials say the same thing or, at least carry a consistent message, they might be boring but there would be little of the confusion that some people have experienced. Rather, there would be a profound understanding or appreciation of the phenomenon we call 'leadership'. However, as Shashkin and Shaskin (2005, p31) observed, "it was clear that seventy-five years of research and application [beginning from 1900] had yielded little definitive or practically useful knowledge about leadership". In fact, scholars nearly gave up on leadership studies at that time because of the confusion around it. For, as James MacGregor Burns who inspired a renewed interest in 'leadership' at that time put it, leadership was "the most observed and least understood phenomenon on earth" (Burns, 1978).

A few years later, Bennis and Nanus (1985) noted that "multiple interpretations of leadership exist[ed], each providing a sliver of insight but each remaining an incomplete and wholly inadequate explanation". Meadows (1988) put it this way: "leadership is a perfect word for a campaign. It sounds wonderful, it requires no concrete promises, and no one is quite sure what it means. Whatever it is, we are supposed to want it, and to want it strong".

By the 1990s, the situation had not changed much in terms of clarity over the subject: "everyone talks about it; few understand it. Most people want it; few achieve it... What is this intriguing subject we call 'leadership'? Ask 10 people to define [it] and you'll probably receive 10 different answers" (Maxwell, 1993, p1).

Myles Munroe captured the difficulty with leadership as he personally experienced it: "I had read hundreds of books, articles, journals, and research papers on the subject of leadership; I had attended countless seminars, conferences and summits dealing with leadership development, yet I was never able to identify, define, or fully understand the mystery that separated and distinguished the leader from the follower" (Munroe, 2005, p14). This is akin to Peter Senge remarking that "the reason we find it difficult to talk about leadership is that we don't know what we're talking about" (quoted in Thayer 2010, p11).

In more recent times, John Maxwell tried to flesh out why the subject of leadership can be overwhelming and confusing, but ended up raising more questions: "Where does leadership start? What should we do first? What processes should we use? How can we gain influence with others? How can we develop a productive team? How do we help followers to become leaders in their own right?" (Maxwell 2011, p4). By the time you start interrogating such concepts as 'influence', 'productivity', 'performance, and 'team' which are prominent features of leadership, the issue of clarity becomes even more challenging. So yes, there is substance to the reaction about leadership being a confusing phenomenon.

Mysterious and scary

Apart from the confusion (or as somebody put it "really knowing actually almost nothing") about leadership and notwithstanding the dozens if not hundreds of leadership models and books that now 'explain' what constitutes leadership, some people find the phenomenon also mysterious and scary. Even Munroe a widely published writer in this area, at one time, acknowledged the mysterious nature of leadership with some explanatory note: "leadership will always remain somewhat of a mystery because it consists of an array of diverse qualities, qualifications, components, skills, capabilities, and even unquantifiable elements" (see Munroe 2009, p33).

There is the view that, unlike some subjects/objects which you can break down into their component parts and then predict outcomes from different configurations (as in the natural sciences such as physics), leadership is not that discernable – not amenable to a scientific approach. For these people, the reason is that "the world in which leadership has to be performed is too dynamic, too complex, too random, and too uncontrollable" (Thayer 2010, p13). Hence, the mystery about it subsists.

To those for whom "leadership [is] a mystery", says Maxwell (2011, p3), "leading people is like walking down a dark corridor. They have a sense of where they want to go, but they can't see ahead and they don't know where the problems and pitfalls are going to lie". Notwithstanding that in recent times "science has taken a significant interest in leadership and its development[3],... nevertheless, leadership remains an enigma, and what constitutes an effective leadership is still a matter of considerable debate" (Kilburg 2012, p6).

Bascal (2013) takes this further. For him, the subject is not just mysterious; it is also scary because

> the only thing we know about leadership is that it all depends on context. We simply are not able to predict, with any success, what person will thrive in one leadership role and not in another. That's because not only are there so many contextual factors involved in determining that fit but we don't even know what they are or, more importantly, how those factors interact with each other.

With too many such unknowns in critical aspects, people can justifiably find leadership mysterious and scary.

Non-existent

Reflecting "a profound sense of frustration with the concept of leadership and the enormous and ever increasing body of research and pontification about it", some writers have gone so far as to say "there is no such thing as leadership" (see Washbush, 2005). Extreme as it may sound, such views are not surprising considering the perceived ongoing failure to define leadership as a coherent construct and the perspective that "continuing along this omni-directional path is not likely to produce anything truly useful for those who study, teach about or work in organizations".

According to such views, with endless discussions and perspectives of a word that simply sounds great and with the tendency to call almost everything leadership, "logically nothing is leadership". The adherents of these views counsel that "abandoning the concept altogether and emphasizing a focus on improving decision making in organizations [or any other human entity] may prove more fruitful". Ironically, though, even 'abandoning the concept' of leadership (if it were possible) and 'focusing on improving decision making' would require some leading to generate a community of thinkers and practitioners to make it a sustainable perspective.

Paradigms: branding leadership – an overview

I'm afraid this leadership thing is here to stay. Abandoning it doesn't look like a feasible option for the foreseeable future. So, we must engage with it in all possible ways to make it work well for us, both in understanding and application. In spite of the senses of confusion, mystery, scariness and existential nihilism that abound, 'leadership' remains such a fascinating subject. Like a colossus, it is an <u>expression</u> that towers high in everyday life of people whether or not they are conscious of it. It shows up on all forms of mass media (newspapers, television, radio, internet, books, journals, etc), especially when matters of destiny for human entities take the centre stage of conversations, discussions and intellectual discourses.

Thus, I hold leadership simultaneously as a ubiquitous force, a contestable subject, and a definer of life. I do not attribute everything to leadership (e.g. saying 'well, the answer must be leadership'), like some scholars do simply to throw their hands up in frustration thereby preventing themselves from gaining deeper or more scientific understanding about the phenomenon (Collins 2001, p22).

In fact, despite my belief about leadership as a destiny-changer, I have maintained an ongoing study of it. From this, it has become clear to me that one way to make a good sense of leadership generally is to view the phenomenon in categories of its varied expressions and images. In Chapter One, I present my effort in this direction as "Paradigms: branding leadership". Although there are various ways to distill these categories[4], the most illuminating in my view is that which aggregates leadership thoughts and practices around the core themes of its philosophies, behavioural patterns and outcomes.

Based on this criterion, I have chosen the framework of 'defiant leadership', 'compliant leadership', 'authentic leadership' and 'virtuous leadership' brands to discuss the relevant intellectual and practical outputs on this phenomenon[5]. After arranging these models or patterns (which is basically what paradigms are) in a staircase format, I outline in that Chapter their characteristics and argue the essential place of virtuous leadership as the apogee of this phenomenon. Against this backdrop, I argue in the branding exercise a radicalizing agenda in which *leading right* is a cornerstone.

Leading right

Beyond the conceptual understanding of the paradigms, I have consciously made a judgment that the value of any of the brands of leadership lies in its capacity to deliver a sustainable 'leading right' project. This judgment is founded not only in my conviction that "everything rises, [stands,] and falls on leadership" (Maxwell 1993, pX) but that "if you want to make a positive impact on the world, learning to lead better [and righter] will help you do it" (Maxwell 2011, p1).

Drawing from my study of exemplary leadership, together with my own personal experiences, I have distilled what for me constitute the core contents of '*leading right*'. Though several, I will outline here those ones that have guided my experiences to date and, *ipso facto*, provided me with the framework for the telling of the story of my personal odyssey in this book.

Leading right requires a call – necessary for beginning well

No one can lead, let alone lead right, unless he or she understands and comes into leadership as a calling to be obeyed, and not a position to be grabbed. A calling is distinguished by its intrinsic lack of selfish interest. At its core, a calling is like some kind of powerful, magnetic force; something one feels he or she is 'born' to be and/or to do. It is not about the pure expression of power, activism or heroism around certain causes or social values, such as championing the fight for independence or equality. It is not about a position, or standing "in an exposed place [to] bring change to the order of things".

Rather, there is a sense of departing from or breaking down inhibiting beliefs, social assumptions, or the status quo and bringing on the possibilities. In the case of *leading right*, such sense is infused with a heavy dose of wisdom, moral courage, justice, temperance and transcendence[6]. It involves "stepping out, stepping up, finding the rungs and handholds that enable [a] person, or a group, or a global tribe, to find its way and know a truer compass [to enduring greatness] against the complexity and confusions of the world itself" (Oestreich, 2009).

What announces the calling dimension of *leading right* is the pattern of behavior or sequence of moments in which a person consistently steps into 'the space' to be counted or to solve problems in an upright manner. More often than not, it is usually a difficult and awkward space. Such a person expresses a refined sense of inner direction that moves him or her very easily (with or without the support of others) toward a principle-based leadership role, no matter what group or space they find themselves within.

Unlike chiefs, presidents or bosses who relish prestige for its own sake or are attracted by positions and for whom the burden of public affairs must produce its own material reward instantaneously, persons with a *leading right* calling are drawn to the act of leading (the moment of truth in itself) sometimes perhaps even with a sense of reluctance. There is no allurement from personal success, social rank, formal power, or instant gratification. Rather, the pull factor usually comes in these words: 'I'm drawn to making a difference. I'm drawn to lifting people up. I'm drawn to helping others achieve their goals and objectives in life. I'm drawn to teaching. And, I'm drawn to wisdom and intellect'.

This and much more is exactly what calling in *leading right* is about. I have tried to illustrate this element with my own personal experiences in Chapter Two with the caption: "Call: beginning well". I outline some of the leadership responsibilities that I have been drawn to from my secondary school days up to my sojourn in Australia. The bulk of the Chapter then documents the process of the 'call' to me to assume leadership at Salem University in Nigeria as the pioneer Vice Chancellor. It is a story of the 'powerful, magnetic force' that impelled me to return from my well settled life of over 20 years in Australia to an 'imperiling' Nigeria – a country which was at that time quite notorious internationally for all the wrong reasons.

Leading right involves giving meaning to vision - clarifying tasks

Next to receiving the call, an important element of *leading right* is about identifying or clarifying the task inherent in the vision one is called to handle. This is to do with giving meaning to the vision with which the leader must set or establish direction and define the job to be done. It is a fundamental responsibility that must precede the other living dimensions of *leading right* such as: uprightly aligning people through communicating the direction/job by words and deeds, creating teams and coalitions to understand the vision and accept its validity, and then motivating and inspiring them to get things done (Hooper and Potter 2000, p59).

Coleman (2004, p5) was spot on when he said: "throughout history and in cultures everywhere, the leader in any human group has been the one to whom others look for assurance and clarity when facing uncertainty or threat, or when there's a job to be done". It falls to leadership to step out when there are visions (pictures of the future) to be defined, goals to be articulated, and strategies to be outlined in a clear *plan* that the team can understand, internalize, and work to make happen.

It is ironical that even though the subject of leadership has struck some persons as confusing and/or mysterious, ultimately it is the leaders that "help reduce ambiguity and uncertainty in our lives… Leaders make meaning… they provide clear and positive reasons for [personal or organisational] aims, actions, and accomplishments… [In other words] leaders add clarity and direction to life and make life more meaningful" (Shashkin and Shaskin 2003, pp8-9).

In many respects, vision is a living thing. Whether it is communicated directly to the leader or it is handed over from another source, it is an essential part of *leading right* for that vision to be kept alive; it must be interpreted or clarified. In so doing, you provide an 'understanding' of which way the human entity that owns the vision is supposed to be heading and what must be done rightly along the way to get to the imagined future.

"Even things without life, whether flute or harp, when they make a sound, unless they make a distinction in the sounds, how will it be known what is piped or played? For if the trumpet makes an uncertain sound, who will prepare for battle?"[7]. Fundamentally, giving meaning to vision is akin to 'making a distinction in sounds' or clarifying what work is involved in any given picture of the future so that stakeholders can 'know what is piped' and properly 'prepare for war'.

In Chapter Three, I present what vision of Salem University was handed over to me and how we went about clarifying that vision. My emphasis there is to show how we understood that vision, what the vision called us to do, and how we had to communicate it to the stakeholders. Our focus in that assignment was to take the vision out of the pages of the relevant documents and give life to its inherent task for all the members of the University community to feel, handle, and make the University happen.

Leading right needs an empowering software - shifting values to principles

After receiving the call to serve and interpreting the vision to set the direction or clarifying the task to define what is to be done, the next element of *leading right* is to establish your personal as well as the organisational values and to shift those values into principles. This is critically so, particularly if the vision entails building character or integrity as Salem University in our judgment was meant to be. In fact, strictly speaking, it is impossible to lead right without moral character or integrity because that trait is central to the credibility factor which in turn gives you the right to expect anyone to follow you (Hamm, 2011).

Values and principles, together, constitute what I call the empowering 'software' (the moral dimension) for *leading right*. The issue of "right" is a matter for morality, ethics and virtues, all of which start with 'values'. Principles, on the other hand, are moral rules (built on values) that influence actions or practice. They are the products of shifting values into enduring behavioural guidance for navigating the leadership territory with all its delicate topographical features towards personal or organisational goals. As Covey (2003, p19) put it, "correct principles are like compasses. They surface in the form of… norms, and teachings that uplift, ennoble, fulfill, empower, and inspire people".

In Chapter Four, captioned 'Software: shifting values to principles', I present the values set for Salem University as we met them in the pages of the originating documents. Then I show how, in combination with our own personal values, we shifted those values into principles. Consistent with the established vision, philosophy and mission, we used these principles to drive the building of the University. Specifically we focused on the core areas of the identity for the University, proprietor's interaction with the University, financial management, student admissions, and the overall academic programmes implementation.

With this software (values and principles), we were able to effectively handle most of the dilemmas (ethical in particular) that came our way in our determination to lead right! The software helped us to deploy what I call the IPPLE compass for wading through such dilemmas:

- Identify 'trigger' situations early on
- Predict probable scenarios,
- Prepare relevant responses in advance
- Listen to your 'inner voice', and
- Evaluate your decisions before you act.

Leading right involves travailing - creating vision ownership

The next core element of *leading right* is the 'travail' to get your followers and other leaders around you, individually or as a team, to <u>buy into the vision</u>. The aim is to get these followers and leaders into the place or mindset where they would make the vision happen not because they are **told to, but** because they **want to!** And if the focus is on leading right, as was our preoccupation at Salem University, you must create a culture where the stakeholders especially the frontline participants (staff and students) develop the sense of owning the vision. That is: they see in the vision a stake to live and, if necessary, die for; they look forward to coming to your human entity to work or study (rather than "coming to work to avoid working or studying"); and they are not looking forward to leaving the human entity as soon as they can.

The leadership effort that is required to achieve such level of engagement is nothing short of travailing. It is hard work; resilience is severally tested; character and competence are constantly tried; and the focus on legacy is relentlessly taxed. In the end, you gain the 'resonance' – a reservoir of positivity - that frees excellence (the best in people) to manifest. People who accomplish such an outcome for their human entities are greeted with tributes such as this one:

> Great leaders move us. They ignite our passion and inspire the best in us through vision, powerful ideas, strategy, and emotions. They motivate and inspire or energise us to overcome barriers and achieve results; they produce useful changes that help us and the organization to develop. We are blessed because they came this way (see Coleman, et. al. 2004, p3).

Such leaders come on the scene in times of great change; they understand their calling as change agents; and they work deliberately to create 'a taste for change' or 'receptivity to further change' with values and principles that they make to permeate every level of the human entities.

As I outline in Chapter Five, the pioneer situation at Salem University presented us with new terrains and new adventures in which we bore the brunt of the danger and thrill of travailing to create 'vision ownership' for all. We delivered as best as we knew how: we recognized the 'Valley of Baca' in which the vision was born; named the 'Goliath' on our way that must be removed[8]; lifted the vision high enough for all to see and appreciate; called upon all the members of the University to appreciate change and become change agents or positive livewires; trained them in the tenets of excellence, timeliness, performance management; and challenged them to bear the pains of the 'journey to the high table' which the vision demanded.

In all of this, we were guided by the principle that leadership is more about persuasion and unlocking human potential than it is about command and control; and that leadership is best practised in a context in which the people are active participants and not merely recipients, spectators, or victims of leadership (see Jinkins and Jinkins 1998, pxiv).

Leading right produces edifice - turning vision into reality

Turning a vision into reality is at the heart of *leading right*. I call this the 'execution' element, which Bossidy and Charan (2002) characterized as "the discipline of getting things done". Hybels (2002) called it "Getting-It-Done Leadership". More often than not, leaders are judged mainly by the decisions and actions they take which determine how much of the reality that the vision forecasts is accomplished. After responding to the call to lead, casting/interpreting the vision or clarifying the task, developing the operating software, and getting a buy in or vision-ownership, the leader comes face to face with addressing the challenges of decisions and actions; and taking advantage of opportunities to produce the edifice that is fitting to the vision.

Leading right in this regard demands that what is in the mind's eye (vision) must be the right thing, given a concrete expression in the right way, at the right time, and for the right reasons. The frameworks for achieving such a unique outcome are many. The one by Ayers (1994), which teased out four phases and their corresponding foci, remains particularly straight forward and was helpful to us in raising the Salem University edifice:

1. Analyze your organisation in order to recognise its current and future capabilities, in terms of the required core competencies and activities.

2. Develop your organisation by crafting the decisions that need to be implemented and the changes that must occur in light of these capabilities.

3. Value and develop your people starting with recognising the importance of people in achieving the vision, then showing a firm belief in teamwork and a commitment to result-orientation through personal integrity and credibility.

4. Maintain and develop your sphere of influence in line with established values and principles. This involves, inter alia, developing judgment to know when to fight and when to back off; pursuing the areas where you can be successful and have the greatest impact; applying flexibility only on style and

no compromise on principles; and over-communicating in a 360° fashion.

In all of this, the leader must make the time to give the members of the human entity all the attention they need – the primary function being to support these people and then guide them to actually make it happen. In return, the leader must develop accountability in the people, namely "the recognition and acceptance that one is answerable for whatever happens within a given area of responsibility, regardless of the cause".

The ensuing edifice must satisfy: the 'engineering specification' where the product measures against the design work; the 'client requirements' where the product hits the technical points that make the reality of the vision adorable; the 'functional requirements' where the product matches the technical goal of the approval authorities; and, above all, the 'verification specification' where the product matches the core philosophy, vision, mission and values of the human entity.

I have captured in Chapter Six our efforts in building the Salem University edifice to the requirements and specifications of the vision, using the Ayers processes outlined above. I show progressively how with the support of the proprietor, the Board of Trustees, and the Governing Council we took the systems and physical infrastructures[9]   virtually from 'ground zero' to the high point of achieving 100 per cent accreditation for all the academic programmes which we built these infrastructures to support. For the verification aspect, you will need to read about our efforts as I have documented in Chapter Seven dealing with 'trophies'.

Leading right produces trophies - leaving footprints in hearts

The high point for, in fact the crowning element of, *leading right* goes far beyond the systems and physical infrastructures. It is about leaving **footprints (better still, visionprints)** not merely 'in the sands of time', but **in the hearts of people**. Footprints in the sands of time can be momentous, no doubt. Indeed, almost all the literature of note on leadership counsel people with such responsibilities to ultimately 'leave their footprints in the sands of time' (Okorie 2011).

However, the audacious processes necessary for *leading right* must result in something more enduring than the sands of time can bear - for it to be worth the pain. This is the 'legacy' dimension. Yes, "leadership is about the emotional impact produced upon the led which transforms their behavior so that they can each reach a higher level of performance" (Hooper and Potter 2000 p9). What *leading right* does is in the direction of transforming (better still, transfiguring) the whole being (not just the behaviours) for those who encounter it – something akin to this quote from an unknown author:

> Some people come into our lives and quickly go. Some people move our souls to dance. They awaken us to new understanding with the passing whisper of their wisdom. Some people make the sky more beautiful to gaze upon. They stay in our lives for a while, leave footprints on our hearts, and we are never ever the same.

Dave Kraft who wrote *Leaders Who Last* (2010) relates how, in the office of his daughter's high school counselor, he read this quote and it changed his life. It compelled him to pray in his heart, "Lord, make me a person who leaves footprints in people's lives. I don't want to be a person who comes and goes with no lasting impact. Because of contact with me, may people never be the same again. May I be a person who intentionally and lastingly influences others". As Leighton (2012) put it, "the best footprints we leave are from when we help people to transform their own lives. Transformed lives are a good set of footprints to leave in this broken world".

For us, it is such transformed lives resulting from our effort at Salem University that I characterize as our 'trophies'[10]. I have presented these trophies in Chapter Seven of this book under 'performance trophies', 'love trophies', and 'lifestyle trophies'. Of particular significance in our leadership endeavours, and this is what I concluded this Chapter with, are the futures that our work has created in the wombs of the carriers of these trophies.

Leading right gives freedom: finishing well to aim higher and righter

A book of this nature, which is substantially anchored to the personal experiences of the author and is intended to challenge readers to a higher and righter leadership ground, following the path that the author has tread, can easily be misconstrued as an exercise in self-adulation. In the Epilogue captioned 'Freedom: finishing well to aim higher and righter', I have reiterated that this is not the intention here, in case this fact is lost on the readers up to that point. Hence, my note that I wouldn't like to be the Pharisees in the time of Jesus Christ in the Palestine of the first century *anno domino* who practised righteousness for show, and Jesus condemned them as 'whitewashed tombs' and 'hypocrites'.

Rather than drawing attention to ourselves, the primary essence of the narration of my personal odyssey is to point attention towards something far greater than our own journey, namely: the power of *virtuous leadership* to arrest and arrest for good the decaying state of our world. When a particular call in such a tasking odyssey to lead right comes to an end, the leader experiences 'freedom' rather than 'loss'. This is the experience of those who come to leadership as a call to service rather than a position to be grabbed.

Ending that service is a double-edged freedom in which one responsibility finishes well and suddenly, the leader becomes available to take another one that may pop up.

The manner of my disengagement from Salem University as Vice Chancellor and the commitment we have made subsequently, as narrated in this last section of the book, illustrate this 'freedom' situation. When I ended my appointment, I felt incredibly free. But it wasn't long before I had to take up another responsibility which has been challenging me to aim higher in my leadership journey. What I emphasise with both events is that not only does *leading right* require sensitivity about the time to finish, it also retains the possibility of challenging one to aim higher (upwardly directed) beyond whatever level of excellence at which the leader might have served. Thus, in the leading right genre, 'getting from here to there'[11] is normally an 'aiming higher and righter' phenomenon.

At this point in the story behind this book, it became clear to me that we must embark on a radical agenda for the right leadership if we must make a difference in our current world. Most of the writings and practices of leadership have, until recently, presented 'transformational leadership' as the apogee of the leadership phenomenon (Sashkin and Sashkin 2004; Omaji 2010). And, that all efforts in this field would culminate there. James McGregor Burns who introduced the concept of 'transformational leadership' in 1978 (while distinguishing the emerging thoughts about leadership from the then prevailing ideology of 'transactional leadership'), presented it as such.

After examining a number of national and social leaders, he concluded that the exceptional ones were those who transformed their followers into more capable, self-directed leaders. For him, a leader:

> looks for potential motives in followers, seeks to satisfy higher needs, and engages the full person of the followers. The result… is a relationship of mutual stimulation and elevation that converts followers into leaders and may convert leaders into moral agents (Burns 1978, p4).

Since that time, many writers or commentators have used various concepts or adjectives to illuminate what transformational leadership represents: 'effective', 'great', 'courageous', 'intelligent', 'primal', 'authentic', 'servant', 'resonant', etc. I subscribed to this view and, indeed, was contented to take my leadership assignments – personally and organisationally - to the 'transformational' level. That was the height I aimed for at Salem University.

Then, in 2012 I came across some materials that made me realise there is another level of leadership that I must explore and aspire to. That other level, as shown in Chapter One of this book, is 'virtuous leadership'. Fully cognizant of my own thoughts and practices of leadership to that point, what I have explored since then about this virtuous leadership has shown me that, indeed, there is a much higher and righter altitude we (leaders or leadership-minded individuals) can aim for in our aspirations.

The superiority of the virtuous leadership paradigm over other paradigms has grabbed my attention so much so that I have presented it in this book as the apogee of leadership to which our rotten world must aspire, if we must turn around radically from decadence. As Havard (2007) contends so appropriately, there is no <u>grander</u> purpose in life than 'personal excellence' which is at the heart of virtuous leadership. In Cameron's (2011, p28) rendition, virtuousness in leadership consists of "the most ennobling behaviors and outcomes, the excellence and essence of humankind, the best of the human condition, and the highest aspirations of humanity".

Concluding remarks

Leadership is not as elusive as it may seem. Yes, so much has been written about it. The approaches in those writings mirror the proverbial nine blind people who touched one elephant at different parts and described the animal based on the part they each felt. That such a description would come to us in volumes taller than the Mt Everest, does not make it "a tale told by an idiot, full of sound and fury, signifying nothing"[12].

"So, why the mountainous literature on leadership?", asks Clark (2009). His answer to this question simultaneously reveals the 'what' and the 'why' of the book you are holding in your hands right now, *Audacity of Leading Right*: "leadership is the animating force that moves us forward. It brings meaning to our lives, in spite of our challenges… [The one main problem] is that [virtuous or at least principled] leaders are going extinct". Any contribution towards a better appreciation of this force, and toward reversing this 'extinction' trend is immeasurably worthwhile, considering the dire consequences of living in a world in the grip of amoral and immoral rulers.

As a prelude to telling the story of my own journey with leadership, I had to determine the framework that covers the quintessence of this phenomenon as I have personally experienced it – specifically in a <u>steering</u> capacity. That framework focuses on the contents of what I call '*leading right*'. In this configuration, I came to see leadership as possessing the capacity for creating a unique culture – a way of life, which defines in a very profound way the destinies of all human entities.

How leadership defines destinies is very much tied to the kind of paradigm within which its practitioners engage. You will see in the narration of my own story that there is no greater need in our twenty-first century world than what our audacity to lead right at Salem University has significantly foreshadowed, namely virtuous leadership.

Apart from our greatest challenge being that of a leadership vacuum (or extinction as Clark puts it), I have tried in this book to alert us to the reality that it would take a higher and righter form of leadership to really deliver our world from the level of decadence it has sunk to. Munroe (2005, p18) presaged this when he said, "the number one need all over the globe today is not money, social programs, or even new governments. It is quality, moral, disciplined, principle-centred leadership".

For me, *virtuous leadership* is it. And I hope that what we did at Salem University, and the narration of its story in this book, constitute a significant pointer to the fact that this ultimate leadership brand is needful and possible. Because of the context of the main story - being a Christian University with the philosophy that its students be modeled on the teachings of Jesus Christ as you will see in Chapter Three, the coloration of our language is profusely Christian with Biblical textual references. However, this does not in any way detract from the universal applicability of the analysis and agenda on the radical leadership that the book presents.

To avoid much of the dissatisfaction with many books on leadership (all the how-to books, books that offer easy steps to effective leadership, etc), I have endeavoured to locate the narration in "the vagaries and subtleties of real-life situations" (Jinkins and Jinkins 1998, px). Like Bill Hybels (2002, p11) said, "the words and ideas that fill the pages to follow are not abstract concepts to me; they represent the activity and passion of my life". Bon voyage!

---

[1]   The 4th Vice Chancellor of the Federal University of Agriculture Abeokuta, 2007-2012, who is said to have embodied 'transformational leadership' (see UNAAB Alumni Association, 2012).

[2]   Pioneer Vice Chancellor of the Federal University of Agriculture Makurdi, 1988-1995, who is said to have embodied 'purposeful' and 'merit-based' leadership (see Idachaba, 2013).

[3]   Richard Kilburg made this observation even with after 70 years of study that has enabled us to "now know a lot more about the components and process of leadership and how to measure it".

[4]   E.g. see Kurt Lewin's categories of 'authoritative or autocratic leadership ("I want you to…"), 'Participative or democratic leadership

("Let's work together to..."), and 'delegative or free reign' leadership ("You take care of..."). To these, Evanson (2011) has added 'servant' leadership ("How can I serve you...").

[5]   See Lee and Roberts (2010) for the first three brands; and Havard (2007) for the fourth brand.

[6]   These are the cardinal and supernatural virtues that underpin 'virtuous leadership' with transfigurational impact and are discussed in Chapter One of this book.

[7]   1 Corinthians 14: 7-8, Holy Bible. New King James Version.

[8]   The metaphors of 'Valley of Baca' and 'Goliath' are explained in Chapter Five.

[9]   Corporate administrative system, physical infrastructural development and maintenance, academic management system, and stakeholder management system.

[10]   Maxwell (2000, p354) identifies what leaders leave behind as 'souvenirs', 'trophies', and 'legacies'. What I have described as our 'trophies' in this book are interchangeable with his own 'legacies'.

[11]   This is a metaphor that Bill Hybels used to define 'Leadership' in his address to the 2011 Global Leadership Summit at Willows Creek.

[12]   Shakespeare's Macbeth describing life: "Life's but a walking shadow, a poor player that struts and frets his hour upon the stage and then is heard no more. It is a tale told by an idiot, full of sound and fury, signifying nothing" Act 5, Scene 5.

1 Paradigms: branding leadership

At some stage in my recent life, I felt I needed to have additional historical and epistemological grounding in this leadership phenomenon. This was in spite of the views I had heard expressed to me that my leadership experiences have been notable. And, yes, there are persons I had modeled for, or mentored, along the way who are now exhibiting very prominent leadership personalities. Nothing in this regard assuaged my felt need to study more on leadership.

Like it had become my custom, even in this 'latter day' passion, I aimed for perfection in this study. Knowing fully well that I wouldn't get that far, I set my hope at landing on 'excellence' (my best)[13]. Joel Hawes one said: "Aim at the sun, and you may not reach it; but your arrow will fly far higher than if aimed at an object on a level with yourself." And, not knowing how far I could go even with this lower scale, I started anyway. All that is necessary for a leader to start anyway is a picture of the imagined future. I could see the study steering myself to the point of saying, "I am getting more insight into some aspects of leadership that have troubled me". And I could see a book enriched by such a study that would stir some hearts towards a higher and righter way of leading their world. That was enough to get me started.

It is the finding of that 'short life of study', imperfect as it may be, that I share in this Chapter. I present it in terms of 'paradigms' because that approach has helped me to make a better sense of the leadership phenomenon. Out of a plethora of thoughts and practices, which some have found to be confusing or mysterious, it is possible to identity models or archetypes. The most illuminating in my view is the framework which aggregates leadership thoughts and practices around the core themes of: philosophies, behavioural patterns and outcomes[14]. Based on this criterion, I have chosen the paradigms of 'defiant leadership', 'compliant leadership', 'authentic leadership' and 'virtuous leadership' to discuss the relevant intellectual and practical outputs in this Chapter.

To me, the finding has been as humbling as it has been exciting in more ways than one. First, I came to realize that my personal journey (odyssey) in leadership up to the time I commenced the study was actually recognizable in some high level conceptual frameworks dealing with the leadership phenomenon. Further, I found out that there is still a level of leadership higher and righter than everything I had known and practised about visioning, setting goals, developing strategies and mobilizing people to go for the imagined future in various facets of life.

The first opportunity I had to start sharing my finding was at the Caleb Leadership Academy of Caleb University, Imota, Lagos. In an address titled "Raising authentic leaders: A clarion call to Universities"[15], I discussed the importance of leadership and the role of universities in producing it. I also showed how the various conceptual frameworks for leadership had evolved over time; outlined the kind of leadership framework that typically characterized the First, Second and Third Worlds; and then focused on what needed to be done to raise authentic leaders. By that time, it had become clearer to me that even authentic leadership, highly effective in tackling complex challenges as it was, was not the highest rung on the leadership staircase that can be conceived. There is another level (virtuous leadership) which I captured in the leadership staircase that I presented in that address. That staircase is reproduced in Figure 1.

Figure 1: Leadership Staircase

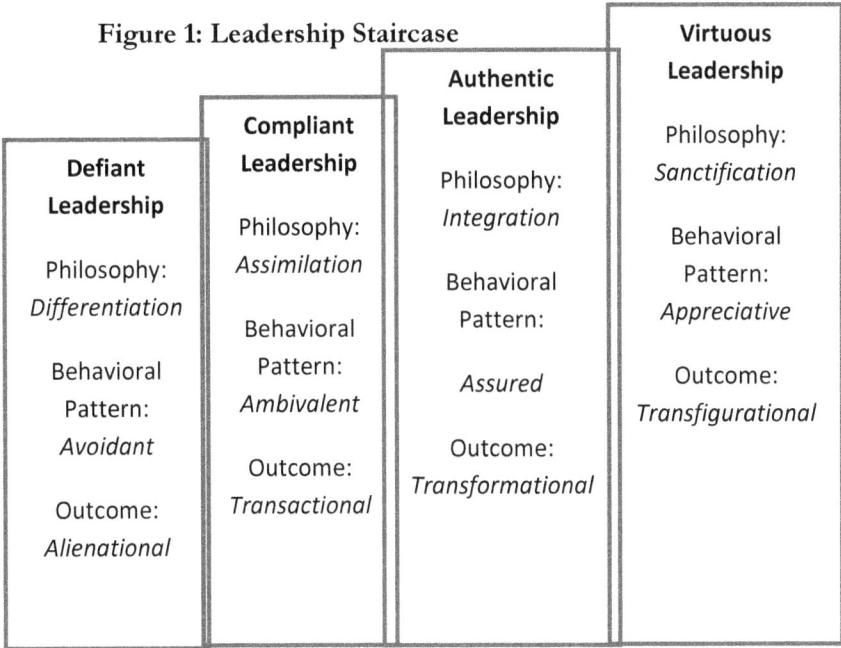

Defiant Leadership	Compliant Leadership	Authentic Leadership	Virtuous Leadership
Philosophy: *Differentiation*	Philosophy: *Assimilation*	Philosophy: *Integration*	Philosophy: *Sanctification*
Behavioral Pattern: *Avoidant*	Behavioral Pattern: *Ambivalent*	Behavioral Pattern: *Assured*	Behavioral Pattern: *Appreciative*
Outcome: *Alienational*	Outcome: *Transactional*	Outcome: *Transformational*	Outcome: *Transfigurational*

More than the issue of style, these paradigms are defined by the quality of consciousness and the level of reflective and integrative awareness that inform the leader's judgements, choices, and interpersonal behaviours on each rung. For the first three rungs of this staircase, I found the analysis by Lee and Roberts (2010) to be most profound and pertinent to the focus of this Chapter; and have therefore summarised it fairly extensively. Their write-up aimed at showing how the concepts can be used "to achieve significant and enduring transitions in leadership performance through coaching". This is part of my next focus in life.

The fourth rung has been variously articulated, especially in the last decade. However, I found the works of Havard (2007) and Cameron (2011) to be quite exceptionally profound and useful; so, I have drawn heavily on them in the course of formulating the key characteristics for the virtuous leadership paradigm in a manner suitable to this Chapter and the light that this entire book will shed.

Let me quickly address a relevant sensitivity that Kilburg (2006, p11) captured in his view that:

> When any scholar attempts to add substance to a well-established discipline like leadership [even if still enigmatic in some quarters],

he or she is faced with a monumental task. How can one create a different way of seeing something that every other scholar in the field knows well? How does one offer a perspective that will be seen as at least useful, if not establishing a wholly new paradigm?

By way of delimiting the scope of this Chapter and by extension this book, let me state upfront: neither my passion nor my ambition at this stage is sufficient to make me set out to establish a 'wholly new paradigm'. My effort here is very modest. From my research into relevant intellectual discourses and my participatory observation of the leadership phenomenon, I have merely analysed categories of leadership thoughts and practices, and constructed them in rungs of a 'leadership staircase'. In doing this, I paid particular attention to the philosophies, behavioural patterns, and outcomes around which these categories have emerged. For, it is in these three dimensions that the personality or essence of every leadership is established.

We see this clearly when we relate these dimensions to the unique and instructive conceptual framework in Hamm's work (2011) which presents credibility, competence and consequence as the core of the leadership phenomenon. The philosophies (i.e. underlying beliefs about, or attitudes to, leadership) address the issue of 'credibility' which earns anyone the right to lead. The behavioural patterns (i.e. consistent outward manifestations of attitudes) raise the issue of 'competence' which gains for the leader the respect of his followers and other leaders around him or her. Lastly, outcomes (i.e. impacts or legacies) relate to the matter of 'consequence' which the leader bequeaths in terms of culture and reputation. As the outline of each of the paradigms below will show, although some elements are common across the board, the gulf between the paradigms is quite wide, especially between the defiant and compliant on one side, and the authentic and virtuous on the other.

Defiant leadership

Some writers refer to this paradigm as the <u>classical</u> or the old command-and-control approach, which involves obsessively telling others what to do. The approach usually depends on fear or morbid respect to get things done, exemplified for centuries by the military and religious organisations. Of late, some members of the political class particularly in Africa and Asia have practised this form of leadership under the guise of democracy.

The philosophy that drives the people in positions of power within this paradigm is one of **differentiation**. They always make themselves stand apart and away from the followers. They are patently unattached, even to the vision that they say they are driving. And so, in their behaviours, they avoid responsibilities when things do not go as expected and continually shift blame to 'others', especially the followers.

Look at the classic case of the Enron Company whose Board Chairman, Ken Lay, was convicted on multiple charges of fraud. "During his entire trial, Lay maintained that he was completely innocent of all charges… he laid most of the responsibility for the disaster at Enron on the shoulders of a few rogue employees while eschewing any culpability for the problems that occurred during his term of office" (Kilburg 2012, p86).

As Lee and Roberts (op cit) put it, the paradigm takes:

> a self-assertive stance at the expense of the other-awareness; [it is] controlling, critical and confrontational; decisive, [but] individualistic and idiosyncratic; [driven by] implicit fear of failure… and regulates emotions through unconscious disassociation and ignoring others' needs. Interpersonally, [it is] awkward, emotionally distant and inflexible".

This traditional paradigm of leadership focuses on the individual and runs on the basis that "we're hard-wired into thinking it's all about one person telling others what to do"[16]. Historically, this is called the 'Top Dog' leadership whose ideal followers were known as 'organisational men' embodying conformism and working without complaint to fulfill the boss's every desire. The 'Top Dogs' spend most of their time barking orders at their drone-like followers and taking all the credit for their loyal followers'/employees' ideas. The prevailing catchphrase in this paradigm is: 'It's my way or the highway'.

Because the paradigm evokes self-serving competitiveness, it generates either resistance or forced obedience. The outcome of that kind of leadership is **alienational**! The practitioners systemically send people away from themselves, lock themselves into their own cocoons where they feel they are tin-gods who can do and undo with no qualms about the impact of their 'leadership' on the people around them (Omaji, 2013).

A close look at most master-servant, autocratic and third world rulers, would show that they are predominated by defiant leadership - mainly so-called leaders ruling for themselves: so self-absorbed; so egocentric! They focus on their immediate families and friends. In more contemporary times, *their focus is predominantly on* how to beef-up their 'bank' accounts for the rainy day or stifle opposition to preserve their political advantage. And they give no hoot if the whole society over which they preside goes up in blazes – Caesar fiddling when Rome burns.

For instance, it is in this regard that Usman (2012) - tying the 'beginning of crisis leadership in Nigeria' to the military rule, argued that a particular regime was responsible for the:

> deconstruction of Nigeria and death of value system… leading

to irresponsible leadership, institutionalized corruption, favoritism and indiscipline at all levels of government. The system was turned upside down and the public psyche was changed... The nation's great endowments were turned into misfortune... the government artificially created poverty and insecurity... Leaders started acting arrogantly like prince and lords; using government as a personal empire (Usman 2012, pp107-108).

This is narcissism par excellence – extremely self-absorbed, to the point of turning public institutions into private empires. Such leaders show an exaggerated sense of self importance and a strong desire to be admired by others through fear and intimidation. They hold the view about coercion of others as being a sport. They raise impression management to the level of an art – adept at scheming ways to enhance their own image by emphasising the importance of personal allegiance to themselves as the leader, rather than to the greater organisation (Pearce, et. al, 2006).

Compliant leadership

This leadership paradigm is all about 'everything goes'! The people in positions of power have little or no mind of their own as 'leaders'. They have no convictions. People don't know where they stand on issues. They have nothing to live and, if need be, die for. Nothing close to the likes of Jesus who said "for this cause I was born and for this cause I have come into the world" (John18: 37). Nor, even on a lesser (and human) scale, do they have anything resembling Nelson Mandela who said that the ideal of a democratic free society "is an ideal which I hope to live for and to achieve. But if needs be, it is an ideal for which I am prepared to die"[17]. Such people knew why they came. They had convictions. Compliant leaders on the other hand have nothing like that (Omaji, 2013).

Interpersonally eager to please others, every wind that blows pushes them around. Their overriding philosophy is **assimilation**. That is to say, so morbidly 'other-focused', they lack self-expression and spontaneity both of which make genuine leaders stand out and come into their own. Appearing to be collaborative and/or responsive, they are in effect timid and driven by the 'fear of abandonment' and the 'longing for safety'. Thus, compliant 'leaders' 'regulate emotions by unconsciously matching to others' and evoking 'process compliance rather than inspiration'.

It's like becoming a chameleon, flowing with the air or the colour of the environment – embracing everything in their domain except fundamental/necessary change. The behavioral pattern of such people is at best ambivalent and at worst manipulative. They may disguise this as being flexible. At core, it is actually a perversion of 'adaptability'[18], akin to the perversion of 'authority' by those in the defiant paradigm.

The outcome of endeavours in this leadership paradigm is fundamentally **transactional**. It relies for performance on 'deals' whose terms and conditions are designed to maximize returns for the practitioners themselves: "What will you give me or what will I get if I give you that?" It is the typical 'nothing goes for nothing' mind-set with which rulers (masquerading as leaders) "essentially exert their influence over their staff by reinforcing their behaviours either positively or negatively, depending on whether or not their staff perform according to the leaders' [selfish] expectations and desires" (Alban-Metcalfe and Mead, 2010).

Authentic leadership

In contradistinction to the paradigms of defiant and compliant leadership, there is the wholesome and progressive paradigm of authentic leadership. Here, responsibility holders work by **integration** as their philosophy. They endeavour to bring all the various parts of their human entities together because they belief in the power teamwork and hold the value of synergy very strongly. In their behaviours they show they are very secure and very assured. They have nothing to fear. Why? Because they have nothing to hide. By the drive to consciously balance the needs of self and others, they are in their conducts 'adaptable, self-disclosing, and motivating'. Thus, they are able to 'regulate emotions through reflection and dialogue', rather than coercion or manipulation.

Under this paradigm, the people in positions of power lead consciously: they are aware of themselves and the situations that they are leading. They are not 'absentee landlords'. They know that they have been put in a position to do something beneficial to their human entities, and that thing they must do. They creatively attune their strengths to their organisational goals. They are true to themselves. They represent or deploy their intentions and commitments with genuineness.

Interpersonally attuned and empathetic to self and others as they are, these leaders evoke 'vitality, collaboration, and creativity'. The outcome of this paradigm is **transformational** because it is associated not only with performance but also with meeting the developmental needs of the people they lead and the goals of their vision. As Alban-Metcalfe and Mead (2010) put it, transformation-generating leadership:

> is named as such because of its effect to transform followers to perform beyond expectations, in part by creating an emotional bond between leader and follower, and by arousing enthusiasm for

a common vision… More specifically, transformational leaders are characterized by being able to motivate colleagues and followers to view their work from new perspectives; be aware of their team and organisation's mission or vision; attain higher levels of ability and potential; and look beyond their own interests towards those that will benefit the group.

Consistent with what James MacGregor Burns who introduced the concept of transformational leadership said, those who operate within this authentic paradigm seek, among other empowering things, to satisfy higher needs as they engage the 'full person of the followers'. There is transformation in 'a relationship of mutual stimulation and elevation' in which followers have an opportunity to grow into leaders and the 'transformers' (authentic leaders) have the opportunity to fulfill their mission of leaving things better than they met them.

Virtuous leadership

When I struck up on the *virtuous leadership* paradigm, during my latest journey towards more historical and epistemological understanding, I shouted like it was an epiphany: "this is the apogee of leadership". Considering that the dictionary equates 'virtuousness' to righteousness and morality, the leadership it qualifies is one that distinguishes right from wrong and, by that fact, influences and enables others to pursue righteous and moral goals for themselves and their human entities with a view to connecting those entities to a higher purpose (Pearce, et. al, 2006).

"Virtuousness is not a common term in scientific circles", says Cameron (2011). In fact, it is rather rashly associated with "social conservatism, religious dogmatism, and scientific irrelevance" and thus relegated to "theology, philosophy, or mere naivete" (id). Yet, it is one term that connotes universal standards of rightness, correctness, and goodness. It possesses an affirmative bias towards (indeed focuses on) elevating, flourishing, and enriching outcomes and pursues the ultimate best – eudaemonism rather than merely avoiding the negative as is the case with ethics (see Cameron 2011, pp26-27).

Locationally, virtuousness is rooted in human character. There, it exercises to bring out 'what human beings ought to be': the inherent goodness, humanity's very best qualities and, ultimately, being in complete harmony with the will or purpose of God for one's life. At core, a leadership that is virtuous is one that is oriented towards <u>being</u> and <u>doing</u> good - not for selfish reasons but simply as an outward working of the inner intersection of the natural and the divine.

Everything I have read about this paradigm suggests that the philosophy that drives it is about **sanctification**. That is, there is the conviction that anything or anyone that comes in contact with a leader of this persuasion has a good chance to be made right or refined. This is because the leader's manner of speech, thinking, action, etc, would invariably confront the limiting impurities in people's lives and/or generate the dynamics to bring out the best in such people. The behaviour of such leaders is always appreciative or empathetic - acknowledging that there is something that can be redeemed even when all looks so bad.

It is the **organic** mold of leadership that pushes the boundaries of possibilities and challenges the basis of leadership as we understand it away from the all-controlling, or conversely all-loose (laissez faire), figurehead leader and towards the shared vision, principle-based, decision-making and mutual-accountability leader (Tarrant, op cit). It is leadership with an arrowhead clearly distinguished by many virtues, key among which are wisdom, courage, justice, temperance and transcendence as outlined briefly below:

Wisdom: integrates experience and knowledge, and then expresses them in action. Its starting point is knowledge of self. Then, it facilitates the art of recognizing and following the most suitable or sensible course of action; good sense in practical or financial affairs, discretion, circumspection, caution, discerning the true good in every circumstance and choosing the right means of achieving it. The leader with the virtue of wisdom is prudent in all his or her ways.

Courage: enables people to do without fear what they believe is right. It is a quality of mind showing itself in facing danger without fear or shrinking, otherwise known as bravery, boldness and valor. It is not about the total absence of fear. In leadership roles, one confronts a multitude of things that terrify people: fear of criticism or embarrassment; fear of poverty or job loss; fear of losing friends or being ostracized—even fear of being seen to be in the wrong. Courageous leaders hold fast to their values and purpose even when there is no certainty that they will prevail. Courage is of particular importance because unlike some other virtues, it is not an end in itself but it supports other moral claims. As such, philosopher Robert Merrihew Adams describes courage as a "structural virtue."

Justice: promotes fairness, equity and common good; respect for the rights of others in the face of conflict of interest, distribution of duties, allocation of resources, or exercising of power generally. It directs leaders to give others their due in executing policies across the board. Justice reinforces followers' trust. Everyone is special even if different.

Temperance: enables restraint in provocation, passion, desire, etc., against instant gratification – for biological or cultural reasons. It provides self-control to leaders when they "encounter unanalyzed opportunities or overindulgence in hedonistic behaviours". They are then able to prioritize organisational gains over self-gain. It sustains a sense of deep selflessness or self-sacrifice, especially in moments of great organisational uncertainty or crisis, thus sending a clear message as to what kind of conduct is needed and how earnestly the leader is committed to the cause of the organisation. It conveys to followers the leader's strong conviction that 'we can do it,' and is an earnest invitation to participate under sufficient self-control.

Transcendence: consists of the supernatural virtues of **faith**, **hope** and **love**. They engender trust or loyalty for living in possibilities; stabilise confidence about expectations; and generate strong bonding towards defined goals. It elevates, strengthens, and ultimately transfigures the bearers of the other virtues into something not just better, but beautiful. No study of the impact of virtue on leadership is complete without taking into consideration these supernatural virtues.

The end (outcome) of virtuous leadership is '**transfigurational**'. The environment and the players therein are changed; they become radiant and show the perfection of relationship as in the pivotal moment when human nature meets the divine nature - the temporal and the eternal finally connecting to display the splendor of righteous governance. Imagine an organisation or a world under a leadership that is informed with the cardinal (human) virtues of wisdom, courage, justice, and temperance; and infused with the supernatural virtues of faith, hope, and love. What a different and rapturous entity that would be!

Some readers would be familiar with the transfiguration of Jesus Christ on a mountain in the midst of three of His disciples – Peter, John and James. When Peter saw what was happening – the radiance of the sanctified or glorified Jesus and the ambience of the surrounding, he said something to this effect: "Oh Master, is this how it looks like to be on this mountain? There is no more need for us to leave here. We are going to build three tents; we are going to stay here". He was so overwhelmed by the gloriousness of that experience he felt that place and nowhere else must be for them[19].

Journey towards virtuous leadership

Here is the dilemma. Virtuous leadership seems too idyllic to be attainable – a pie in the sky that no one can reach. The natural reaction is to leave it alone. Talk about it if you may, but do no more. At the same time, we are so dissatisfied with our present world, excepting those who profit from the misfortune of the world – a world so traumatised by the defiant-cum-compliant leadership complex that even the authentic brand (with all its transformational potentials) seems incapable of radically turning the trauma around.

My take is this. The situation is such that even the fatalistic would, with a modicum of encouragement, wish to reach out to a more liberating brand of leadership. In the circumstances, aiming for the virtuous leadership brand seems imperative if not inevitable. But it has to be a journey not a jump. The distance from where our world is now to where the desired leadership brand can take it is enormous. Nevertheless, as the Chinese adage goes, a journey of a thousand miles starts with one step and builds up from there. In the remainder of this Chapter, I offer three of such steps.

1. *Start with history*

History is not just the repository of the past. It uniquely shows when journeys in life began and how they got to the present in the manner that they did. In this regard, therefore, history is above all a conveyor of 'the art of the possible'. In the stream of leadership and management history, what we see is that the four paradigms we have outlined in this Chapter are indeed symptomatic of their times.

Take the last 60 years, or so, for instance. The period of 1960s to 80s witnessed a concerted war on values. The result was wholesale descent into decadence and other cultural problems linked with moral irresponsibility. Then, in the 1990s there arose a nearly universal condemnation of the war on values – calling for a return to traditional and family values as the surest solution to the nation's woes ranging from crime and drug abuse to poverty and illiteracy.

However, like in several social movements, 'value vendors' quickly emerged as entrepreneurs. They created 'values boom' in which not only did the lines between values and virtues become blurred; ironically even values became an inherently vitiated term – turned into a business commodity, embodying no more than a relativistic ethic. As Himmelfarb (1995) argued,

> morality became so thoroughly relativized, that virtues ceased to be 'virtues' and became [mere] 'values' … with… the assumptions that all moral ideas are subjective and relative, that they are mere customs and conventions, that they have a purely instrumental utilitarian purpose, and that they are peculiar to specific individuals and societies.

Not surprisingly, leadership research during this period exalted the situational or contingent and transactional leadership models. In organisations, the mantra was about total quality management and system flows. 'Doing the right thing' was only to ensure the organisations were efficient. Leadership was seen to be formal with the shared view that people were led from the top – clearly an artifact of the defiant or classical command and control leadership paradigm.

This held sway until the 1990s when the focus shifted to ethical (but still predominantly transactional) leadership. Ethics, as we know, places emphasis "on avoiding harm, fulfilling contracts, ensuring compliance, and obeying rules and laws" (Cameron 2011, p27). During this period, 'doing the right thing' for organisations for instance, meant downsizing, adding to the bottom-line, judging a company's health and wealth by the size of its profit and surplus, etc – all within the bounds of rules and laws. Leadership was rules-based but mainly about increasing assets and shareholder value with transactional ethos by whatever means conceivable, not minding the attendant huge human costs.

As from the mid-2000s, virtues re-emerged as critical antidotes to the toxic societies that the previous leadership paradigms had foisted on the world. Virtues came to be seen as holding "considerable promise for understanding and fostering exemplary leadership" that the world needed so badly (Manz et al, 2008). By the end of that decade, 'doing the right thing' came to be seen as delivering outcomes (individual or organisational) while carrying along, and caring for the needs of, all stakeholders even in the face of incredible velocity and rates of change. Consequently, the authentic leadership paradigm with all its transformational promises as we saw before came into vogue.

Today, it would seem that the state of the world is such that even this authentic leadership paradigm - wholesome, humane and honourable as it may be, would struggle to effectively and profoundly turn things around for good. This realization has given rise to the current hunger for a higher paradigm of leadership which, for me, is the virtuous leadership. The literature on this approach to leadership is still very much as limited as it is inchoate.

Of about 70 million entries on leadership in the wide world web, less than 10 per cent (about 5 million) deals with 'virtuous leadership'. This means that this brand of leadership is still grossly under-explored in a world that desperately needs *virtuousness* to be enthroned in all facets of society to save it from self-destruction. Genuine leaders are increasingly becoming conscious of this need. This is what Lorenzen (2009) was alluding to when he said: "the crucial issue of leadership may not be how much power leaders exercise but how well their presence has been able to preserve that society from decay. By the integrity and audacity of their own self-possession, they keep societies from disintegrating".

Writers about the USA, for instance, generally note that it is a world that has seen countless quick fixes and instant solutions that swept through its culture only to give way to the next fad. In such societies, "only a virtuous man can uphold an oath' and that 'if the leaders upheld their oath to the Constitution, the mess [they] are in would be much smaller or nonexistent" (see Friedman, 2007; Stallard, n.d;)

This is like going back to the spirit of the founding fathers of the USA. For, John Adams once wrote to Thomas Jefferson in words that are eerily resonant with the need of our own times today. He said: "have you ever found in history, one single example of a nation thoroughly corrupted that was afterward restored...? Will you tell me how to prevent luxury from producing effeminacy, intoxication, extravagance, vice and folly...? I believe no effort in favor of virtue is lost" (October 7, 1818).

Nearly 200 years later, keen observers of the American life are invoking this same spirit, albeit in commercial terms: "all the economic stimulus in the world will not save America if we fail to stimulate virtue and virtuous leadership. If we do become intentional about developing **virtuous** employees, leaders, and organisations, then America's productivity, rate of innovation, and global reputation will soar" (Stallard, op. cit; emphasis, added).

In making a case for virtuous leadership, Kaak and Weeks (2013) argue that:

> many institutional failures and disappointments within Western culture are due to [vicious] leadership [in] the era of modernity [which] was inclined to attribute credibility to incredible leaders, to the celebrity heroes of politics... Today, the confidence and surety once placed in those who lead has perished in waves of corruption and duplicity. Expertise, charisma and competitiveness, elements of... modernity's "moral fiction", have been unveiled as insufficient (at best). Organisations need leaders who are good,

leaders whose vision and performance are an outgrowth of their **virtue** (emphasis, added).

Needless to say, this argument applies with equally strong force to the rest of the world, and especially those countries where institutions that check human vices are either too weak or non-existent to yield virtue-based leadership. In these countries, the 'strong man' syndrome is pervasive and thoroughly corruptive. And, it leaves a needless trail of desecration in all facets of life.

The book by Havard (2007), apparently the "first systematic and holistic attempt to relate the classical virtues to professional leadership in modern times", is particularly instructive regarding the capacity of virtuous leadership to **sanctify** the world. In the 10-point summary of this book in Wikipedia[20] one can see how *virtues* uniquely interface in enabling and ennobling processes to produce a new breed of leadership that is epochal and transfigurational in its impact. I present this summary below, with necessary changes as the context requires.

1. Virtue is a sound habit of the mind, the will, and the heart that helps us achieve personal excellence and professional effectiveness. Leadership is all about virtue. Why? (1) Because virtue instills trust, the sine qua non of leadership; and (2) because virtue is a dynamic force, which enhances our capacity to act (the word "virtue" stems from the Latin word virtus, signifying "strength" or "power").

2. **Magnanimity** and **humility**, which are virtues principally of the heart, are the essence of leadership. Magnanimity is the habit of striving towards great things. Leaders are magnanimous in their dreams, visions, and sense of mission; and also in their capacity to challenge themselves and those around them [away from base life, and towards greatness]. Humility is the habit of service. Humility means that leaders pull rather than push, teach rather than command, inspire rather than berate. Thus, leadership is less about displays of power than the empowerment of others.

3. The virtues of **prudence** (practical wisdom), **courage**, **self-control** and **justice**, which are virtues principally of the mind and the will, are leadership's bedrock virtues. Prudence enhances our ability to make right decisions; courage - to stay the course and resist pressures of all kinds; self-control - to subordinate passions to the spirit and direct them towards the fulfillment of the mission at hand, and justice - to give every individual his due.

4. Leaders are not born, but trained. Why? Because virtue is a habit acquired through practice. Leadership is a question of

character (virtue, freedom, self-improvement), not temperament (biology and genetics).

5. Leaders do not lead by exercising the *potestas* (power), inherent in their office *unless it is absolutely necessary to do get the right things done*. Instead, they lead through the *auctoritas*, the authority that stems from character. Those who lack genuine authority and succumb to the temptation to exercise unalloyed power are leaders in name only. In fact, they are non-leaders.

6. In order to grow in virtue one must (a) contemplate virtue so as to perceive its intrinsic beauty and desire it strongly (a matter of the heart); (b) act virtuously habitually (a matter of the will) and (c) practice all the virtues simultaneously with special attention to prudence (a matter of reason.)

7. Through the practice of virtues, leaders achieve maturity in all its aspects—judgmental, emotional, and behavioral. The unmistakable signs of maturity are self-confidence and consistency, psychological stability, joy and optimism, naturalness, a sense of freedom and responsibility, and interior peace. Leaders are neither skeptical nor cynical, but realistic. Realism is the ability to maintain the noblest aspirations of the soul even as one remains beset by this or that personal weakness. This is not giving in to weakness, but transcending it through the practice of virtues.

8. Leaders reject a utilitarian approach to virtue. The leader's motive in striving for virtue is not simply to become good at what he does. Rather, it is to realize himself fully as a [redeemed] human being in doing what he does well. Effectiveness is not the aim of self-improvement; it is merely one of its manifold (happy) results. Excellence comes first, effectiveness second.

9. True leaders live by **virtue ethics**, rather than by rules-based ethics. Virtue ethics does not deny the validity of laws and rules, but it does insist that rules cannot be the ultimate foundation of ethics. Laws and rules must be at the service of virtue. Virtue ethics redound to original and creative leadership.

10. **Christian** life has a formidable impact on leadership, because the supernatural virtues of **faith**, **hope** and **charity** (which are the heart of Christian life) elevate, strengthen, and transfigure the natural virtues, which are the foundation of leadership. No

study of the impact of virtue on leadership is complete without taking into consideration the supernatural virtues.

Cameron (2011, p28) also captures this point quite well. He argues that "virtuousness associated with leadership refers to the most ennobling behaviors and outcomes, the excellence and essence of humankind, the best of the human condition, and the highest aspirations of humanity... That is, virtuousness in leadership is less a means to another more desirable outcome than an ultimate good itself".

Reading both works (especially Havard's) itself was a riveting experience for me. I came to understand that in all serious consideration, genuine leadership is synonymous with virtuousness. Havard illustrated this understanding by the lives of some of the greatest political, intellectual and religious leaders of modern times, even making allowance for bias in the citation of those personalities[21]. With their lives, he "emphasizes that this mode of leadership is more than a technique for increased 'productivity' but one which brings about something greater, that is, the creation of working environments and communities that retain their essential humanity while increasing fruitfulness in the forms appropriate to... the intended purpose" (O'Brien, 2007). In such environments and communities, "the authority of a true leader stems from the character they display which gives rise to trust". Consequently, "the natural tension between leaders and followers dissolves because followers know that their leader has their best interests at heart and they recognize in the leader a role model for their own character [and professional] development"[22].

For me, the overall signification of Havard's work lies in its pervasive message that leadership is about "the call of all human beings to serve mankind, the search of personal excellence to help others, and - at the end of the day - the struggle to become - and help others to become - fully human" (Soria, 2010). Across time and space, such leadership holds the promise to completely change the form, appearance, and operations of human entities not only so that they **be better** (ala transformation), but that they **look more beautiful** (ala transfiguration). This is what makes the *virtuous leadership* paradigm tower far above all other leadership paradigms known so far to humanity.

2. *Articulate a radicalizing agenda of 'leading right'*

If a radical picture of leadership has emerged in your mind from the foregoing analysis about the paradigm of virtuous leadership, that would be understandable and gratifying. Having reviewed the literature fairly extensively and having lived through several leadership experiences (Salem University inclusive), I couldn't help but challenge most of the manifestations of leadership I have come to know. On the canvass of virtuous leadership, those manifestations are quite dim indeed.

So, on the journey towards virtuous leadership, another step that we must take urgently is to change the leadership DNA that has brought our world to its current undesirable state. This is not merely to democratize leadership by hook or crook. It must be about going somewhere together and chasing shared goals, virtuously. Recall the 10-point summary of Havard's work in the preceding section. Leadership must become a reciprocal relationship, with a radical DNA - one whose manifestation would be morally comprehensive, action-oriented, and virtues-based.

Insofar as my understanding to date goes, that DNA is *leading right* whose core elements I outlined in the Prologue of this book. It calls for a redefinition of, and an unusual commitment to, the leadership phenomenon. Based on further studies and my experiences to date, I am led to put forward a view which redefines leadership as "influencing volunteers to become stewards for the responsibility to do the right thing, in the right way, at the right time, and for the right reasons" (Omaji, 2014).

It is a radical thought to view followers as 'volunteers'. In settings where power and influence are deemed to be unidirectional – as in public bureaucracies and private empires that dominate the landscape of the world, such a notion would an anathema. But the reality of life is that, although we have the power to influence, "those we lead can choose… to follow or not. They have the power to grant or withhold support" Clark (2009). If we force or deceive them into obeying us, then all we have are automatons at best not followers.

It is not enough, as Clark (2009) rightly observed, to say "leadership is the business of influence", which is the view many have proffered previously. Such view of leadership has inadvertently provided a banner under which many have wreaked the havocs of defiant and compliant leadership brands. We must grapple with the question of what kind of influence: whether it is 'manipulation'[23], 'persuasion'[24] or 'coercion'[25]. I agree with Clark that on this spectrum of influence, "only persuasion is leadership":

> Only persuasion really helps people. The other two hurt people. Manipulation exploits. Coercion controls. Both can produce results, but not the best results, and not lasting results, and more often than not, very bad results.

At core, persuasive influence of the *leading right* genre is about creating the right vision, setting the right goals (using logic, data, and creativity), demonstrating the right interest and concern for the vision/goals, and mobilising people in the right way to participate at the right time, and for the right reasons (Omaji, 2014).

However, once the 'volunteers' accept responsibilities assigned to them, based on persuasive influence not coercion or manipulation (implicit or explicit), then they transform into 'stewards' and can now be held accountable for what they do with those responsibilities. So, 'accountability' which is sorely lacking in several leadership regimes today is inherent in our radical view of leadership.

Over and above all this, the radical redefinition of leadership extends the role of leaders to modeling virtuousness and to helping their followers (ala stewards) to develop and deploy a morally grounded character. Both the leaders and the stewards must subordinate their selfish interests to the morally valid collective ones, a capability which develops only from consistently doing the right things rightly. Kilburg (2006) called 'executive wisdom': "doing the right thing, in the right way, at the right time, and for the right reasons"; and I have interfaced it organically with Clark's notions of 'persuasive influence' and 'volunteerism' to postulate my radical concept of leadership.

3. *Paint the quintessence of leading right*

Within the context of our decaying world and the provocative (stimulating) canvass that we have laid for the virtuous leadership paradigm to help us out, two key actions are imperative. They are actions that (a) enable human entities to drain away the bad blood (vices) and (b) ennoble them to rehydrate with the good blood (virtues).

In this regard, 'enabling' and 'ennobling' become the two sides of righteous empowerment which is at the heart of virtuous leadership. The capacity to cultivate, nurture and activate the underpinning virtues (which is like a rebirth of the original good nature) is simultaneously reinforced by the regained willpower to detest, challenge and correct vices wherever they show up in the daily lives of leaders *qua* leaders. This, then, is the lifestyle of habituated virtues - holistically manifesting to produce *virtuousness*, far beyond the accidental display of strength in one or two virtues in given circumstances.

For example, Hitler displayed the virtue of courage but violated several other virtues and thereby dislocated his world. This is the practice you would expect within the defiant and compliant paradigms of leadership. As the following portraits will show, the daily manifestations of leading right as a journey towards virtuous leadership are quite antithetical to the viciousness of many of our past (and indeed present) leaders.

Consider the portrait that Cochrane (n.d.) cited from *Towards a Meaningful Life* by Simon Jacobsen and you can feel the aura of daily *leading right*:

> a leader sees his work as a selfless service towards a higher purpose. As the sages say, 'Leadership is not power and dominance; it is servitude.' That doesn't mean that a leader is weak. He derives great strength from his [timely] dedication to a purpose that is greater than himself. Every generation has its Moses — a leader who inspires absolute trust — one who is totally dedicated to fulfilling his unique role. He understands and appreciates each person's role in perfecting this world and guides him or her accordingly. He rises above any individual perspective to take a global view, seeing how much each individual person and issue fit into the whole scheme of the contemporary world.
>
> A leader shakes people from their reverie and tells them: 'No, you don't need to live a life of desperation and confusion. Yes, you do have the ability to find meaning in your life and the unique skills to fulfill that meaning. You're an important link in a chain of generations past. You have a legacy worth preserving and a future worth fighting for.'
>
> A leader shows us that our world is, indeed, heading somewhere and that we control its movement. That we need not be at the mercy of personal prejudices or prevailing political winds. That none of us is subservient to history or nature. That *we* are history and nature. That we *can* rid the world of war and hate and ignorance — obliterate the borders that separate race from race and rich from poor…
>
> A leader does not seek followers. He wants to teach others how to be leaders. He doesn't want control. He wants Truth. He doesn't impose his leadership on others, nor does he take away anyone's autonomy. He inspires by love [and persuasion], not coercion [or manipulation]. When it becomes time to take credit, he makes himself invisible. But he is the first to arrive at a time of need. And he will never shrink away in fear… [He is audacious].

Here is another portrait – that of the proverbial 'Virtuous Wife'[26]. In it we see virtues translating into uncommon behaviours with potentially transfigurational impact. It is a powerful metaphor for *leading right*. Substitute 'virtuous wife' with 'leader', 'husband' or 'children' with 'people', etc; and you will find a very radically confronting personality – antithetical to the indolence, corruption, decay, mass penury, insecurity, and other shenanigans of our contemporary world.

> An excellent wife (read, *leader*), who can find?
> For her worth is far above jewels.
> The heart of her husband (read, *people*) trusts in her,
> And he will have no lack of gain (anything of value).
> She does him good and not evil
> All the days of her life.

> She looks for wool and flax,And works with her hands in delight…
> She rises also while it is still night
> And gives food to her household…
> She stretches out her hands to the distaff,
> And her hands grasp the spindle…
> She extends her hand to the poor,
> And she stretches out her hands to the needy.
> She is not afraid of the snow for her household,
> For all her people are clothed with scarlet.

> She girds herself with strength
> And makes her arms strong…
> She makes coverings for herself;
> Her clothing is fine linen and purple…
> Strength and dignity are her clothing,
> And she smiles at the future.

> She opens her mouth in wisdom,
> And the teaching of kindness is on her tongue.
> She looks well to the ways of her household,
> And does not eat the bread of idleness

> Her children/youth rise up and bless her;
> Her husband also, …praises her, saying:
> "Many daughter have done nobly,
> But you excel them all."
> Charm is deceitful and beauty is vain,
> But a *leader* who fears the LORD, she shall be praised.
> Give her the product of her hands,
> And let her works praise her in the gates.

Such portraits, as the two presented above, call all of us to the quintessence of *leading right*: providing selfless service towards a higher purpose or a new city as in the Biblical Book of Revelation[27]; shaking people from complacency by raising the matter of legacy before their eyes and making them accept that they are history makers; modeling optimistic engagement with the world (decadent and troubled as that world may be); and focusing on raising not followers but other leaders through genuine delegation and empowerment.

With particular attention to the 'virtuous wife' metaphor, you have a leader that is: good, supportive, trusting, and hardworking; making right decisions; serving others out of the excess of her work and the leaning of her heart; educated about the worlds of governance, business, security, etc; having a tremendous influence on her people's productivity; freeing her people to serve with her established reputation; partnering reliably with her people; looking out for everyone's interests; and giving her nation a sense of security that is greatly lacking in the world around.

Not all individual leaders currently exemplify these characteristics. This may present the leadership paradigm that the portraits reveal as 'too near perfection' to be realizable. Nevertheless, they are metaphors of the daily manifestations of *leading right* by which we must judge our prospective and self-proclaimed leaders so that we can aim higher and righter than where we have set our individual or corporate leadership bars to date.

As Cochrane (n.d) observed, "this nation, and indeed the whole world, has come to its current sorry condition because we have set our bar too low. We have expected too little. We have excused indiscretions and fabrications as necessary evils. We have demanded selfish objectives for ourselves" rather than demand selfless and transfigurational (ala virtuous) leadership for our world.

Leading right (and the virtuous leadership that it points to), though still a tall order, requires no more that bringing together in a rather unique way the shepherding (people-oriented), visionary (goal-oriented) and administrative (disciplined and resourceful) responsibilities – aimed at producing a transfigurational impact. Such leadership becomes extremely critical in situations where our world (like sheep) has become disoriented, confused, frightened, unable to ward off hungry predators, and incapable of finding its way back to the fold of a right-living existence.

The shepherd in this situation leads, feeds, nurtures, comforts, corrects and protects – doing all this by modeling goodness and uprightness in his or her own life and encouraging others to follow his/her example[28]. The leader feeds and nourishes the people with the only food which will produce strong, vibrant people[29]. S/he does the comforting with the balm of compassion and love: "binding up the injured and strengthening the weak in his organization or nation"[30]. S/he corrects and disciplines those in their care when they go astray – not with rancor or an overbearing spirit, but with a "spirit of gentleness" - according to the value-based principles for their human entities[31]. And, s/he protects from predators who take people astray from the truth - they come in sheep's clothing, but inwardly they are ferocious wolves[32].

The visionary dimension provides direction and development, establishing teams that can take initiatives at every point on the journey out of the disorientation, confusion, fear, helplessness in the face of predatory enemies, and incapacity for right-living. All of this requires planning and coordination (of appropriate programmes and procedures) which the administrative dimension is best suited to provide.

Properly deployed, these responsibilities can save the human entities from loveless interaction, stagnation or going nowhere, and floundering or having everyone doing what is 'right' in their own eyes. Such conducts, we know, are carried out at the expense of the collective success. Only a radicalized agenda of leadership, intent on instituting and/or carrying out the shepherding, visioning, and administrative responsibilities can change the destiny of human entities for good.

Concluding remarks

The leadership phenomenon becomes generally demystified and, by that fact, more accessible when considered in its paradigmatic expressions. In philosophy, behavioural patterns and outcomes, each of the four paradigms reviewed in this Chapter shows unique traits. They also produce different state of affairs in the human entities where they are practised.

In one camp, there is the defiant paradigm that shows the overbearing power which people in positions exercise over followers. They extract from these followers forced obedience and, invariably, reap diminished performance at best or, at worst, dysfunctional and rebellion-prone entities. There is also the compliant paradigm that lacks decisiveness and resorts to manipulative 'deals'. The resulting 'contingency' leadership produces 'everyman-to-himself' state of affairs and a human entity going nowhere.

In another camp, we have the authentic paradigm in which leaders are attuned to individual and corporate needs, strengths, and purposes. These leaders, while focused on results-orientation, seek to transform their followers through social bonding and professional development. In return, they get the community that is well engaged and willing to make their corporate vision happen. We also have the virtuous paradigm in which leaders pursue goodness, correctness, and rightness in all that they do. By character, they have a refining effect on things and people that they come in contact with. Being virtues-based in their practices, these leaders produce radiant and splendid human entities, with enviable relational beauty.

Of the four paradigms, the virtuous brand seems to suffer the greatest paradox of being the most needful for our troubled world and the one easily rejected because it is seemingly too idyllic to be realisable. By presenting it as the apogee of leadership in this book, we have raised it as an 'ideal type' in the Weberian[33] sense. That means, it is the type of perfection (though seemingly abstract and unattainable) to which people can (indeed, must) aspire and towards which they can journey. To embark on this journey, we have encouraged us to start with history and the insight therefrom, articulate the radicalising agenda of *leading right* whose core contents we have outlined, and give life to the brand as exemplified in the two portraits.

In the Chapters that follow, I will narrate how we have demonstrated possibilities in the direction of this agenda – anchored to our experience at Salem University and using the framework of the core elements of *leading right* as outlined in the Prologue to this book. The socio-economic and political realities at the time of my leadership as pioneer Vice Chancellor of the University were symptomatic predominantly of the defiant and compliant brands of leadership in the land.

So, when we turned up with a call, discipline, determination and dedication to lead right (in the camp of authentic and virtuous brands), we came up against a fierce battle. The full story of that battle would be for another project. Suffice it to say here, we courageously stayed the course. Against all odds, our team made the University happen – of course with the help of the Proprietor, the Board of Trustees and the Governing Council! Thankfully, testimonies are that we did this in the direction of *virtuousness*. And this, in our view, not only makes the story worth telling. It also makes it pleasant to tell it from an overcoming angle and to use it to promote the *virtuous leadership* brand which I believe is the hope of our world.

2 Call: beginning well

On 2 May, 2012, the African Command Office of the Mission for Africa International came to Salem University, Lokoja, Kogi State, Nigeria and conferred on me the *Outstanding Leadership (Executive Chaplain) Award* at the rank of Major-General of the conventional army. The Award, according to the Command Office, was in recognition of what they described as my "dynamic and purposeful leadership that has affected lives positively and worthy of emulation by others".

At the time, I just entered my fifth year as the pioneer Vice Chancellor of that University. This was the leadership responsibility I returned from Australia in 2008 to assume, after a sojourn of over 20 years in that country. In the lead up to my travel to Australia, I was already severally involved in responsibility roles both in the community and professional arenas alike.

An overview of these roles (in terms of how I came into them and how I actually discharged them) suggests to me that 'calling' is vitally essential to beginning (and indeed, finishing) well a leadership journey worthy of its name. For each of these roles, I felt some kind of 'powerful, magnetic force' drawing me to service and simultaneously driving me to a state of intrinsic lack of selfish interest about the role. On each occasion, my acceptance of the role felt more like an act of obedience than an opportunity to be grabbed. In hindsight, I could see a sequence of moments in which I just stepped into 'the space', no matter how awkward the space was, and did so because of the desire to make a difference.

Role recollection - Nigeria

During my secondary school years at St Peter's College, Idah (1971-75), I served as the Prayer Secretary and, later as, President of the Fellowship of Christian Students (FCS). Because of my love, passion and commitment to sports, I was also elected the Captain of one of the four sports groups in the College (Attah House). Then, for reasons unknown to me at the time, I was appointed as the Head Boy of the College to lead a population of about 400 students, beginning from the second half of my fourth year at the College. Over 30 years later, at the Golden Jubilee celebration of the College, I ran into the Principal of the College, Mr J.F. Aduku, who appointed me. I was then in my Vice Chancellor role. He said: "I saw a unique leadership character in you back then in those days of St Peter's College. Not only was I proved right then, I am glad you have kept that character".

After I completed my studies from the College in 1975, I headed to the Federal School of Arts and Science, Mubi in the then Gongola State, where I did my Higher School Certificate (1975-77). In that School, I served as the FCS Secretary-General, coordinating ecclesiastical and pastoral care activities, along with planning and leading outreaches and community concerts in the Executive Council. Also, I was appointed a class leader to liaise with lecturers on academic and welfare matters. In the School Drama Group, I served as a leader and also played lead roles in most of the plays that the Group staged, including *The Gods Are Not Blame* (by Wole Sonyika) where I acted the part of King Adewale.

In my undergraduate years at Ahmadu Bello University, Zaria (1977-80), I was an active leader in the FCS Drama Group; became the Bible Study Secretary of the FCS; and served as the Secretary to the Bus Fund Committee which raised money and bought buses for the Fellowship. At the community level, I was an amateur lead guitarist starting with a musical Group called *The Messengers*. Together with a brother and friend, Attah Haruna, we ignited the musical fire at Idah that has now engulfed the Qua Ibo Church (now known as United Evangelical Church). Within that period also, I became a founding member and one of the leaders in the Board of Trustees of *The Reconcilers Ministry*, a group dedicated to the uplift of Igalaland to enable it enter its positive purpose in Nigeria.

Upon graduation, I went for the National Youth Corps Service (1980-81) at Ikirun in the then Oyo State (now Osun State). In addition to my official duties as a Corper, I served as the Secretary-General of the State Corpers Fellowship. When I returned to Ahmadu Bello University to take up a teaching appointment, I was appointed to the position of Acting Head of the Sociology Programme at the School of Basic Studies of the University (1982-83).

I later moved over to the Faculty of Arts and Social Sciences of the University and served in several capacities including, the Departmental Representative on the Faculty Admissions and Registration Committee (1984-87); Departmental Examination Officer, Sociology Department (1985-86); Departmental Students Registration Officer (1986-87); and Acting General Secretary of the National Anthropological and Sociological Association, Nigeria (1985-87). In the community, I became the Secretary-General of the Graduate Fellowship (1983-85); and subsequently served as the Secretary-General of the Chapel of Redemption in the University (1985-87).

In all of these roles (from St Peter's College to Ahmadu Bello University), I was constantly driven by the values of integrity, accountability, and professionalism. For instance, my appointment as the Head Boy at St Peter's College brought me in to replace the student government 'leader' who became mired deep in some moral failings. I completed that tenure enviably and on an exemplary note. In the other subsequent roles, the character and competence which my electors/appointers saw never failed me all through those periods.

Role recollection - Australia

Then I left for Australia early 1988 for my doctoral studies at the Australian National University, Canberra. Same year, I became a *pro bono* liaison officer for the postgraduate students housed in the estate of the University on Canberra Avenue, in the Forest suburb of the capital city. In the period of 1989-91, I served as a Member of the Council of Elders of the O'Connor Uniting Church (later Grace Ministries), Canberra, which was responsible for the high level strategic leadership. I also established and led the African Fellowship - a group dedicated to helping students to focus on their goals effectively in the Australian society. From 1995 to 2000, now in Perth (Western Australia), I established and led as President another African Group to raise and empower members to attain their leadership destinies.

During much of the period between 2001 and 2007, I travelled widely as a motivational/intellectual speaker on social issues in Australia, Nigeria, South Africa, UK, the US, Canada, etc. I also served on the Executive Council of the International Society of Victimology, and in a position akin to Deputy Vice Chancellor in a tertiary institution devoted to the education of Indigenous Australians in the Northern Territory of Australia. For the latter, my responsibilities included strategic planning and organisational accountability; managing all the Institute's operations regarding prudent financial and human resource acquisition/allocations/acquittals, developing and maintaining property/facilities, managing students & staff wellbeing, and coordinating complaints resolution. I had the fortune of being a senior member of a management team under an able leader.

Halfway in the same period, I made a foray into the Australian Commonwealth Government Public Service at the Senior Executive Services level where I led the Branch that had carriage for Leadership Policy, Repatriation, Human Rights, and Land Policy services. In this role, my responsibilities included: developing advice for the Ministers who oversighted the Departments that housed Indigenous Affairs; leading overseas representations and negotiations for the return of Indigenous human remains; and managing human and financial resources to perform Branch functions. In one instance of these negotiations, I represented as policy person on the Australian Government team in an arbitrated case that resulted in Aboriginal Australians securing the return of the human remains of their ancestors from a British institution in London[34].

This was 2007, and it marked a major breakthrough in a matter that had lingered for several years. In June of that year I was still in the euphoria of that unique success, when I sensed that my time in Australia was up for the time being. When exactly, where to, and what next, I did not know.

Midnight call

The following month (July, 2007), I received a phone call from Nigeria (night time in Australia) asking me if I had heard about Salem University, to which I said: "No". "But you know Bishop Samson Amaga", the caller further inquired. I said "Of course and what is the matter with him"? "No problems", he said. "It's just that he has developed the vision of establishing a new private university and we are led to approach you to become the pioneer Vice Chancellor". The caller then gave me an overview of the vision, particularly the focus of the University on raising global leaders with integrity that would change their world in a Godly way, against the backdrop of the rot in the university system at the time.

Although the overview immediately struck a strong cord with me and with my pre-existing burden for Nigeria (my fatherland), I told him to give me time to seek clearance about this calling before conveying my response. By and large, I received a positive nudge to this effect: "Nigeria needs this vision; there is a task that must be done, and you have been prepared over time for this". Thereafter, I shared the calling with my family who gave their blessings - sort of, considering that this meant leaving the children behind in their various engagements. I subsequently notified my mentors and work colleagues. They all expressed reservations for good reasons, but conceded that I should go if I felt strongly about it, knowing that in the past I had not discussed any matters that way without following through.

I eventually conveyed to the proprietor of the University around October 2007 my agreement to consider the offer. Even then, when the details of the offer finally came, I was still struggling with the whole thing; wondering why I should not be left alone to "enjoy" life a little bit more in Australia at the level that I had reached; and certainly the fact that our last two children were still schooling at the time weighed heavily on my mind. My main mentor counseled that I should not resign my work with the Australian Commonwealth Government but go try it out – in case I decided to return within one year.

Other friends (including a Vice Chancellor of one of the universities in Nigeria) counseled that I must see evidence of at least N2.0 billion in a dedicated bank account for the University before accepting to go and pioneer, considering that some universities had been started by private proprietors who could not sustain them. This counsel came from people who cared deeply about me.

Finally, in my study of the book of Jeremiah 1: 1-19 in the Bible, I got a fresh insight into the nature of the calling that had come; the task involved; and the protection that would be available to me. The calling was going to be as tough as that of "a prophet to the nations" (v5). The task would involve rooting out and pulling down disempowering mindsets, destroying and throwing down uncomely practices, and then building and planting rightful standards (v10). There would be a personal fortification against opposing kings, princes, priests and people of the land over which they could not prevail (vv18-19).

All this was meant to address the fears that I was entertaining about leaving the now familiar and safe ground, to return to a land that was reportedly infested with evils too numerous to list and being unduly exposed to insecurity. In the end, I felt 'commandeered' to go; helped by the miraculous way in which the dilemma over our house in Canberra was resolved within an unbelievably short time. I was convinced and freed to go; and I left Australia in the company of my wife on 8 March 2008 to begin a new leadership journey at a University that existed virtually on paper in Nigeria at that time.

This return to Nigeria in 2008, and assuming office as the pioneer Vice Chancellor of Salem University, opened up another vista for me to experience different intricacies of leadership. In my first meeting with the University Board of Trustees on the night of our arrival (9 March), I got from all the talks the impression that the vision was indeed a very tall order. Recall the information from the caller while I was in Australia, that Salem University was conceived for the sole purpose of "raising global leaders with integrity that would change their world in a Godly way".

The Board of Trustees made that information clearer: the University would be a vision-driven institution, with a corrective and standard-setting mission mandate which was tagged *Transformational Academic Revolution* Mandate. I understood from the enunciation of the philosophy, goals and objectives of the University that night, that the task was "to run a university of the highest standard" (Academic Brief Vol. 1, p3) – academically and morally.

In the words of the Chancellor, "the University [would] operate a governance system that provides an enabling environment for the establishment of a citadel of learning of exceptional distinction"[35]. The building of this University was to be pursued in strict observance of the eight core values defined for the University, namely: Godliness, Confidence, Mental Empowerment, Integrity, Accountability, Diligence and Resourcefulness, Sense of Priority, and Synergy.

Both these expectations and their undergirding values were virtually non-existent in most institutional arrangements in Nigeria as at that time. So, what magic would perform this feat? I wondered. Nevertheless, in my response, I reiterated the commitment I had expressed in my acceptance letter, and that I had come for good and would, with the grace of God and the help of all present, give my best.

In the next four months, I stayed at the Chancellor's residence in Abuja, getting to know more clearly his heartbeat as the Visioner, while commuting between Abuja and Lokoja in the full swing of work. By the time I relocated to Lokoja around July 2008, I had no illusion as to what the vision bearers wanted and the challenges ahead. It became particularly clear to me that resources would become a major issue – too early for comfort in the take-off days of a new university, but that was the reality I perceived. At the same time, speed was necessary as we had to race against time to get ready for the full take-off within six months from that point.

Thus, in the assumption year and against the backdrop of this sense of a tall order and restricted resources, we started laying what I determined would be an enduring foundation for a unique university. We progressed the establishment of the governance bodies, commenced recruitment for staffing, pursued infrastructural development (one became an "expert" in buildings and constructions overnight), established the framework for admission practices, and concluded the curriculum development, consistent with the vision and in readiness for take-off.

Pew! The University did commence academic programmes on 30 January, 2009; and for the next four arduous years, we continually labored to build the University of this unique vision. "Look, the vision was a dream before you came, but now we have a University. No one can ask more from you!" (emphasis added). That was a comment by a member of the University Governing Council (also a highly regarded member of the Board of Trustees) after the meeting of the Council on 4-5 August 2012. Incidentally, it was at that meeting that the Council, among other matters, approved my request to disengage from the University as Vice Chancellor with effect from September 2012. We were coming out of the meeting, and the member was still wondering why I had to disengage at that time. Suddenly, that member stopped and made the comment. Though humbling, it gave me a perspective on the reality of where we had arrived.

Fortuitously, the following day this University that we now had, captured the attention of the renowned Professor Peter Okebukola. He led to our Campus on 6 August 2012, the Independent Corrupt Practices and Other Related Offences Commission delegation on University System Study and Review (ICPC Team) to examine what had announced Salem University to the world as an exemplar of anti-corruption management and leadership. At the end of that day, he wrote in our Guest Book: "Highly impressed with the 'A' grade take-off and efforts to lower/eliminate corrupt practices ravaging other universities. We urge the Chancellor and the other officers of the University – Chairman BOT, Chairman Council, and VC to keep up the good work".

Considering that Professor Okebukola was a former Executive Secretary of Nigeria's National Universities Commission (NUC) during whose tenure the application for the licence to operate Salem University was lodged, and considering that he was at that time the Pro-Chancellor and Chairman of Governing Council in about three Universities in Nigeria and a prominent quality assurance guru in African universities who had drawn on standards from Harvard, Yale, Oxford, Cambridge, Covenant, etc, his view on the state of Salem University on the eve of my departure was weighty and instructive indeed.

This book tells the story of the kind of leadership with which we built the University that was judged to have demonstrated "the 'A' grade take-off and efforts to lower/eliminate corrupt practices ravaging other universities". I can call to mind that the Command Office that gave me an Outstanding Leadership Award had described my leadership as transparent and transformational over time. However, it was what others (especially some of my fellow Vice Chancellors) had described in relation to my time at the Univesity as me "leading right" that has continually exercised my mind. Hence, the title for this book.

Among the several congratulatory messages I received on the completion of my tenure, the one below was quite illustrative of that sentiment:

> ... I felicitate with you on the successful completion of your glorious and eventful tenure as the pioneer Vice Chancellor... We appreciate God for the wisdom and grace bestowed on you for the great pioneering work of building a solid foundation for Salem University. The giant strides made by the University within the short period of its existence is quite validating and evidently points to your passion and drive for excellence. Without doubt, you have engraved your name on the sands of time not only in Salem University but in the entire history of University Education in Nigeria... We hope you will be returning [from Australia] home shortly to Nigeria, noting the enormous task of building a great nation for our God and humanity...

These messages suggest that people saw something more than ordinary leadership at work during my tenure. Perhaps, as I sketch in this book, what we actually did might shed more light on this leadership characterisation.

Concluding remarks

While many hands were involved in the main life story to which I have anchored this book, and their own contributions merit a narrative in their own right, the focus here is on my **personal odyssey**. I have captioned it the "audacity of leading right" because most of the circumstances of the University's take-off would have provoked a different leadership complex and produced contrary or less salutary results but for the tenacity and focus of purpose with which we carried out our leadership responsibilities.

I could have packed my things and returned to Australia when confronted with the reality of a tall-order vision with a highly constrained funding base to execute it. The sense of being called held me back. And, we audaciously refused to be co-opted by the highly reactive, often regressive atmosphere of chronically anxious and dysfunctional society in which we worked. The responsibility for this atmosphere lies squarely at the feet of the defiant and compliant brands of leadership in vogue at the time.

Since stepping down from the Vice Chancellor position, I have had more time to reflect on what it was that we did which made the difference. Along the line, I have become so eerily aware of the fact that there is so much about leadership that people who accept responsibilities still do not understand. Yes, the world is awash with literature on leadership and yet the subject remains puzzling as we saw in the Prologue to this book.

It is not just that there are different paradigms of leadership some of which we have identified. Moving from one to the other actually entails a paradigm shift or, more accurately, moving up or down a 'staircase'. As I have come to understand, the greatest accomplishment of any human entity is to shift or move progressively towards a brand of ultimate leadership which, as I have argued in this book, is *virtuous leadership*.

Although the telling of this story is predominantly anchored to my Salem University experience, I would not suggest that what we did there demonstrated the full scope of this ultimate brand of leadership. It is just that, in the rear view, one can see that the experience falls squarely in line with what I came to understand after I left office to be the trajectory of this brand.

Significantly, the experience has reinforced my very strong belief that considering the level of decadence to which societies around the world have descended in the last five decades or so, particularly on the African continent, it would take that ultimate brand of leadership to turn things around for good. This makes it more imperative that we explore this brand of leadership, and to do so, anchored to some reality that people can relate with, such as my Salem University experience.

It is a privilege for me to have been part of this reality and to now have you come along on this journey of discovery about what virtuous leadership stands for. The audacity with which we practised the rudiments of this brand of leadership in the Salem University context should be a pointer to what it would take to deploy it in the lives of nations, particularly those that are steep deep in decadence.

---

13   My best. This is the core criterion of excellence I espoused for the University community. See Chapter Five of this book.

14   Kurt Lewin, focusing mainly on behavioural patterns, constructed 'authoritative or autocratic', 'participative or democratic', and 'delegative or 'free reign' brands of leadership. To these three, Evanson adds the fourth one: 'servant' leadership brand.

15   Occasional paper to the Caleb Leadership Academy, Caleb University, Imota, Lagos State, 13 March 2013.

16   Professor Gayle Avery of the School of Management in an Australian university, quoted in Tarrant (2007).

17   Mandela, speech at his Rivonia Trial, Pretoria Supreme Court, 20 April 1964.

18   'Adaptability', as a strong trait of genuine leadership, means 'getting to level in order to rescue and not getting to level in order to avoid responsibility or, in certain circumstance, the pain of making hard decisions.

[19]   Matthew 17: 1-9, Holy Bible.

[20]   http://en.wikipedia.org/wiki/Virtuous_Leadership

[21]   Jerry Kearney, in his review comments posted on 26 May 2009, is of the view that "the meritorious commendation of fundamental virtues [in Havard, 2007] is compromised by the biased citations of contemporary personalities".

http://www.amazon.com/ss/customer-reviews/1594170592/ref=cm_cr_dp_synop?_encoding=UTF8&ref_=cm_cr_dp_synop&showViewpoints=0&sortBy=bySubmissionDateDescending#R1QVZE9QM1WRIW

[22]   Review of Havard's *Virtuous Leadership*, posted on 28 January, 2008 – no author named.
http://www.amazon.com/review/R37HRUWXGWDT1R/ref=cm_cr_dp_title?ie=UTF8&ASIN=1594170592&nodeID=283155&store=books.

[23]   Consists of bribery, kickbacks, graft, embezzlement, cronyism, unholy alliances, deception, etc.

[24]   Consists of belief, conviction, agreement, willing action, etc.

[25]   Consists of raw power or force, extortion, threats, intimidation, harassment, discrimination, etc.

[26]   Proverbs 31: 10-31, *Holy Bible*. New American Standard version

[27]   Chapter 21: 1-11, Holy Bible, New King James Version.

[28]   The Apostle Paul understood this in his saying: "Follow my example, as I follow the example of Christ" (1 Corinthians 11:1)

[29]   "Man does not live on bread alone but on every word that comes from the mouth of the LORD" (Deutronomy 8:3; Matthew 4:4).

[30]   Ezekiel 34: 16.

[31]   "The LORD disciplines those he loves" Proverbs 3:12; Galatians 6:2.

[32]   Matthew 7: 15.

[33]   Max Weber was a German sociologist who constructed 'ideal types' as a conceptual tool with which to synthesise many diffuse, discreet and concrete individual phenomena into analytical units that are neither too specific nor too general for intellectual discourse

[34]   For these services, our efforts had been recognised with Departmental Secretary's Awards: Australia Day 2005 Secretary's Citation for Excellence in Managing Outcomes (Indigenous human remains from Sweden); Australia Day 2006 Secretary's Citation for Excellence in Managing Outcomes (Land Policy); and Australia Day 2007 Citation for Excellent results in the repatriation of Indigenous human remains (from the United Kingdom).

[35]   See "Foreword" in the University Academic Brief Vol. 1.

3 Vision: clarifying the task

After confirming a leadership calling in any given situation, *leading right* must begin with rightly discerning the task at hand. A vision that is not made plain cannot be pursued; and a vision that is not pursued cannot be possessed! So, a lot of successful leadership depends on this segment of vision-based projects.

A leader must give meaning to the vision he or she has been given to handle and, by so doing, establish direction to go and define the job to be done along the way. Unless this is done effectively at the beginning and on an on-going basis, it would be difficult to align people by words and deeds to the big picture, create teams and coalitions to understand the vision big picture and accept its validity, and then motivate and inspire them to get the right things done. In the circumstances, conventional leadership would struggle to make any headway, and *leading right* would certainly fail.

At Salem University, I led the team to whom it fell to give clarity to the University community concerning the vision that the Proprietor gave and enunciated for us. We needed to take the vision out of the pages of the relevant documents and give life to its inherent task for all the members of the University community to feel, handle, and make the University happen. It was a responsibility we took seriously from the word go. Considering the nature of the vision, ambiguity and uncertainty – by omission or commission, would have compromised it in our hands. "For if the trumpet makes an uncertain sound, who will prepare for battle?"[36]

University business ideology[37]

A member of the Governing Council[38] of Salem University once quipped in a meeting: "the task we have given the Vice Chancellor and his team is like asking them to raise saints in Sodom". Quite insightful! The infamy of Sodom and Gomorrah (two cities where no 10 righteous people could be found) is legendary. So, impossibility - as the quip implied - starred us in the face in our calling to build a unique University. And, as the arrowhead or the person on the driver's seat, the enormity of the task of building a university of the kind envisioned in a decadent society that Nigeria had become was not lost on me. My first responsibility was to make my co-travellers appreciate this crucial aspect.

As evident from some salient documents of the University, the vision, mission, mandate, philosophy, etc., all attest to the extraordinary nature of the task given to us to do. The Academic Brief (Volume 1) stated that "the vision of Salem University is to be a center of excellence for the production of graduates who are worthy in learning and character as well as sound in mind, body and spirit for outstanding leadership and global impact", (emphasis added).

The first portion of being a centre of excellence for the production of graduates that are worthy in learning and character is more or less generic in Nigeria. Almost all the Universities have that in their books. If the vision of Salem University stopped there, it would not have been any different. I expatiated on this issue in one of my several addresses to the University community. Focusing on the underlined portion of the vision, I demonstrated in that address that the task given to us to accomplish was more than the ordinary:

"Daring to be different: reflections on Salem University"[39]

... If the vision of Salem University stops at being "a centre of excellence for the production of graduates that is worthy in learning and character"...[t]here is no daring in that... *There are several* Universities in Nigeria that have that part *in their vision statements*... but have become... centres of excellence *allegedly* for the production of thieves..., armed robbers, ... rapist, ... looters, ... pen robbers, etc.

Not long ago I read a story about a university... in the Eastern part of Nigeria - *about* some students gang raping a female student. It made international news because I read about it when I was in Australia about three *or four* months ago... The University Management tried to manage that particular situation - several versions of the story are being told.

Also not long ago we had some report about some students from Kogi State University in Anyigba, *allegedly* taking their guns and going to do armed robbery along the road, killing some people and *being killed by Police*. That is a centre of excellence for the production of graduates who are worthy in learning and in character? Learning? Yes, I can see *but what are they learning?* How about character?

Salem University says we are not satisfied with the generic... It is the portion: "<u>as well as sound in mind, body and spirit for outstanding leadership and global impact</u>", that distinguishes your University from *several* other universities in Nigeria that I am aware of. It is the portion that encapsulates the daring to be different. Global staff that are here, especially all of us that came from the public sector where the *generic* part is the vision of those institutions, if you stop at that generic part you will fail not only this university buy you will fail yourself *also*.

You must know that the *vision* committed to our hands is not just making this place a centre of excellence for the production of graduates who are worthy in learning and in character. It must be a place where everyone - staff and students alike - develop a sound mind, sound body and sound spirit. This University believes in the triune nature of human beings. Every human being has three parts. Those who deny that turn themselves into animals...

Salem University is completely committed to all of us that come here - global leaders and staff alike - becoming sound in mind, body and spirit. That is why if for instance you (academic staff) have any *anger*... in your soul or you are troubled in your soul, you should find a way to get some help. Don't carry it to the classrooms and *download* it unto the global leaders. We call it transferred aggression.

...One of the things that surprised so many people including my fellow Vice Chancellors today is, when we tell them that we call our students 'global leaders', they say "Global kini?" – *a colloquial for* "What do you mean? Are they global leaders?" In fact one parent was bold enough to ask me that question. And I said, "oh you woman of little faith. You worked hard, struggled, prepared your child and brought him here. *Also*, you had read in our vision mandate that we are to raise global leaders and, after bringing your child here, you're still doubting? Is he really a global leader *right now*? Not yet. [To the participants, I said] In your thinking, in your mind and action, you may not be a global leader or a global staff, yet.

That particular concept [of global leader] is an aspirational label. It is the vision of the University for you. That is what we see you becoming. Anything else is unacceptable to the vision... The only person standing between you and that future is yourself. Nobody else!

The accompanying mission statement for the University was also extraordinary. In brief, the University was to "empower generational leaders for global impact; promote and enhance the talents and skills of the [students]… through the provision of quality education that guarantees balanced comprehensive curricula for the full development of the spiritual, intellectual, physical and social character of our future leaders; equip its students with the knowledge and skills necessary for… responsible and responsive leadership; and promote research both for its role as service to society in finding solutions to its problems and also as a means of enhancing intellectual development and confidence".

Anchored to both the vision and the mission, was the mandate of "Transformational Academic Revolution (TAR)" which was articulated in terms of the University being out to achieve the following:

1. Take academics from just cramming to pass examinations to the level of imparting knowledge and practical skills, thus equipping our students to be nation builders.

2. Produce graduates who will combine intelligence with integrity for we know that smartness can take a man to the top but only integrity can keep him on top.

3. Produce graduates who are sound in spirit, mind (intellect) and body thus creating wealth and making outstanding global impact.

4. Empower our students to be global leaders through promoting their natural abilities and enhancing their practical skills, making room for creative learning and cutting edge research intentionally targeted at proffering solutions to specific human needs. We will not just teach students what to do but how to practically solve human problems.

5. Raise global leaders with royalty and prestige who are simply change agents who will not:
   - settle for average, but strive for distinctive achievement in their area of calling;
   - be saturated with complacency, but shall stir up compassion for change and results;
   - rationalize their disappointment, but will go on to realize their dreams;
   - be governed by their darkest mistakes and deepest

regrets, but by their finest thoughts, greatest optimism, highest enthusiasm and their important experiences, knowing that God can turn their mistakes into miracles.

They will be leaders who seek out and create opportunities for others to excel.

In philosophy, Salem University was to "empower and transform her students to be spiritually alive, intellectually alert, physically disciplined and socially adapted to enable commitment to service for self-reliance". For this, the University was to develop an "educational system geared towards self-realization, better human relationships among all categories of people, and national and global unity as well as social, cultural, economic, political, scientific and technological progress".

And, in consonance with the name "Salem" which means "peace", the University was to provide "a peaceful learning environment to guarantee the continuity of academic programmes, instead of incessant strike actions that truncate academic programmes... and [the]... raising of leaders who shall be peaceful at home, work and in the society at large despite the chaos, troubles and challenges in the world". The University's graduates must be raised "with such peace in their spirit and soul to reflect in their physical behavioral pattern of non-violence to their fellow human beings".

As a church sponsored University, the philosophy was also to "model the students on the teachings of Jesus Christ in which love for God must translate into love for the fellow man and peace at heart which makes the man unruffled by circumstances; for a leader must not waver in the face of challenges." The commitment of Salem University is to help raise leaders that will promote peace in our world.

Even the logo of the University was meant to convey the uniqueness of the task. In its oval shape, the logo consists of an open book sitting on a golden pillar, flanked by yellow sheaves and nine white stars underneath. 'SU' being the acronym for Salem University is on top of the open book. A rising sun from a dark blue sky illuminates the background. The name of the University in purple color symbolizes royalty and prestige. The blue background is a symbol of peace requiring the University to be "a peaceful learning environment using the art of conflict management that enhances continuity of academics [and the raising of] ambassadors of peace".

The golden pillar is the symbol of strength and character: When a leader is trained to be competent and has no character, chaos is inevitable. We are raising leaders from Salem University who shall show character and integrity in the world that cries against leaders who lack integrity. This generation of leaders will stand out at work, at home and in society.

The nine white stars and the rising sun symbolize light to the world: Graduates of Salem University shall be as stars shining into the dark path of the earth in character, knowledge and wisdom that change things in their environment. The nine stars represent the fruits of the Holy Spirit namely, Love, Joy, Peace, Patience, Kindness, Goodness, Faithfulness, Gentleness and Self-Control.

The open book and the sheaves symbolize continuous attention to learning and knowledge as instruments of change and empowerment, as well as representing fruitfulness as in harvesting the wheat corn fully ripe in its season. Both demand that products of Salem University be not half baked or deficient in their disciplines. They shall be fruitful and a worthy reward for their generation and the world at large, creating impact wherever they go. And, as the motto of the University is "Knowledge, Empowerment and Self-Reliance", all graduates of Salem University will be equipped through training and education for creativity and self-reliance.

It is a paradigm shift from graduating job seekers to raising job creators with skills; a shift to raising quality leaders strong in wisdom, strong in character, priceless in integrity and excellence, who will be able to think for themselves and contribute to making the Nation and the world a better place.

Similarly, the University Anthem which was composed by the Chancellor of the University encapsulated the vision, mission, mandate and philosophy - all of which as we have seen above convey uniqueness and extraordinary responsibilities. As can be seen from the lyrics, Salem University is about raising Global Leaders, anointed to be bold for education yet untold; to proclaim transformation with power to all as 'end time soldiers', sent by the Lord.

The Global Leaders are the battle axes, and as ministers of great change they proclaim transformation with power to all. They are the change agents, telling others to rise, speaking and living bold, and with 'integrity…change our world'.

This Anthem was another potent directive in what was nothing short of a comprehensive intellectual and moral re-engineering task. Significantly, this task was enunciated at a time in Nigeria when socio-political and economic realities or demands were in a very bad shape. There were political assassinations, incessant labour unrests in the University system, inadequate and mismanagement of funding, dilapidated facilities on campuses, inadequate academic staff resulting from brain drain and failure of the postgraduate system, and other vices.

At that time, the Federal Government of Nigeria decided to involve the private sector in the establishment of universities because of the problems faced by many prospective students who could not gain admission into the limited places available in the existing public universities. There was also the fact that competing demands on the finances of the country did not allow for the establishment of more public universities.

In the rationale for the proposal to establish Salem University, the following background issues relevant to understanding the task of the vision were identified among several key constraints of the existing Nigerian universities:

1. Existing universities do not emphasize the total man beyond the disciplinary focus..., and they fail to stress the empirical fact that most graduates will be judged 15 years after graduation not by their major (discipline) in the university at the first degree level but by how their "total man" entity has performed in the market place, the polity and the society.

    As a corollary, existing universities have failed to emphasize the fact that their products are going to be judged decades after their graduation not so much by the specific contents of their disciplines at the first degree level but rather by their character, and they have failed to develop the learning environment and course content that will impart those desirable attributes that make the "total man" who will positively transform society.

2. Existing universities impart knowledge in the various disciplines in a value vacuum. Because no core values are transmitted, students graduate from these universities without a set of shared values with the result that on graduation, they join the larger society with its legacy of corruption, instability in the home, poor leadership qualities, lack of patriotism and poor work ethics, among other vices.

Interpreting the Task

How did we understand this Task? What did it call us to do? How would we communicate it to the stakeholders? These were some of the questions that confronted us early on as we grappled with the vision and sought to give life to what was obviously a heavy-duty assignment.

The earliest interpretations of this task featured in the Chancellor's first Charge and my first Message as the Vice Chancellor, both of which (excerpts only) are reproduced below from the maiden Salem University Students' Handbook:

Chancellor's Welcome Charge

Welcome on board.

Salem University Lokoja, is out to achieve the vision of raising leaders who are spiritually alive, mentally alert and intellectually developed to change their world in a Godly way. Our mission is to spark a Transformational Academic Revolution.

We have admitted you as work in progress but you will be released as a global leader empowered to be a positive change agent – a catalyst for change that will not settle for the average, but strive for distinctive achievement in the area of your calling; will not be saturated with complacency, but shall stir up compassion for change and result; will not rationalize your disappointment, but will go on to realize your dreams.

… Our core values are meant to help you combine intelligence with integrity – for smartness can take you to the top, but only integrity can keep there.

You may have read the histories of many. It is easier to read a history than to make a positive one. This is your time to prepare for a great and impactful life. Nothing is as difficult as it first appears… Success is not a mystery but a predictable outcome based on positive attitude, habits and proven principles. You have all it takes to succeed and be a positive difference maker in our negative world.

… Doing the same thing and expecting a different result is one definition of insanity. Globally, nations are doing the same thing and expecting different results especially in governance. Everything rises and falls on leadership. That is why we are embarking on this vital process of raising you as a global leader to do things differently and rightly, and to make positive influence in our world.

…You will emerge a leader God and humanity will be proud of in Jesus name.

You shall set the pace for others to follow in Jesus name.

No evil shall befall you on this destiny journey in Jesus name. The covenant of God's presence shall abide with you all the days of your time here in Jesus name.

Welcome to Salem University where global leaders are raised.

Archbishop Sam Amaga
CHANCELLOR

....

Vice Chancellor's message

There is something special about favoured firstborns. They lead the breakthrough for subsequent generations.

... By reason of being in the pioneer sets, you also carry the unique responsibility of setting for the Campus the standard for academic and spiritual excellence in leadership for nations. You will have succeeded if you become a flag bearer in the University's transformational academic revolution, designed to raise leaders that will combine basic knowledge with entrepreneurial skills, and intelligence with integrity, to positively change their world.

Most leaders of yesteryears promoted, tolerated, or bowed to poverty, corruption and insecurity. Today's leaders are asking questions about these ills – a welcome progress. Tomorrow's leaders from Salem University will not only ask questions; they will take action to right these wrongs and put nations on solid paths to prosperity, civility, and security. We expect you to do or endure whatever it takes to be one of such leaders starting from today.

Study the lives of pioneers! And, you will see how they experienced challenges of different kinds – some good, others bad – but all were life transforming. Their perseverance bequeathed to posterity the essence of their dreams.

... On behalf of the entire University management and community, I welcome you to this noble vision. Our history, mission and mandate, which you will read on the pages of this *Handbook*, show that there is a rich heritage from which you can successfully launch your university education and future role as a dedicated, devoted, disciplined, and God-fearing leader.

... We are committed to your success as a leader, because we believe in the power of Godly leadership in shaping destinies for good. I echo the prayers of the Chancellor for the God of Salem University to help you succeed as you commit your ways to Him.

Enjoy your University!

Professor Paul Omojo Omaji
VICE CHANCELLOR

Subsequently, we took every appropriate opportunity to continually interpret the task so that the University community could understand and buy deeply into the project. For instance, in my maiden matriculation ceremony address on 9 April, 2009, I emphasized the reason for being for the University:

...This is a very special day in the life of our University. It is our maiden matriculation day. When the day is done, there will be students that we can formally call our own: our firstborn children; our global leaders in the making. They will become fully inducted into our academic and character molding community. A unique history will have been made by this ceremony.

...When I took up the reins as Pioneer Vice Chancellor of the University in March 2008, I had very little idea of what laid ahead. This much I knew: that it would entail crafting from ground zero the systems for the academic and administrative operations of the University.

...All we have done to date, and will continue to do, has been defined by the task given to us by the Chancellor, namely to raise transformational global leaders who are thoroughly grounded in learning and character to change their world for good in a Godly way. The University Anthem conveys this mission...

We have set out pursuing this task, guided by the core values of Godliness, Confidence, Mental Empowerment, Integrity, Accountability, Diligence & Resourcefulness, Sense of Priority, and Synergy. Along the way, we have been helped by key external stakeholders...

Now let me turn to the matriculants... Apart from the academic knowledge, you will also acquire moral values to help you with your own future development. We will make faith, integrity and excellence very real to you in your studies. Your colleagues in the wider world should be able to tell the different values that you would have acquired after the programme. We are very confident that when you complete the undergraduate programme, you will truly be an agent of positive change that we as a University desire.

...In all your pursuits on this campus, remember what the Lord has said in Isaiah 41:10: *"So do not fear, for I am with you; do not be dismayed, for I am your God. I will strengthen you and help you; I will uphold you with my righteous right hand"*. Stay blessed.

Professor Paul Omojo Omaji
Vice Chancellor.

A few months later, the University entered into a partnership arrangement with Kogi State Government to train about 300 of what the Government framed as "restive youth". At the flag-off of this arrangement on 13 October, 2009, which brought the Kogi State Governor to the University for the first time, I also interpreted the task given to us in an address titled: "TOGETHER WE CAN RESTORE: Pro-active Partnership for Youth Productive Citizenship".

...On behalf of the Chancellor of Salem University, Archbishop (Dr) Sam Amaga, and the entire University community, I welcome you all to our young, vibrant, enviable, and destiny-making Campus.

The occasion that has brought you here today is unique both in our short history and the more extended history of university education in Kogi State. We are here to celebrate the official flag-off of the youth entrepreneurship training programme which Salem University has developed in partnership with Kogi State Youth Empowerment Scheme.

...Amazingly, Salem University had independently and from inception nursed the essence of your [Excellency's] vision about the youth. From the Chancellor, through my humble self, to most of the Management and the generality of the University community, there is a river of aspiration to make global leaders out of young people.

...You [the Governor and his Government] will receive at the end of their studies young dynamic leaders who combine intelligence with integrity; who are strong in wisdom by means of renewing their spirit, soul and body. They will simply become unstoppable change agents.

... The restoration of the youth is non-negotiable and is everybody's business. The youth are not only leaders of tomorrow, they are leaders of today!!! *They already have too many bad things to die for. They must be given something to live for.*

You [the youth] and your community do not need to tolerate or bow down to poverty, corruption, violence and insecurity. As a participant in this empowerment programme from Salem University, you will be equipped and expected to take action to right these wrongs. By so doing, you will put your community, Kogi State, and indeed the nation on solid paths to civility, security, and prosperity... Enjoy our University! And God bless.

Nearly one year after this event, I was addressing the University community during the Founder's Day Celebration (6 August, 2010) and reminded them about what I understood we had been called to do. Among other things, I said:

...Friends! We live in a globalised world. It is insane to continue with approaches that have produced localised and self-serving leaders *and expect different results*. That is why the Founder of Salem University we are celebrating today, was given the vision mandate of transformational academic revolution which is meant to train people to become global problem-solvers and leaders that their generations, right now and the ones to come, will be proud of. For those people who have *recently* come into this vision, the Founder is sustaining this University for a number of reasons and I'm going to just outline a few. He is sustaining a University that:

1. believes in you to become a global leader and will treat you as such - in spite of your, let me say, infirmities. In spite of your short comings, we still refer to, and regard, you as global leaders. We treat you as such. We want you to become global leaders;
2. challenges you to bring out the best from your innate potentials and possibilities;
3. is committed to academic excellence for you;
4. pursues character-molding based on the core Godly values that define our existence;
5. stands firmly against cultism, examination malpractices, staff malpractices and other vices that have debased tertiary education in Nigeria; and
6. works in partnership with you and your sponsors and parents to attain the shared common goal of raising a well-rounded graduate prepared to transform your world for good.

That is our vision. Such a Founder is worth celebrating and this is the person that we are gathered today to celebrate. Happy Founder's Day. And God bless.

Three years into my tenure, I gave the most extensive interpretation of the task as I still understood it on the prestigious Nigerian Television Authority One-on-One Program. The NTA presenter, Mr Bayo Adewusi, interviewed me for one long hour. Although the resonance of the program is better felt in the DVD format, I have endeavoured to reproduce here some excerpts as faithfully as possible.

Presenter: My guest is a Professor of Criminology who has spent twenty (20) years of his academic and professional life in Australia. He is the pioneer Vice Chancellor of Salem University Lokoja. Please welcome Professor Paul Omaji.

VC: Thank you very much; nice to be here...

Presenter: Now, Salem University - there have been in the recent past the proliferation of private Universities and now there is Salem University. What unusual qualities does Salem University bring into the educational sector?

VC: Thank you very much. Let me tell you what Salem

University stands for. It is a University with a vision to raise Global leaders; these are people that would impact the world positively; those that would combine intelligence with integrity; those that would combine knowledge and character. So, the University is fundamentally committed *in a unique way* to the two planks or platforms of higher education that we talk about in this country: worthy in learning and in character. The University has tried as much as possible to bring these two elements together in a very pungent way.

Now, the context is very simple: there was a time in this country when tertiary education, particularly University education was good. Go anywhere in the world, carry the certificate of any University in Nigeria and you were respected. They knew the power and the knowledge behind the certificate. Then came a time when the certificate never represented anything (worthless). Why? Because there was a lot of decadence in our educational system. And we are all talking about a situation where over 80% of those who applied for the University never had any access to go in. And lastly, we had a situation where there was only one and one choice; you either go to a public University or there was nothing else for you to do. Quite different from what you have in developed countries.

So in that context, the Government began to realize the need to bring other partners in, to help develop in lifting University education to a higher level where it can be respected again. Salem University was born in that context. The visioner of the University, Arcbishop Dr. Sam Amaga received a vision of setting up a University that would raise global leaders; University that would bring in Christian ethos, Christian values (the core values) that drive quality education... This is how Salem University came to being.

Presenter: Yes sir! But you must be very aware of the fact that there were other Universities that run on the Christian ethos. So, what makes Salem University... exceptional? Why would I rather send my child to your University as opposed to other Christian Universities?

VC: Other Christian Universities that uphold the core values of the faith are in the same boat with Salem University. Salem University holds them in very high regard. But what Salem University does which in my view is unique is focusing on raising leaders. In other words, we have identified where the crunch of the issue is - the need of the hour, and it is about leadership. Our country for the past fifty-sixty years has been groping in the dark.

We've had leaders before but when you talk about leaders today, we go back to the fifties. What happened in-between - between the sixties and now?

Salem University says there is a need to focus on bringing into being a crop, a new breed of leaders. That is why for example when the Chancellor of the University was granted the licence to start the University, and some people went to him and said "thank you so much; now that you have gotten the licence, go to Obajana - a cement factory close to the location of the University in Lokoja, go and get empty containers, cut doors and windows into them and start running your own University; the Chancellor said no! This University is about raising unique leaders and you don't raise leaders from containers. Anybody you bring up in containers would develop container mentality. So, Salem University is about establishing the platform where quite a number of these global leaders would indeed lead and lead effectively.

...

Presenter: What are the qualifications; is it the same basic qualification that would get you into any other University in Nigeria?

VC: Yes, well! The qualifications required to get admission into our University are published in the Joint Admissions and Matriculation Board brochure; so if you go to that brochure you will see all of them there. In addition to that, the University does its own post-UTME screening.

...

Presenter: Now, what is involved in your screening?

VC: In our screening, we get *candidates* to go through some aptitude test; basic aptitude test. We get them to reflect on life; we get them to express themselves orally and in some cases in writing so that we can see the potential they are bringing in. Remember, we have lived in this country where a number of ways has been devised to beat the normal *process* of assessing the capability of students. So what Salem University does is to find out who... well, if you tell me ...

Presenter: Well sir! Sorry to interrupt you right now. In this screening exercise, are you able within such a period to determine character?

VC: That is what we look for! Are we 100 per cent certain at that particular aspect...? No! But we look for potentials; that is why I used the word "potentials". And all the University needs is to locate the potential in the person and then we build on that potential. We refer to our students as global leaders right from day one of entering into the University.

Presenter: But you haven't graduated?

VC: No! We haven't. What we are doing is to put on them an aspirational label. You have come in here, your destiny is very clear to us as a University management. You are a global leader. So, we now work with you to build on the potentials that you have brought until you graduate from the University *as a global leader*.

...

Presenter: Sir, let's go to, this is of particularly interest to me, this College of Regional Integration and Diplomacy.

VC: It's a Department.

Presenter: What's the student population?

VC: At the moment, in fact, it is one of our popular courses and we have the numbers ranging from fifteen to thirty. For a program we started barely two years ago, this is a very good subscription; the number is growing. Recently, we actually took our global leaders *studying in that program* (those in 300 level) for a tour. They visited the National Institute for International Affairs here in Lagos, they went to Accra in Ghana to interact with people on ground.

So, it is our own way of vocationalising our programs. And this is the instruction given to all academic staff regardless of what they are teaching: whether it is English or it is Mathematics or it is Physics; they must vocationalise. *I use to challenge them regularly with this:*

"If any person passes through your class they must be able to do something with the knowledge they have got to sustain them, to develop self-reliance and to be able to create job for others. So, when they leave the University they don't depend on government - running around from office to office with the certificate in their hands looking for jobs. They would be able to think about something creatively and positively to do and become self-reliant. The motto of the University is Knowledge, Empowerment and Self-reliance".

Presenter: Knowledge, empowerment and self-reliance?

VC: Yes!

Presenter: But that hasn't been put to test yet because you haven't graduated the students. So we have to wait to graduate the students, let them go into job market, let them go into the world and then we would be in a better position to assess their contribution. Don't you think so?

VC: Here is the good news. Some of our global leaders have already established their own businesses. Let me give you an example: one of our global leaders went on holidays (a student of our ICT), and while he was there somebody wanted to develop a website but looked down on him, saying "what do you know?" The global leader said, "Sir, I can help you... Well, you don't need to pay me, just give me a chance." He did the website; *the man was so impressed and paid him handsomely*. The global leader came back to the University with five hundred thousand naira (N500,000.00) - for just one effort. And many of them have set up their own businesses; they have their business names, they have developed their websites. So, we are not waiting until they graduate.

Presenter: So you also teach them to be business literate?

VC: Exactly!

Presenter: You teach them; you equip them to be self-sufficient when they leave school?

VC: Yes! Entrepreneurial spirit is what we are building into them. Now, we have a lot of ways to go in terms of actually establishing most of the facilities we need. But right now we are focusing on one cardinal or prime element of entrepreneurship and that is attitude. You have knowledge, you have skills and you have attitude.

Presenter: Attitude is everything?

VC: Oh yes! Attitude drives every other thing that you do. And the University is focusing on that. We have as a matter of fact a program that we call TLTC-Total Leadership Training Concept. This develops activities to help our global leaders establish foundational character upon which they can build their businesses; upon which they can build their knowledge. So, it's a holistic approach that Salem University has taken to University education. I went through university education in this country. I did my first degree and my master's degree in Sociology and Criminology, respectively.

Presenter: Before you went to Australia?

VC: Before I went to Australia; and I know the difference between what I experienced then and what Salem University is offering to global leaders now.

... Short break

Presenter: Yes Mr Vice Chancellor, shortly before we went on break, we were talking about leadership issues and entrepreneurial issues. You know, students who have not yet graduated from the University have already - some of them distinguished themselves with the entrepreneurial savvy that they have picked up from the University. Now, when the students graduate, what do we look out for, to say: "Yes! That is a student from Salem University"?

VC: Well, when you see them, you will see the people we refer to as "unstoppable" change agents.

Presenter: Unstoppable?

VC: Unstoppable change agents! These are…

Presenter: Very optimistic?

VC: Very optimistic! These are graduates from Salem University that have picked up the basic resilience or the basics of resourcefulness, the basics of integrity, the basics of accountability. They have not only learnt it in the class room; they have seen it demonstrated. One challenge we posed to ourselves is leadership by example. So, if we are telling our global leaders that you are destined to be a global leader, a change agent; all the lecturers, all the administrative staff must display and model those behaviours. Challenging! But we are getting there. Quite a number of people in our community are responding effectively.

So, when they move around on the campus we tell them, "you are a global leader". Look! Come to the campus, you don't see pure water sachets; you know … pure water sachets dropped everywhere as you will see in a number of other places. Why? Because we tell them that cleanness is part of global leadership. Timeliness is also part of global leadership and being able to be relied upon without anybody coming to harm - that is global leadership. You give advice your advice must be sound; your advice must lead to development. And it must be done selflessly.

Presenter: Ok Sir, quiet a number of these issues you have raised need to be determined and tested in the real world. The parameters for doing those tests to a large degree are very subjective. But let me go back to the train of thought we were pursuing; that if you for example were a Muslim student or belong to any other faith apart from the Christian faith, how do you fit in to this large resource called Salem University?

VC: Ok! Number one: unlike some faith-based institutions, we allow our Muslim students to pray on Campus in their own Muslim way. Every global leader is informed clearly that regardless of your religion, you are on equal platform here and you must respect one another. So, Muslim global leaders on our Campus do not feel intimidated; do not feel isolated; do not feel discriminated against.

As a matter of fact, they are among the very resilient and also very intelligent global leaders we have. And I can also assure you that most of them have never showed up on our disciplinary radar. They comport themselves very well. I am very proud of the Muslim students we have. They understand what the policy of the University is.

They understand the drive of the University and the focus on leadership regardless of their religion. And they have come to appreciate that the University values them for who they are and the University is prepared to give them resources that would make them transformational leaders. So, they are very much at peace.

Now, this is important, because some people are saying, "But you let them come to the chapel?" Of course! Because our chapel is not just the conventional religious service you know. It is about developing key three leadership themes: developing the leader in you, developing the leaders around you and using the leadership spirit in you. These are the things that inform our Total Leadership Training Concept activities that I mentioned before and they are delivered in the Chapel, in the class rooms and everywhere on the Campus.

Presenter: So, why would you use the Chapel as a pulpit for leadership training? I thought what goes on in the Chapel or in the Mosque should be principally religious and spiritual.

VC: Isn't that the problem we have as a nation? What goes on in the mosque or in the chapel should be principally religious and spiritual? But what they don't realize is that in these very centres (mosques or churches), "leaders" are raised. Many of these "leaders" return to these places to give thanks for whatever blessings come their way. And I can tell you that some of these people are actually supported in their own ungodly ways from these places.

So, we have actually turned our own Chapel activities into leadership training ground. Yes! Our foundation is the Bible. Yes! Our model is Jesus Christ… because of what He has modelled for us: the leadership qualities, the care for the nation, development focus, etc. These are the things that we build into our Chapel activities and our Muslim global leaders have come to see this very clearly and they appreciate what they are getting from the Chapel activities.

Presenter: To what degree do you think from this kind of integration we can sustain critical mass? Ok, you are turning out four hundred students; but if we have sufficient leaders - sufficient transformational leaders - for whom religion is a blur; it doesn't matter what your beliefs are. There are certain things that need to be done in terms of nation building; so, let's do that. To what degree do you think like I said earlier on we can get the critical mass that can begin to change the situation in Nigeria?

VC: Well, I said before that the focus of the vision of Salem University is about transformational leadership for nation building. And we need people that are groomed in this kind of environment to be able to take our nation forward.

Presenter: So you've answered the questions that I have asked consistently. Sir, leaders must be trained.

VC: They must be trained!

Presenter: You can have leadership qualities but you need to…

VC: But you need to have those qualities honed, trained…, and given a sense of direction. Everyone is a leader within but not everyone becomes an effective global leader. Some fall by the way side; some use their innate potentials for leadership for wrong things. We have "leaders" among armed robbers; among pen robbers; among some of our politicians that have brought this nation to shame; they are there! But it is about letting them (the University students) realise that they can be distinguished.

Presenter: What about political leadership?

VC: Political leadership is also included in our University training. We have the Student Leaders Forum where we encourage *global leaders* to show or practise leadership. We encourage them to show community orientation, making sure that they live beyond their individual selfish interest.

Presenter: Fifty years from now, you believe that Salem University would still be standing. What is your futurist picture for Salem University fifty years down the line?

VC: Our futuristic vision for the University is not only fifty years. Eight hundred years from now. Harvard University started just like Salem University started; it is still standing. The vision and orientation might have changed but the University is there. Our own conviction is this: so long as we have people who will be the carriers of the vision, the University would last beyond fifty years and into hundreds of years.

Fifty years from now, I would like visit the Aso-Rock (Presidential Villa) and see a graduate from Salem University as the President of Nigeria. I would like to be able to go to the UN either in New York or Vienna and see a graduate from Salem University as the Secretary General of the UN. Fifty years from now, I would like to see a graduate of Salem University proffering solutions for basic challenges that we have in the country: water, electricity, transportation. Some of these things are... I told you that I have been overseas for several years...

Presenter: I will come to that...

VC: ...and our vision for this University in fifty years' time we would have global leaders spread all over the place. Let me tell you this, thankfully, there are a few Universities that are similarly committed. Covenant University is a sister University; we appreciate what they are doing. And they are releasing graduates into Nigeria that would help create this critical mass we are looking for.

...

Presenter: Sir, you are the helms man right now at the Salem University. You have your discipline - you are Professor of Criminology. You started out here in Nigeria at Ahmadu Bello University, Zaria. You did your first degree and second degree; and then you were away for about two decades and transposed back to Nigeria at the helm of an academic community. Do you think realistically, you were in torch with what is going in Nigeria today after having spent such a long time in what most Nigerians would consider fairer climes?

VC: Thank you very much *for that question*. During the period of my sojourn away, I maintained constant torch with my homeland; my parents were still alive, my siblings are here. On average, I was visiting Nigeria once every two years. Number two, when we were there, we were constantly consumed with the passion to serve our fatherland. Let me give you one critical example. During the time of President Obasanjo, all the Nigerian High Commissions and Embassies abroad were asked to set up what is called NIDO - Nigerians in Diaspora Organisation. The Nigerian High Commissioner to Australia at the time took up this challenge and called on some of us to help him set up the organisation.

I can tell you now that I was able to mobilise a few Nigerians that were there; we drafted the constitution and set up the organisation. And if you read everything we put in there, it demonstrates very clearly that we were very much in torch with what was happening in Nigeria. That was where I further developed the passion about this problem of leadership. When the call came to me to come back to Nigeria, yes, I was disposed to come and assist. Many of my colleagues said, they wouldn't come back even if they were called upon because of the horrible experiences they had with the country. But I made up my mind and I was persuaded that it was time to go back and put in just a little to a place that raised me up.

As I said, I went all the way to the masters *degree* before I left the shores of this land and here we are. Where we were living (in Australia), everything was working well. That was developed by their own people. So, if you stay away from your own land, it is going to remain very horrible. Some of us have decided to come back. Those who are there are still contributing; you don't have to be back here physically to contribute... But there are different areas and levels. At this point in time I chose to come back, responding to a call to help lift the University off the ground.

Presenter: Now, so you have been a Professor of Criminology; we have a situation in Nigeria today, particularly at this point in time, there seems to be a lot of insecurity. What is your view or thought?

VC: Nigeria is a nation that is searching for its soul. And any nation in that situation would confront the issue of insecurity. How Nigeria was born and how it has been led up to this time, have not helped in establishing clearly her identity. And so, many Nigerians try to develop their own individual, regional, and ethnic identities. I tell you right now that, the future is looking brighter because Nigerians are waking up to the fact that what we have is not what we are destined to have. Well, there was a time in this country - this is not about nostalgia, when you could go to bed with your doors opened...

So, what has happened is that, by and large, our development trajectory has taken us into a way that is dysfunctional; that is criminogenic - it generates or causes crime, i.e. making people disposed to criminality...

We have a lot to do as a nation to bring ourselves back into a trajectory where we are *truly* developmental in our mind-set; where we care for every Nigerian. What makes the developed world what it is today? Every citizen is valued.

But we are getting to a point and this is part of the vision of Salem University to raise leaders that would cherish accountability, cherish integrity and make sure that they treat each other Godly. I believe that criminality is not in nature bound to be a Nigerian product. Criminality is generic. Ok, I don't believe in the theory that people are born criminal and then they stay criminal. No!

Criminality is socially constructed and can also be socially deconstructed.

Presenter: Sir, you know, very many great leaders in the world both past and present have gone through some degree of personal hardship. I know of some United States President who when they started out as kids, had trekked miles to school. You know, there had to be some sense of sacrifice; some denial, some crucible of hardship that you went into that developed your character for the long term. Now in your talking about your University- Salem University- you have a lot of emphases on leadership but I haven't heard you talk of some denials. When you have power supply 24/7; all the conveniences are at your beck and call. Are you really building strong leaders?

VC: That is a very wonderful question. I agree completely with you that challenges of life actually build character. I can tell my personal testimony. But let me start from Salem University. When our first set of global leaders came in, our hostels were not ready. The Chancellor of the University Archbishop Dr. Sam Amaga, was on ground with us; I conferred with him; I said what do we do? We have three options: we can send the global leaders and their parents back home because we are not ready; we can put them into hotels in town; or we can put them in some classrooms *temporarily*.

These options, under the guidance of the Chancellor, were put to the parents. And the parents said: "what are you talking about? Let them stay in the classrooms". So, our global leaders started in the classroom as their dormitory. So, they know what it means to have an accommodation that is not the ideal. They experienced that before they went into their hostels. Some time we have challenges of water.

There was a time I went to the campus and I saw them trooping out with buckets in their hands. "What is happening?", I inquired. "Our VC there is no water in the hostels", they replied. And I said, "so, what are you doing?" "Well, we wanted to go fetch water but there is no water here". Then I said, "As leaders, what are you supposed to do?" So, we went through the scenario *of problem-solving*. There is water down the track - about 200 meters away. "Oya! Let's go. All of us, I'm going to follow you now", I said. And it was a joy *all around*. I told them my story. I grew up in a polygamous family; with several children and in lack. We had to go through so many *difficult* things. I carried load on my head when I was growing up as a young boy; look at where I am today.

Presenter: Professor Omaji, thank you very much for coming on the program. We wish you and Salem University the very best in all your endeavours.

VC: Thank you so much. I appreciate the opportunity and I encourage the parents in this nation and beyond to send their kids to us so we can work with them - so that we can produce leaders that Nigeria and the world would be proud of.

Presenter: Thank you Professor.

Among other things, this interview encapsulated the essence of the understanding, aspiration, and drive with which we approached the task we were given to build a unique University. No one determined to lead rightly should step out without continually articulating what she or he understands the task to be.

The NTA One-on-One interview was broadcast at least three times on different days and at different times. Most of the stakeholders must have heard the articulation of our understanding of the task. Indeed, many called me to say they were most delighted.

Our Destiny: Leadership Development and the Chapel of Peace

One of the highly misunderstood aspects of the task given to us was our use of the Chapel of Peace to anchor the moral transformation dimension of our leadership development focus. The query of the Presenter in the NTA One-on-One program was typical of this misunderstanding. So, at some point, I decided to interpret this issue in greater details in one of my addresses[40] to the University community:

> …On behalf of the Management of the University and all the staff of this community, I say a big welcome to all our returning global leaders and staff [and the new members of our community – staff and students alike]. It is a major privilege to live to see members of this community coming back to engage with destiny. You don't know how much we prevailed on our knees for all of you to come back safe and sound. Over the Christmas break there were many people that came so close to the year 2012; some could even feel or *smell* it but they never entered into the year 2012.
>
> With some pain in our heart and nevertheless in deference to the sovereignty of God, I announce to the University community that one of us - one of our global leaders went to be with the Lord during this break… [*We observed a minute of silence in her honour during which I challenged the participants to reflect as global leaders on: "God, if I have one more day to live, what would you have me do?"*].
>
> *In rounding up the introduction, I shared some challenges we had with*

completing our new hostel projects; the national security challenges that delayed our resumption in the year with its attendant pressure on us to work harder to still deliver fully the curriculum for the academic session; and the fact that some old staff had moved on and we had employed some new ones. Then, I stated three salient leadership nuggets: (1) Leaders always lead with hope. Where there is no hope, you cease to have the will to lead. (2) When pressed for time, leaders don't waste time; leaders redeem the time. (3) Every organisation is dynamic; it is a golden rule of leadership that you rejuvenate your organisation by ensuring that there is a new fresh air that comes in as some old air goes out.

...Today I just want to emphasise... that we have one and only one destiny to fight for, to defend, to protect, to promote and that is raising global leaders; nothing more, nothing less. And if anyone is here that has something less in mind, the honourable thing for you to do is to quietly pack your things and leave. This University will not subscribe to anything less than raising global leaders, in spite of the challenges that we face.

I am anchoring the presentation for today to 1Timothy 3: 1: "This is a faithful saying, if a man desires the position of a bishop [in the place of bishop, put a global leader], he or she desires a good work". *Note* in particular the two words: "desire" and "work". If a man desires the position of a global leader, he desires a good work. *The writer* did not say it is a good dream. To be a global leader takes more than a dream. It is work, not play, not deception, not playing to the gallery, not wanting to be like the Jones, not care-free relaxation or going on holidays. It is a good work.

We take it prima facie (i.e. on the face of it) that everyone that comes here desires to be a global leader and we follow the tenets of Paul to declare to you it is a good work. Whether you will acquit yourself well in that work, is what all of us are concerned about. Because in the end, your work will be tested. If it is made of wood and hay and stubble, guess what happens to it? It would burn off; nothing would stand. But if your work is made of silver, gold and metal, let come what may, let the fire rage: your work would stand. If anything, it will be purified. Job said, "When I am tried [even with fire]; I shall come out as pure gold".

...This year I perceive in my spirit that all of us have to work harder than before to defend our destiny... Every activity on the Campus must contribute to the realisation of this destiny. And if anything does not play that role, that thing does not belong in this University. I want to take the *Total Leadership Training Concept*

(TLTC) activities in particular tonight *and interpret its role in our leadership development project*, especially as anchored and mediated by the Chapel of Peace. These activities are designed to stand on three pillars (to remind those who are already aware and to inform those who are new to this community):

1.   They are designed to develop the leader within you. We have made efforts to let everyone know that you have been born with the potential to lead. Every human being is born with the potential to lead. The Scriptures tell us in Genesis that God made man in His own image and gave them dominion over everything that He had created: have dominion, subdue, lead, cultivate, look after, protect, give sense of meaning, bring hope where there is no hope, bring light where there is darkness, bring life where there is death all around, etc. Let there be a sense of meaning in your environment; that's what it means to be a leader.

And in developing the leader within you, this particular Chapel emphasises the need for you to be a positive influence in your generation...

...In our TLTC activities, the Chapel of Peace works hard to bring to us an understanding of the most important ingredient of leadership which is integrity. Integrity is a value; it is a characteristic of generating honesty, trustworthiness and consistency in everything that you do. In our work with global leaders we see quite a number of people struggling with being honest - honest to themselves and honest with their environment. We see quite a number that are struggling with trustworthiness: nobody can depend on what they say without coming to harm. It is an integral part of the activities of the TLTC to ensure that you grasp the essence of integrity as you become the global leader that God intends you to become.

The activities of the Chapel are also geared towards creating in you that person, that authority, that instrument for positive change. So when you desire the office of a global leader and the Bible says is a good work, it is about you becoming a positive change *agent*...

The activities of the Chapel of Peace are designed to ensure that you are problem solvers; that you develop that imaginativeness, the power for innovation. You will notice that there is a difference between craftiness and innovation. Many of you here already manifest craftiness. Craftiness is not innovation; craftiness is not even intelligence. *It is certainly not a value we countenance in this place...*

The Chapel of Peace TLTC activities are designed to make sure that you develop the right attitude... It is ok for challenges to come. In fact leaders are formed in the crucibles of challenges. That's where you know who a leader is - in the crucible of challenges, in the furnace of fire. When the furnace of fire comes, followers that are not properly led die; leaders walk out and proceed. That is what the activities of TLTC are designed to do. And in doing this the Chapel of Peace values you as people not as objects – as human beings endowed with the virtues of God so that if anyone touches you that person touches life.

... It is imperative that I have given a disproportionate amount of time today to the pillar of "developing the leader within". That's where the battle is actually won or lost. Let me go over the other two pillars briefly.

2.   The second pillar is "developing the leaders around you". Having helped you to operationalize and develop the leader within you, you become an asset to develop the leaders around you. The way you interact with people, the help you give, the understanding you bring, the communication you make, the word you speak - all of these things are to develop the other leaders around you. *This includes you* challenging your fellow global leaders or staff members that are not doing things that will advance their own lives. You make sure that you step in there and guide and help and encourage.

3.   The third pillar of the activities of the Chapel of Peace is to ensure that you actually put your leadership to practice. Apply the leadership within you. As I said at the beginning, in this year 2012 we must defend our destiny. The first weapon that you need is making sure that you desire to be a global leader. Let there be an unquenchable thirst in you. When anybody comes close to you, asking you to do things that would derail you from that destiny, defend your destiny with every *leadership* might in your body, soul and spirit.

... Let me conclude with this. There is a choice we must make this year: defend or defile the destiny. I pray that everyone who is under the sound of my voice now will make up his or her mind to defend her destiny. There are many forces at play to defile this destiny. But those forces cannot succeed unless you and I allow them to succeed. We have a lot of work to do if we desire the office of a global leader, which as we said before is to desire a good work. I believe that the God of this vision will help us to do this work effectively. I believe that as we have come back this year with all the zeal and all the desire to do the right thing, God will never abandon you. Amen. You will succeed; you will overcome; you will stand tall among your peers. Just make sure nobody defiles your destiny. Nobody! And it shall be well with us in Jesus name. Amen.

The Imagined Future

As can be seen from the foregoing, there is a lot of idealism in the vision of Salem University and this would be a delight to any genuine leader any day. So also are the tasks that must be performed in order to realize the vision. For instance, the tasks of developing the leader in and around you, and deploying that leadership can be overwhelming unless there is a tangible object to which these efforts are directed. Thus, as part of constantly casting the vision, we endeavoured to paint a picture of an imagined future in several aspects of life and the world as a way of sustaining the engagement of the University community with our calling. In one of the orientation sessions, I used Nigeria as an example as can be seen in the excerpts below.

Ｔhe situation report before us is heavy and grave. We are all familiar with the "prophecy" in a CIA report that by the year 2015, Nigeria would be a failed state. "God forbid", I hear you say? Yes God will forbid if we seize the time; if we seize the moment; if we know that we have been called upon to be end-time soldiers; if we know it is time to take a stand for transformational academic revolution; a stand for the core values of Salem University; if we know that God is depending on you and me to bring about the fulfillment of that phrase, "God forbid".

Our own world as a whole is in disarray at the moment. If you want to know the state of affairs of any nation or society... look at what happens to their educational system. The state of education tells you clearly - demonstrates beyond any shadow of doubt - what that society has come to be. When Salem University was conceived, it was at a time of not only educational decay but indeed educational coma. Our educational system was comatose.

No wonder Nigeria was what it was looking like. No wonder intelligence and integrity had gone out of the way and people were just using human smartness. Smartness and intelligence are not the same. Train a rat over time and the rat becomes smart but it is not intelligent. Those of you who are interested in psychology you will like to know that one of the foremost experiments in psychology is the Pavlov experiment. Pavlov trained a dog to salivate anytime, *using* food; there was smartness but there was no intelligence.

The state of education in Nigeria at the time and dare I say up to this moment - with some minimal improvement, meant that our nation was nose-diving. Why wouldn't it? Yesterday I said that it came to a point in this nation some Professors were rumored to be selling potatoes along the road to survive [*at that time salaries were not paid to lecturers*]. So who cared about education? As if there was an agenda to <u>de-educate</u> all Nigerians so that we would become morons and therefore some people (particularly in government) could take everyone else for a ride. They made everyone else fight for survival. A Professor that had to sell potatoes to feed his family, what does he care whether you are attending classes or not?

… As I was praying and reflecting on the Salem University Anthem, …I saw an imagined Nigeria of the future…

Suddenly we are on the New Year's Day in 2020. You opened your eyes and you saw a Nigeria still intact despite the CIA prognosis of disintegration; the social contract is largely upheld; everybody knows his or her place and his or her responsibilities for the survival of the society. Everyone is working with everyone else according to their positions *in life*. Nigerians as a whole are better fed. There are no more beggars on the streets. You look around, people are no longer praying for one meal a day. Our hospitals are empty.

You are back to Salem University, not as a student or staff but as *an august visitor – to your alma mater.* The health centre of the University is empty; all the beds have been removed and turned in couches that are spread around the hostels *for relaxation.* Our doctors and nurses have been given another assignment to do all together: instead of health crisis managers they have become preventive health educators.

Back to the national scene again. The economy is booming; instead of growing in one digit, Nigeria has joined and indeed overtaken the likes of China and is growing 17 per cent per annum. That is 2020 Nigeria. Crime rate is gone down to almost zero per cent… The mineral deposits under her soil have been properly exploited and the economy is well diversified; there is enough money for every Nigerian to live above poverty level.

There is distributive justice in the country so much so that when you ask somebody, "do you know about the Niger-Delta militants"? He will say: "what are you talking about? You mean there was a group that existed like that before"? In other words it has become a thing of a distant past. You travel to Maiduguri or the North East and you ask them, "how are you living with Boko Haram"? And they reply: "What is Boko Haram"? It is no longer part of their consciousness. And then you (those… who were studying Criminology) are now Professors of Criminology, with one of you leading the United Nations Commission on Crime and Justice. As you were flipping through the archives, you came across an institution called EFCC Nigeria and you ask: "by the way what is that"? And Nigerians tell you… "we don't know anything about EFCC". It no longer exists. And so on, and so forth.

Every aspect of the society you turn to, the challenges have become not only things of the past but the consciousness of them is no longer there.

That is the imagined Nigeria of the future. *You have seen something… a new city. Now consider John* on the island of Patmos where he saw a new city[41]: "And I saw a new heaven and a new earth: for the first heaven and the first earth were passed away [*The first Nigeria that you knew, passed away; we are still in the year 2020… Nigeria is a new 'city'. And you say "oh my God this is my country". You visit the United States of America - by this time Nigeria has overtaken them. The US President asks you: "how is your country"? And you respond: "My country is a bride; as sparkling as a bride, as majestic as a bride, as sincere as a bride, and as gorgeous as a bride. Nigeria my country, oh what a feeling!"*]…

And I heard a great voice out of heaven saying, Behold the tabernacle of God is with men, and He will dwell with them, and they shall be his people, and God himself shall be with them, and be their God. And God shall wipe away all tears from their eyes; and there shall be no more death, neither sorrow, nor crying, neither shall there be any more pain: for the former things are passed away…

Come hither, I will show you the bride, the Lamb's wife And he carried me away in the spirit to a great and high mountain, and showed me that great city; having the glory of God: and her light was like unto a stone most precious, even like a jasper stone, clear as crystal. And the city had no need of the sun, neither of the moon, to shine in it: for the glory of God did lighten it, and the Lamb is the light thereof. … And the nations of them which are saved shall walk in the light of that city: and the kings of the earth do bring their glory and honour into it".

This is my imagined Nigeria of the future. What is your

imagined Nigeria? What is your imagined world? I imagine all the surrounding countries both in Africa, in Middle-East and the farther away countries in the West and Asia coming to Nigeria entering into the glory of the land. Wouldn't you be proud? …

The imagined future we have talked about now (*too idyllic to be true and realizable as it may*), happened because of Salem University alumni - graduates of Salem University - had gone all through the system and taken charge of Nigeria's political economy. The new city I painted did not happen by accident; it happened because you (global leaders of tomorrow) were now in charge. Everything that we have been saying since yesterday translated and transformed you into a person of the right influence (*exemplary global leader*) that could change the course of the destiny of the nation as a whole.

The question is, what must we do today to make the imagined future possible? Today is the time! …If we do something today, we will wake up to a wonderful and blissful dream. If we don't do something today we will wake up to a terrible nightmare...

Such is the scope of the task of the vision that we clarified for the University community.

Concluding remarks

During my tenure, very few (if any) members of the University community would be in doubt as to why we were there. For all intents and purposes, the vision handed over to us was extraordinary both in scope and in value-orientation.

Making the vision plain, so that the University community could pursue and possess it was a responsibility we took seriously from the word go. For this, we deployed several forms of communication. For instance, we used every 'rite of passage' occasion (such as welcoming students, matriculation, external partnership, and mass media interactions) to propagate and reinforce what we understood our task to be. As demanded of purposeful and righteous leadership where the arrowhead must show the way, we made our persons the 'town criers' for the vision.

As every authentic leader knows, a vision on the pages of documents is not as powerful as the one that finds body in the lives and voices of the carriers. For there, it takes on its own life and defines the way things must go. Pictures of the future properly imagined, no matter how far-fetched its realization may be, provide the necessary energy and election to forge ahead with a vision of raising Godly global leaders who are directed at fulfilling enviable destinies.

---

[36] 1 Corinthians 14: 7-8, Holy Bible. New King James Version.

[37]   Every human entity's business ideology comprises of its philosophy, vision, mission and core values.

[38]   This member was representing the University Board of Trustees on the Governing Council.

[39]   Vice Chancellor's Address on the Founder's Day, 6 August, 2010. In this excerpt, as in the other excerpts from my addresses/speeches, I use square brackets [ ] and/or *italics* to indicate words or phrases I have added in the course of writing this book to make the contexts or meanings of the excerpts clearer.

[40]   Address to the first TLTC session in a new year, 1 February, 2012.

[41]   Revelation 21: 1-24, Holy Bible. New King James Version.

4 Software: shifting values to principles

"To create [a different] future, we will need a huge shift in thinking, values, and action" (Albert Einstein)

Building a University that would raise global leaders, strong in character or integrity, wisdom and doing exploits in a decadent environment, was not only a lofty task; it was a major departure from the prevailing reality. I realized from the word go, that such an edifice, no matter how elegantly designed and/or built, cannot stand or operate well without a foundation held together by a proper mortar (software).

The more audacious the edifice (as in the case of our task of raising "saints in Sodom"), the greater the need to ensure the mortar was capable of sustaining a foundation that is solid, firm and deep. I was very conscious of the fact that where a foundation is mishandled or destroyed, not even the 'righteous' can achieve anything good. The revealed truth is that the righteous can do nothing[42] in such circumstances. This is true for individuals as well as for organisations and nations.

The Prince, written by Nicolo Machiavelli, not only illustrates the importance of foundations but also counsels that nations or states must have their foundations "fixed in such a way that the first storm will not overthrow them…". Since the proprietor charged me with the responsibility of leading the team to build the Salem University edifice whose foundations should not be overthrown by the first storm, I decided to start early on with appropriately 'softwaring' what we were about to do.

That is, we must create the mortar that would be bold and strong enough to hold together the foundation stones and the superstructure bricks.

Leading right in this circumstance, as in any other intellectually and morally driven projects, required us to establish our personal as well as the organisational values and to shift those values into principles. Above all else, such values and principles would underpin the credibility with which any leader can legitimately and rightly call and expect anyone to follow him or her. As we stated in the Prologue, the issue of "right" is a matter for morality or value-oriented ethics. And, principles must provide the moral rules (built on values) that can help leaders navigate the leadership territory with all its delicate topographical features towards personal or organisational goals.

Core Values

My take-off place was to understand and deploy the University's eight core values which were outlined in one of the University's foundation documents. These values were expounded as follows.

1. ***Godliness*** forms the bedrock of our existence as a University and defines every aspect of our operations and context. The Christian ethos guides our activities and conduct at all times and every student of Salem University is expected to exhibit character traits and dispositions of Jesus-centered heritage. The Jesus centered approach to all issues is non-negotiable and central in the pursuit of our mandate in raising a new generation of leaders and in the realization of the objectives of our purpose. Therefore, students will be committed to maintaining a high level of godliness and shall act in such manner as to facilitate their spiritual growth as well as work out ways to evolve and implement a spiritual development plan. Attendance at Chapel Services is part of students' spiritual development. Students are expected to demonstrate a deep reverence for God at all times. The aim is to eliminate occultism and other vices in society.

2. ***Confidence:*** Students of Salem University are expected to exhibit character, attitudes and habits exuding self-confidence and dignity at all levels through communication, interaction and general conduct. They are expected to see themselves as persons of worth and value, taking pride in their uniqueness as individuals with a positive mindset devoid of any trace of inferiority but a strong belief in self and nation as well as articulating their core purpose as individuals and a possibility mindedness directed towards positive achievement and contribution.

3. *Mental Empowerment:* We are committed to raising students who themselves show commitment to a life style of continuous academic and personal development, striving to be continuously relevant to the overall vision requirement of the University as well as its core mission, goals and objectives. Students are encouraged to constantly seek paths for self-improvement. Openness to learning new skills and taking on board new information are traits expected of Salem University students in order to cause a robustness and depth in the quality of their output.

4. *Integrity:* A man may rise to the top by craftiness, but only integrity can keep him there. Students of Salem University are therefore expected to demonstrate qualities of honesty, uprightness and trustworthiness at all times. They must ensure that they are accountable persons, whose word is their bond, transparent and open in all their dealings and flagging truth as a virtue at all times, particularly, in conduct branding the core values of the University. Integrity in matters of conduct during examination, obeying the rules and regulations, being spiritually sound, morally upright and having a good conscience.

5. *Accountability:* Doing the right thing at the right time and for the right reasons is one of the values of life we want our students to hold dear. We are committed to inculcating a sense of accountability in our students. We expect them to do what is right at all times. We believe in the place of discipline for effective leadership, responding to issues as demanded not as convenient. Here, at Salem University, our students are not permitted to do what they like but what is right. Punctuality to lectures as well as prompt response to assignments as demanded are desired traits of accountability. Doing what is right, not just what you like is a mark of honor.

6. *Diligence and Resourcefulness:* Only the diligent eventually stand before Kings. Therefore, students of Salem University are expected to be strongly committed to their assignments. We expect that they will demonstrate the virtues of hard work and deliver qualitative output and constantly strive towards excellent attainment of high standards, in all they do. They must be resourceful, doing everything to improve on themselves and their performance. We believe that commitment is the greatest

qualifier for attainment, hence, our celebration of this trait in preparing students for leadership responsibilities after graduation.

7. **Sense of Priority:** Going up requires giving up something. We want our students to know that life is in phases. The phase they are in as students requires giving up pursuit of some extra-ordinary pleasures so they can go up in their intellectual pursuit. This is where priority comes in. Sacrifice is the ultimate price for outstanding leadership. It is the quality of right placement of priority that defines great leadership. We expect students of Salem University to go the extra mile, paying the extra price in the attainment of their set goals. Raising an altar of sacrifice in pursuit of their dreams is what must distinguish and define the Salem University students. If you play now, you pay later. Priority says *"pay now and play later."*

8. **Synergy:** It takes a team to make the dream work. One is too small a number to achieve great results. As an individual, you are only a voice, but together we are a force. Synergy is basically achieving more together as a team than the sum of all working as individuals. Our students will understand and celebrate the individual uniqueness of their fellow students with the view of harnessing and harmonizing them for geometric results. When effort is combined, effort is multiplied. That is the product of effective synergy.

Laying down some key principles

Values are personally and/or organisationally held strong beliefs: the "constructs representing generalised behaviours or states of affairs that are considered by the individual or the organization to be important" (Dubrin, et. al. 2006, p.127). We took it then, that the values we found in the documents were beliefs that the Proprietor said they held strongly about things they considered important regarding their University.

There can be no leadership worthy of its name except insofar as it gets the stakeholders' community to behave in a way that is consistent with the stated values set for that organisation (Hooper and Potter 2000, p7). These values provide the map of the territory that the vision covers, showing all the major features of the moral topography.

However, values on their own like the ones we met on ground, mean very little. They can be put on and off depending on the convenience of the moment. At the commencement of the assignment we found that the core values, though very endearing, were practically impotent in some areas. I observed, without prejudice to how they were deployed before I arrived, that not much of these rivetingly espoused values was seen in the lives and activities going on around the University project. Thus we felt we needed to shift them, along with the ones we had imbibed independently over the years, into broad or general principles and nurture them to become a steadying force in the turbulent world of leadership that we were called to.

Leadership is about working with principles, not merely values. The reason, as Covey (2003, p19) so vividly captured, is that:

> correct principles are like compasses: they are always pointing the way. And, if we know how to read them, we won't get lost, confused, or fooled by conflicting voices and values. Principles are self-evident, self-validating natural laws. They don't change or shift. They provide "true north" directions to our lives when navigating the "streams" of our environments. Principles apply at all time in all places. They surface in the form of… norms, and teachings that uplift, ennoble, fulfill, empower, and inspire people. The lesson of history is that to the degree people and civilisations have operated in harmony with correct principles, they have prospered. At the root of societal declines are foolish practices that represent violations of correct principles."

Covey, in this work, empirically demonstrated the fundamental difference between values and principles:

> In a talk show interview, I was once asked if Hitler was principle-centred. "No", I said, "but he was value-driven. One of his governing values was to unify Germany. But he violated compass principles and suffered the natural consequences. And the consequences were momentous – the dislocation of the entire world for years" (Covey 2003, p95).

Thus, in addition to steadying our practices, these principles would help us to define the right things to do, and to communicate consistent messages about them across the expanding community of the University. Further, we needed them to assist us sustain clear focus on capacity-building and value re-orientation for us as the leaders and for all who came in contact with the University.

Broadly, we had to fashion out from our values key principles for virtually all the core areas of the University. As illustration, we reproduce below some of them - particularly those with wider cross-cutting applications.

General identity mantra

Identity is like a dress. It creates the first impression about the wearer. It, therefore, has the capacity to influence the wearer's entire interaction with the outside world. Hence, the popular saying: 'as you dress, so are you addressed'. We started by making sure that our 'dress' projected the University core values by shifting those values into action-oriented statements or mantras.

1. Salem University Lokoja, is driven – in philosophy, vision, and mission – to be a centre of excellence for raising global leaders. As battle axes, change agents, etc in God's hands, these leaders are spiritually alive, mentally alert, and intellectually developed to change their world in a Godly way. At core, we are to release graduates who will combine intelligence with integrity because **we believe that smartness can take a man to the top but only integrity can keep him there.**

2. We must judge all that we do (principally, the intellectual and character transformation for global leadership) with the eight core values of the University. No action taken by or on behalf of the University will pass our test unless it satisfies the values in their specific and broad applications.

3. The administration (management and leadership) believes and practises **leadership by example** anchored on our mantra of 'Doing the right thing, the right way, at the right time, and for the right reasons'.

Proprietor's interaction with the University

The NUC, although promoting the establishment of private universities, frowned on proprietors interfering with the day-to-day administration of these universities. In particular, it was concerned that such interferences would compromise the time-honored traditions of universities worldwide. This matter featured prominently in the reasons the NUC gave for suspending the licences of seven private universities during my time at Salem University.

Interestingly, the ICPC Team that visited Salem University on 6 August 2012, inquired about the level of interference in the University administration from the Proprietor as part of its exit debriefing.

We had developed the following principles to guide us in relation to this matter:

1. Salem University holds the view that Proprietors in the private universities sector occupy a unique position compared to their

counterparts in the public universities. Unlike the President or Governor (Visitors to federal/state universities) who uses public funds to support the universities to which they serve as "proprietors", private Universities' proprietors are obliged to use their own personal resources to fund the universities at least until they become self-reliant. Thus, whether these universities are for-profit or not-for-profit, we recognize that the dynamics of the interactions would be different substantially.

2. Experiences of proprietor's interaction with their universities range from total freedom (very rare) to suffocating control. Salem University management chose to stay faithful to the proprietor's policies as outlined in the approved Law and Academic Brief of the University so as to enjoy the confidence of, and gain the respect of, the Proprietor. We must avoid, if need be resist, the extremes and work hard for a mutually healthy interaction.

3. From experience, when resources become tighter, proprietors of private outfits would pay closer attention to the internal running of their outfits. More significantly, where such outfits are driven by a vision that is an off-shoot of a religious commission, proprietors would be concerned that the personnel in the outfit are such that can carry the vision faithfully. Salem University Management considers this to be perfectly normal but would assist the proprietor to remain professional in instructing on fund utilisation and employment outcomes in the University. So, resource situation must not be allowed to derail interaction into unethical and unprofessional paths.

Financial management

Our commitment to applying the core values to all areas of the University, especially the financial management, led us from the word go to develop critical principles that would enthrone prudence and probity in our handling of the University resources. These principles (listed below) stood the University in a good stead when the ICPC Team visited us to see how we were managing the finances among other things.

Somebody (a visitor) once told me: "Sir, we are hearing what you are doing in this University. In fact the work we see on ground is enough to tell anybody that cares to know that the work is being done. So don't bother about accounting further how the resources are used. So long as people can see the building standing there, Mr. VC the only questions you should care about are: did they give you money to build facilities? Yes! Are the facilities built? Yes! End of story".

Of course for us (the Management under my watch), that was not the end of the story. We made it also critically important to answer these additional questions: How were they built? With what amount? What remains or what are we owing? This takes stewardship beyond merely getting the job done. It extends it to getting the job done faithfully and accountably! To guide us in operating at this higher level, we crafted the following principles:

1. Any organisation/institution that lacks sound financial policies and accounting procedures is doomed to fail because finance is the life wire of an organisation. It is widely believed that a major challenge facing the educational sector in Nigeria is lack of adequate funding. At Salem University, we believe we must be **accountable and judicious in the use of the funds** that are released for various projects aimed at enhancing the quality of education at the University and, by extension, in the country as a whole.

2. We work with the consciousness that the hydra-headed monster called corruption thrives easily in the financial management area and we, therefore, give palpable attention to strict monitoring/supervision of the activities of financial managers to ensure adherence to approved financial regulations and probity.

3. We ensured that we **establish clearly the sources of the University revenue** and areas **where the revenue is expended** in each financial year, which for our University is 1st September to 30 August (the following calendar year).

4. All monies of the University (including internally generated revenues) are paid into appropriate bank accounts opened in the name of the University, and are drawn upon only by means of cheques (or counterfoil cheques in the absence of original cheque leaves) duly signed by authorized signatories.

5. Every financial transaction on behalf of the University must be requested in appropriate format and receive <u>prior approval by the</u>

delegated officer, and must be documented (in the case of revenue) or retired (in the case of expenditure) within a given period with verifiable evidence (authentic receipts or certificates of honor).

6. Officers (including all Principal Officers – VC, Registrar, Bursar, University Librarian, etc) who receive funds (colloquially called 'imprests') for the day to day running of their units (Offices, Colleges, Departments, Directorates, etc) **must, as a general rule, retire with receipts or (where no receipts are obtainable) certificates of honor any money received before a replenishment can be released**. Only in rare cases of verifiable urgency, can this rule be applied with sustainable flexibility, i.e. without breaching the accountability value.

7. **All unexpended monies from whatever transaction (whether it is N5.00 or N500,000,000.00) must be paid into an appropriate University account** and the teller submitted in the retirement or returned to the Bursary and the official University receipts issued by the Bursary for submission in the retirement.

8. **The University frowns against inducement and gratification in implementing all its policies, programs and projects**. Staff, students, and contractors alike are regularly informed that no act of inducement and gratification is tolerated in all matters (admissions, enrolments, appointments, promotions, continuous assessments, examinations, awards of contracts, etc).

9. **All charges** for the University services (fees for tuition, accommodation, post-UTME screening, etc) **are published so that clients know in advance** and cannot be ripped-off at the point of payments.

10. In the award of contracts or employments, the University strictly observes the "Conflict of Interest" principle. **No University staff or member of governance bodies is allowed to participate without declaring their interests and accordingly being excluded from the process of selection**. No "cornering" of any sort (including "contract splitting", etc) is tolerated in the University.

11. **All known infractions of the University financial management regulations must be dealt with promptly, and with appropriate sanctions.** Such "infractors" are to be suspended promptly, processed through the Staff or Students Disciplinary Committee and, if found guilty, dismissed from the services/privileges of the University.

12. Ultimately, corruption-free financial management, like the management of other areas of high probability corruption, is a function of discipline, determination, and dedication to a cause which managers and leaders must pursue transformationally – selfless and focused on institutional/national interest - with contentment!

Student admissions

We had key principles that helped our general success in relation to corruption-free admissions. These principles attracted the attention of the ICPC Team, and so they requested for a copy of the document that guided our exemplary practice. Below are the principles we developed and applied throughout my tenure.

1. The Admissions policy of Salem University is outlined in the Academic Brief that the NUC approved for the University, covering the general requirements for undergraduate and postgraduate admissions, indirect (JAMB process) and direct entries, internal screenings, and the specific requirements for admissions into programmes of study.

2. While the University was building up its enrolments towards the NUC approved carrying capacities, over-enrolment into any of the approved courses would not be allowed, save to the margins that can be normalized by the attrition process. Not even the resource constraints would tempt the University to dabble into any form of underhanded practice "just to fill up the space" in order to beef up the revenue side of its budget.

3. All students are to be admitted on merit using the JAMB national cut-off points and Admission Data Input Layout. Where, despite rigorous process, any students with not enough 'O level' credits are given admissions, such students must be given a prescribed

period within which to remedy their deficiencies or risk having their admission offers withdrawn.

4. Our admission exercises must endeavour at all times to ensure that only those candidates who are ready for excellence and who commit to being transformed into global leaders are brought on board and retained for study. This means that the admission processes have to be conducted in a very transparent manner following laid-down rules of the supervising agencies (NUC and JAMB) and the University's post-UTME regime.

5. All personnel involved in our admission processes must be trained to ensure adherence to all applicable rules including those of NUC and JAMB, our post-UTME screening (which also involves the use of a simple non-academic instrument to reveal the character of persons we bring to the University), and the rules against manipulation, inducement, gratification, rip-off, racketeering, etc.

6. **To avoid any extraneous influence being brought to bear on admission practices at Salem University, there would be no Chancellor's list, Vice Chancellor's list, or anybody's list with regard to anything, including admissions.**

7. Our best-practice admissions efforts derive from our key philosophical convictions that:

   α) **living the life of compliance with legitimate instructions is a major feature of authentic leadership**. A University that fails to follow the policies/rules of regulatory agencies cannot produce leaders of global impact;

   β) the law of sowing and reaping means that **candidates brought into universities through corrupt means would graduate with corruption-prone minds, unless there is an intervening experience that breaks the chain**. In the computer parlance, it's a case of garbage in garbage out;

   χ) there must be equal opportunity and equitable access for all candidates seeking quality university education through private institutions. **Apart from contributing to**

government effort, this is about doing justice which encourages citizens and exalts the nation; and

8) planning for excellence from day one of our actions would enable our post-UTME screening for **potentials in intelligence and character** to assure the University of getting the proper "raw materials" with which to produce quality graduates that would be assets (rather than liabilities) to the nations.

Overall Academic Programmes Implementation

Every activity in the academic management system that we established since assumption of duty was geared towards producing high quality overall implementation of already approved Programmes. We developed the following broad principles to guide us along the way; again these principles attracted the attention of the ICPC Team, and we supplied a copy to them on their request:

1. **Salem University committed itself to running a regular academic calendar,** so that even if the academic operation was delayed for any reasons, Management and staff would task themselves with doing all that was necessary to regularize the calendar.

2. The Senate of the University is rostered to meet once a month; and except during inter-semester breaks or some other exigencies, this roster must be followed. **This is to ensure that no delays would be experienced in clearing all academic matters that required Senate actions, including the approval of semester/session results.**

3. **Management is committed, no matter the odds, to see that funds would be mobilized and judiciously or prudently applied to ensure that instructional materials and other infrastructures** (classrooms, labs, library, powerpoint projectors, lecture notes) are very adequate and in line with NUC prescribed ratios.

4. **It is Salem University position that students must satisfy attendance requirement of a minimum of 85% before they can be allowed to sit examinations in those courses attended.**

5. To sustain quality academic programme implementation all round, Salem University observes **zero tolerance for academic malpractices in relation to illicit liaisons, selling of examination questions or answers, influencing results, projects, practicals, examinations, and any other continuous assessment task.** Any infringement in this area would be met with dismissal or expulsion for staff and students respectfully.

6. All academic programmes at Salem University would be put forward for accreditation by the NUC when due. The success or otherwise of such accreditation would be determined purely on merit, as any contrary process would be inconsistent with the core values of the University.

7. As part of the University's commitment to quality academic programme implementation, and positioning its graduates for professional excellence, Management should also prepare and present relevant programmes to professional accreditation.

8. Salem University considers it imperative to subject its question papers, answer scripts and final year projects to external examination so as to ensure that **the programmes are being implemented at least at the nationally accepted standards**.

9. The moral dimension of the vision of producing graduates that are worthy in learning and character requires that the Management of all Universities be capacity-built in the art of **authentic leadership** which is transformational rather than transactional, selflessly oriented rather than selfishly oriented, and which is **alive to broad national interest rather than narrow and parochial interest**. For Salem University, authentic leadership is our irreducible minimum; and our orientation or capacity building activities must aim to support or, better still exceed, it.

Concluding remarks

Principles, in their activated form, are powerful. As true compasses, they show direction and glue focus on the destination. They are supremely important for those called upon to lay foundations while pioneering a character-centred vision implementation. No one audacious enough to embark on leading right in such an enterprise can ignore to shift values into principles.

But it was not enough to have formulated some broad principles in furtherance of our determination to lead right in the project of building Salem University. We had to hold them constantly on display for all to see. We drove their application in word and deed, getting the University community to be alive to the principles' demands and directions. In this doing this, we adopted Covey's methodology: "I teach them correct principles, and they govern themselves" (2003, p69), characterizing this as an enlightened approach to leadership.

In our own case, I wore the identity of the University for all in our community to see through such things as neatness; pursuit of excellence in all areas; reciting of, and rewarding for, living consistent with the core values; and adopting a hands-on approach to demonstrating leadership by example. I felt that to do any less during the pioneering phase of this extraordinary task was to risk derailment and, worse still, sabotage of the vision.

Regarding the financial management principles, for instance, I was the first officer to retire (or acquit) the first fund I ever took from the University for daily operations. By this action, I established my legitimacy to subsequently demand (and I did demand) all other staff to do likewise. Our peace about the general probity with which we handled the University finances came to the limelight one time an officer of the Economic and Financial Crimes Commission (EFCC) visited the University unannounced. She drove in with a police van with an envelope in her hands and briskly walked pass me, heading towards the Vice Chancellor's office.

That day, there was a visitor I was taking around the Campus. As was my practice with all visitors to the Campus that I met outside of my Office, I inquired from this EFCC officer whether we could be of any help. "No, no, I am looking for the Vice Chancellor", she said. Even my attempt to confirm whether she had any prior appointment and how much time she had, was rebuffed by "Look I am in a hurry, I don't need an appointment to come and see the VC". Noticing that I wasn't making any headway, and that she obviously didn't know who the VC was, I said: "OK. Go up the stairs and the VC will be with you in 30 minutes". Off she went.

Well, I continued with our other visitor – showing him the facilities on the Campus and areas for possible collaboration. Exactly 26 minutes after, I returned to my office and saw the EFCC officer seating in the waiting room. I said to her: "Are you the Officer from the EFCC?" She said, "Yes". I said: "follow me". She must have realized at that time that it was the VC she had rebuffed on her way in. She apologized, narrated her mission, and subsequently left - not only satisfied but accepting to carry the University brochures for distribution at the EFCC headquarters in Abuja.

The significance of this story is that, had we got any financial misdeeds (skeletons in the cupboard, as they call them in the numerous cases of executive malfeasance), the mere sight of an EFCC officer would have sent me escaping with alacrity – especially as her original failure to recognize me provided a perfect 'escape-opportunity'. However, we knew we had no cause to fear; and so, I returned to attend to her confidently.

Regarding the University community members governing themselves in line with our teaching and leading by example, the following story is instructive. A contractor we engaged to complete one of the hostels went to the Bursary to receive the mobilisation cheque I had signed for him. When the Accountant gave him the cheque, he stood there "waiting for the next instruction" as to where to make 'returns' but nothing more was said to him. He inquired: "Please tell me how I can deliver Oga's envelope (referring to the gratification he had packaged for the Vice Chancellor)". The Accountant warned him: "if you don't want Oga to cancel your contract and tear this cheque, please don't attempt to go to him with anything". Then the contractor said: "what about your own (i.e. the 'gifts' he brought for the staff in the Bursary)?".

"The Oga has taught us never to do such a thing. All that we require from you is to go and deliver on the contract", said the Accountant. The contractor stood there, speechless and motionless! He was shocked that there was such an organisation that would give out contracts where the Oga and their staff would not only <u>not</u> demand gratification, but also reject the one offered to them. That was Salem University at home with principles during my tenure.

During my tenure, also, the University complied with our admissions principles and policies to the letter. Some of our students did testify that they would have lost the chance of being admitted if Salem University demanded for bribe or any inducement/gratification before admitting them. Here is one experience I found hilarious. One afternoon, a parent brought his daughter for admission and met me standing in front of the Library.

The JAMB cut-off score for admissions that year was 170; and this parent's daughter had 168. He said something to this effect: "Sir, I am from the Presidency in Abuja. Please give admission to my daughter and you can name your price. In fact, I can make a way for you to get good things flowing from Abuja". You can guess what my response was. He went away, not only disappointed but wondering what manner of place this was. That was Salem University[43].

On the principles for implementing overall academic programmes, the display was strongly consistent with authentic leadership which was "our irreducible minimum". We graduated the first set of global leaders in three and half years. This was because we started their first session late, but we tasked ourselves through reduced holidays to complete the syllabus and, by sacrificial commitment, we thus regularised the academic calendar and maintained it subsequently to the time I disengaged.

Also, several staff and students who violated the University code of conduct relating to academic programmes were disciplined with sanctions, ranging from warning through fines, suspensions to termination and dismissal. That was Salem University. With the unflinching support of the Proprietor, under the leadership of the Chancellor, we developed and applied the empowering software (principles, in particular) and, in consequence, sustained the loyalty of the community and the admiration of the external stakeholders.

---

[42]   Holy Bible, Psalms 11: 3.

[43]   Had our pre-degree programme taken off at that time, I would have persuaded the parent to enrol his daughter into it to help her remedy her JAMB deficiency.

5 Travail: creating 'vision ownership'

There is a tension in the heart of leadership between the need to be true and grounded in one's personal character strengths and the need to tune in to others, understand how to motivate and be sensitive to their environment. Leadership is what is co-created in the space between the leader and the led, the self and the other, to foster a mutual sense of vision ownership[44].

All the prior elements of *leading right* – in relation to the calling to a vision, clarifying the task for that vision and 'softwaring' with values and principles for a solid foundation – should prime up the relevant community towards <u>owning</u> or <u>buying</u> into the vision. Then the leader steps into the space to pull the community to the point of seeing in the vision a stake to live and, if necessary, die for. This releases 'resonance' – a reservoir of positivity with which all stakeholders go on to accomplish excellently.

The cost of achieving this outcome can be high. The leader's resilience must be tried and tested; so also are their character, competence, and focus on legacy. The test of all this, as Jinkins and Jinkins 1998) had observed, is that the people become active participants and not merely recipients, spectators, or victims of leadership.

In the course of our work at Salem University, it became crystal clear to me more than ever before that leaders are formed in the crucible of challenges. I continually harped on this principle to the University community. Our own crucible was like the "valley of Baca" (a place of decadence, drought, weakness and weeping) which we must pass through to arrive at our imagined future.

The journey to deliver on our promises or to succeed at the task set before us at whatever level we were operating required us to turn the valley into a wellspring of decency, good supply of blessings, strength and a joyous workplace. Even in better climes, that requirement would be onerous. To compound the situation, there was also a "Goliath" (a towering, intimidating, and seemingly unconquerable enemy) in the valley that we must conquer as well – in fact as a first order priority.

The condition of the valley was a given, and we needed to appreciate it. Nigeria, or the wider society, was irritatingly mired in malfeasances. However, the foremost need of the hour for us (first order priority, because of its immediacy) was to correctly define and deal with the Goliath. At the first glimpse, it became clear that we needed to challenge ourselves, using all legitimate motivational means, to develop the conviction of the heart to stay the course; even if all we had were a few small and smooth pebbles like the Biblical David had.

Without that, creating a sense of ownership of the vision among the University community would have been impossible. Taking our point of departure from the issue of 'thinking', we pursued our 'vision-ownership' assignment by addressing selected issues: 'the change we must have', the call to be 'change agents', the need to 'free the leader within', the power of being 'positive livewires', the 'spirit of excellence', 'time as a resource', 'performance management', and the 'pain and thrill of leading right'.

What we did, in light of these realities, is what I term the 'travailing'. These were our efforts principally targeted at the 'thinking' of our stakeholders, not only to visualize but to also 'own' the vision. Our aim was to strengthen them to work with us to overpower the Goliath, transform the valley, and then go all out to actualize and promote the vision. We consciously planned it to be that they did so, not because they were told to but because they wanted to. That, to us, was the essence of travailing to create vision-ownership.

In our assessment, the atmosphere on ground when we arrived was patently corrupt and corrupting - among the high and the low alike! As we know from history, such a ground is the graveyard of the corruptible and the battlefield for the incorruptible. The former needed no further encouragement to indulge; and the latter needed no greater 'holy discontent' to step up for action. For us, it was the battlefield; and we had to work hard to make the 'holy discontent' infectious throughout the University community.

Early on in my tenure, I attended a conference organised by the Association of Vice Chancellors of Nigerian Universities at the University of Ilorin. One of the presentations was Professor Peter Okebukola's a paper on "Stemming Corruption, Restoring our Moral Compass and

Sustaining Ethics in our University System". No participant (among my fellow Vice Chancellors) challenged either Okebukola's assumptions or his diagnosis, certainly not to my hearing. Rather, a sense of the situation worsening and engulfing the entire nation was palpable. We were truly in the valley of Baca.

The "Goliath" on our way

Based on the impression you might have formed from reading the previous Chapters of this book, you would be pardoned to think that it was the constraint of resources that was the Goliath on our way. But you couldn't be farther from our reality. Of course, resource constraint was real and could have been debilitating when you consider the task of developing a University from virtually ground zero, the unflinching commitment of the proprietor notwithstanding. However, surprise, surprise, our own Goliath, in my considered judgment, was the **_mindset_** that the people we recruited, admitted or contracted brought along with them to the University community.

Towards the end of 2008, a team from the NUC visited us to monitor our progress in firming up our facilities for the take-off of the University. Curiously, they wanted to know what the biggest challenge was for me. They were shocked that I did not say it was resource constraint. I spent about two hours narrating the battle I was waging against the mindset of those 'building' with me.

We needed "to root out and to pull down, to destroy and to throw down…" that mindset. And then, "to build and to plant" a diametrically different software of the mind before we could cross the valley and turn it into a place of inspiring life[45]. We needed to do all this, leading from the front or by personal example. I recall telling the Chancellor and other members of the BOT that the task and the modus operandi that I was visualising at the time would test all of us sorely. But then, we had put our shoulders to the wheel (or hands to the plough) and there was no going back. I must say, we were already assured of some form of victory which was indescribable, much less comprehensible, to the human mind.

With several capacity-building seminars, we began to drill down to the heart of the matter for the wider University community to catch a glimpse of what we were up against and the endearing picture of the future of it all, should we stay the course. In one of such seminars, I made the point that:

> "… a woman when she is in travail has sorrow, because her

hour is come: but as soon as she is delivered of the child, she remembers no more the anguish, for the joy that a man is born into the world"[46]. That is one mystery we will never understand fully until we get to heaven. Mothers that are here I'm sure you can bear me witness that the pains you go through in childbirth suddenly (as soon as the baby is delivered) go into the recesses of your sub-consciousness or stand completely gone. I have seen a baby delivered and within seconds, the mother who was crying and wailing and kicking and cursing the husband was embracing this baby and smiling. It's a mystery.

And as I reflect upon what the Chancellor has being led by God to do for this University, I see a similar metaphor with my mind's eyes - the travail of a woman giving birth or delivering a child. I think Paul had a taste of this when he said: "My little children, of whom I travail in birth again until Christ is formed in you"[47].

So then, we travailed to burn into the souls of our community the new mindset needed to make the University (with its declared business ideology[48]) a reality even if we had to do this individual by individual. As John Maxwell did observe, "before God could change the world, He had to change the thinking of an individual". As a person thinks, so is he! Thus, the task of raising Godly global leaders ("saints in Sodom"), required that we helped our people to change the way they thought and acted. Several areas were shouting for attention; however, we zeroed in on our conviction that in matters of *leading right*, our people must as a matter of the irreducible minimum shift from:

- impossibility (no, we can't) to possibility (yes, we can) thinking;
- scarcity (not enough, better grab now) to abundance (there is a enough, let's share) mentality;
- mendacity (duplicitous and being averse to truth) to integrity (consistent, honest and trustworthy) behaving;
- simpleton (deceivable) to savvy (thorough) capabilities;
- mediocrity (average is good) to meritocracy (pursuit of excellence) commitments;
- selfishness (me for myself and I) to significance (me for others and us) philosophy; and
- provincialism (locally focused) to cosmopolitanism (globally oriented) thinking.

These seven areas adequately typified the broad dimensions of the challenge (the Goliath) as we perceived it at the time. The first three relate to the matter of <u>credibility</u> in leadership personality – which earns the leader the right to lead. The next two relate to the matter of <u>competence</u> with which the leader gets things done and earns the respect and commitment from his or her followers. And, the last two relate to the matter of consequence - which secures the culture and reputation from the leader's results. Hamm (2011) says, when these three components come together in a positive configuration, you have an 'unusually excellent' leadership.

So, regularly and persistently, we developed and deployed a series of seminars and workshops targeted at producing the mind-shift that must occur in order for us to succeed in our calling. A sample of my presentations at such seminars/workshops is reproduced in abridged forms below.

The change we must have

It was King Whitney Jr that once said: "change has a considerable psychological impact on human mind. To the fearful it is threatening because it means that things may get worse. To the hopeful it is encouraging because things may be better. To the confident, it is inspiring because the challenge exists to make things better". In one of the seminars on our travailing journey, I addressed the issues of thinking and change in a presentation titled: "Lead the Change, Sustain the Vision":

… Whether you and I like it or not, there will be change. *In other words, change is inevitable.* What is important to understand is what type of change, when, and how. And that leads me to what I'm going to talk about this morning. Look at that topic there: "lead the change, sustain the vision". The original topic was, "leading organisational change".

I was reflecting about that around 2.30am today and my spirit says, "change the orientation a little bit". It's not just leading organisational change, it is actually a call to a special duty: lead a purposeful change in order to sustain the vision. If we don't lead change, change will happen anyway but it may not be the change that you and I would like to see *in relation to the vision before us…*

I make this proclamation that "you either lead it or you lose it". [*I asked the participants: "When we say lead change, what change are we talking about?", and variety of thoughts was expressed.*]

… Everything we have said so far comes down to this for me: the change in the way we think and act. Whether is the change we desire, the change to build our future, fundamental change, transformational change, paradigm shift, and a host of other views expressed. They all come down to this simple construction for me, "the change in the way we think and act".

Many of us wondered why everything we've said so far comes down to this simple thing: 'thinking and acting'. The Bible says as a man "thinks in his heart so he is"[49]. Your entire being including *your* identity, modus operandi, way of life, etc., is reducible to that concept of thinking. You can be a millionaire today *but* if you think poverty, poverty and poverty, guess what will happen? You will become poor. It's not *because* you just lie down on your bed, *which of course* continually thinking poverty *can make you do*. No! It's just that your actions will be consistent with your thinking[50].

Thinking invariably translates into some form of action. Now, refusing to leave your bed and staying there until you die is an action - an action anchored to your thinking that "the whole world is bad, *I can't be bothered,* I better be poor, let me be poor". You will die poor. It didn't take me long to grasp the seriousness of this issue when I returned from Australia in 2008.

I went for jugging around in *a neighbourhood* in Abuja; I talked with people; I went to bukas (i.e. local eateries) to eat. Some people say, you mean Vice Chancellors eat in bukas? This VC you are seeing has eaten in bukas…, mama-put, that's another name. Why did I do that? I wanted to know how everybody at every level was thinking. I wanted to experience what everybody at every level was experiencing.

There was a time my driver and I went to one market in Abuja; and I asked somebody where they sold second-hand *(used)* cloths? The driver froze. He said, "what did you say?" I said "where do they sell second-hand cloths"? Was it because I could not afford new ones? No! In fact that very same day, I bought about a hundred thousand naira (N100,000.00) worth of new cloths – *which seemed such a big amount for some people*. I just wanted to go to the second-hand shopping centre *and have some idea about* how the people working there were thinking: how they defined their world. When they talked politics *or other social (local or national) issues*, they did so from their own perspective - from their own place in life. And I did all that so that when I came to engage with our global leaders and staff I could share with them real life *experiences/stories* at all levels…

From such exposures, I have come to see that there is something fundamentally upside down in the way we Nigerians think and act. Underline the word, "we". I'm not preaching to the Nigerians over there and hear people say… this one is not a Nigerian. That's why I love Daniel… When Daniel was praying for his people, he said,

Lord God Almighty, forgive **us** our iniquities[51], Was he among those that sinned? Was he sitting in broken Jerusalem committing all those atrocities and worshiping other gods? No! But he was nonetheless one of them.

This is the leadership 'law of sharing and/or identification' at work. It requires that good leaders take a little more than their share of the blame, and a little less than their share of the credit among those they want to influence[52]. Whatever we go through, wherever God has placed us now, you cannot but be a Nigerian. So when I talk about the way **we** think and act, I mean every word there. We are upside down in the way we think and act.

I came to the conclusion that this must change; if it does not change our destiny is permanently compromised. *I then exemplified this dire situation with many things that defy explanation or rationality which were occurring in Nigeria at the time, e.g. the Independent National Electoral Commission (INEC) failing to conduct simple elections[53].* It defied explanation that INEC *(as we read in the media)* had sent its teams overseas to check about 52 factories where its electoral papers could be printed, contracted five of them - all of them in Europe - to print 75 million sensitive electoral papers, went out for inspection on 26th of December in Europe when everybody would be on holidays. Then *the Commission* wondered why it failed to receive those papers on time for the elections.

Then there was the story of some ambassadorial nominees who could not recite the National Anthem and the National Pledge at the Senate screening, but their nominations were confirmed anyway. This was like saying "go with your ignorance *or negligence* and represent the nation well; go with your mediocrity and represent the nation well". *How do you explain that?*

… If this is where we stop, then we are most miserable... But this is the context in which you and I are challenged to lead change. I know we all have a laudable and lofty vision for Nigeria; we all do. This vision is not just going to happen by happenstance - it will not happen just like that: willy-nilly. It has to happen when you and I lead. Right now God has called us to Salem University to learn to lead.

The change we must have is from scarcity mentality to abundance mentality, from selfishness to significance, from mediocrity to meritocracy, etc. I have seen Nigerians scramble over resources. Towards the end of last year the National Assembly was in the newspapers, on the radios, in televisions - not for the right reasons *I must add.* They were there because of the way they were *alleged to be hovering* over the national treasury *or cake as vultures to the spoil.*

And some reports suggested that the President of the Senate in Nigeria was earning more than the President of America. His own salary, his own take home was much more than that of President Obama of the United States of America. But don't let us take away anything from our National Assembly. They are doing a fantastic job, isn't it? They are serving the nation well, isn't it? They pass laws *as required by* Section 4 of the 1999 Constitution of Nigeria which defines their role to make laws for good governance, peace and prosperity of Nigeria.

It is amazing how our National Assembly has acquitted itself even with reference to that *Constitutional power.* .. I have been waiting to see when one member of our National Assembly will stand up and say: "let us do some self- assessment. Our mandate is this; let's compute what we have done - put them on one side of the scale and put our mandate on another side of the scale to see how they weigh against each other". Not once have I heard that. *It's possible they've done that and I have yet to hear about it. But one hears more about their fight over constituency allowances, etc in the media.*

To me this all stems from (in addition to other complicating factors) the mediocrity, selfishness, scarcity, etc., mentalities which say in sum: "While you are there grab your own now, tomorrow, it will be gone". *They grab inordinately, stupendously and struggle to conceal their loot.* That is why I'm told via the media that in this country we have politicians who no longer use the banking system. Their own banking system is a hole or water tank in their backyard. They dig the hole or mount the tank there and then stack away not naira, but hard currencies: dollars, euros, pound sterling and in some cases franc. ...

We have this mentality of "it is impossible". This is one of the cardinal mental blocks that I battled with when I first came to the University. A Nigerian would give you 15 reasons why something could not be done. When you ask him or her to find just one reason that it could be done, they would scratch their heads and then squeeze out one reason. And you know what? Those of you that have worked with me closely would recall I always said: "that one reason you have found is more than enough; let's start from there then the 15 counter-reasons (i.e. for the view that it could not be done) would take care of themselves". The effort was to shift from impossibility thinking to possibility thinking.

Then there is the need to change from simpleton to savvy... In spite of our claim to smartness, we are very simpleton in our thinking. When it comes to dealing globally, Nigerians appear naïve. *Talking in generalities and from personal experience here,* before a white man or woman comes to the table to discuss something with you, he or she has thought about ten different scenarios and he or she has prepared what his or her action will be in those ten different scenarios. Bring a Nigerian to the same table. Usually it is at that meeting that we begin to think or create options; but in the international arena, that would be too late.

Before you know what is happening, decisions are made. They haven't got time to wait and waste. I have seen the way many politicians here behave. Why would they care about time anyway? If they give 10 am for a meeting or an event, you can be sure that they will get there at 2 or 3 pm and people would still be waiting for them. So why would they care? We take the same attitude overseas. You organise a meeting inviting people – Africans and Westerners alike. The Westerners would be there generally on time, while Nigerians or Africans would take their time to arrive very late. And the Westerners would be sitting there wondering, who are these people? Of course, there are exceptions on both sides.

...We must also change from provincialism to cosmopolitism: it is about your horizon - whether you look so low just around you or you look farther afield... Our leaders today are generally so provincial in their thinking: 'it is the here and now; it is the world around me'. The other day there was a commentary that anytime a politician went to their *electoral* ward, people rushed to mob them and would not let them go until the politician has given them money. So what have politicians become? They are now provincial in their thinking.

When they are *going to their constituencies,* they get some change (currencies in smaller denominations); they are thinking about the people that would be rallying around them. *These politicians* cannot look beyond *these hangers-on* to see the broader developmental needs of their community. As soon as they satisfy the people that are rallying around them, that's it, they've done their bit and tomorrow they are gone. Provincialism makes you to be myopic - short sighted. However, cosmopolitanism lifts your horizon to see globally – the big picture and compels you to act accordingly.

... From mendacity to integrity. Oh Nigerians, we are very

mendacious. We have crafty ways of solving our problems. And these crafty ways are in the long run very counterproductive. We devise a number of ways to solve our problems now. We don't care whether those solutions will become problems in the future. And when you are hell bent on solving your problems *anyhow* now; when you are hell bent on getting out of trouble willy-nilly, chances are that integrity would become a casualty. But we know that in Salem University one of our core values is integrity.

To lead change and to sustain vision is about transformation. This is more than doing something new. As you lead change, you must combine inner shift with the external variations... There *must be* a perspective shift. And that involves the values that you subscribe to. It involves the aspirations that you have or you develop. *All of these must show in* the behaviours that you exhibit. This inner shift must happen for transformation to be brought about and to be sustained...

Your strategies must change, your processes must change, and your practices must change. In all of these, there must be capacity building for doing things in a new way and sustaining that change. None of us is born with the capacity of doing new things in a way that is sustainable. None! We all have to learn.

The day before yesterday I was walking down to the Administration Block; there were about five global leaders ahead of me and two were coming behind me. I saw some rubbish on the path way and walked passed them deliberately. The global leaders ahead of me had already walked pass them carelessly. So I was watching to see what the ones behind me would do. They equally walked pass the rubbish. Then I turned to them and said, "by the way, are you global leaders"? They said, "yes". "Ok! … you [*I pointed to one of them*] go back to the end of the flower bed, you will see something that does not belong there". He went back there and picked up the rubbish. I said, "Good! Look for the next rubbish bin and drop them there". You see, this thing (mindset) doesn't come to us as a natural endowment. It comes by learning or capacity building.

You and I are called to lead so that the vision can be sustained. So where are you in all of this? And what are you doing? … The vision you do not understand, you cannot pursue. And the vision you don't pursue you cannot possess.

… Let's read Psalms 78: 70-72. God chose David from among his people; He chose him from following young lambs. In other words He chose him from being an ordinary shepherd of animals to become a Shepherd of God's inheritance (people). And the

Bible records in verse 72 that David **shepherded them with the integrity of his heart and the skillfulness of his hands**. .. That scripture was given to me, if I'm not mixing dates now, a month before I left Australia. "You must shepherd the vision with the integrity of your heart and by the skillfulness of your hands. If you don't do that you will *struggle*".

That's why I am here. Now, some of us don't understand what it means to be a shepherd. There is a difference between a shepherd and a hireling. A hireling is someone who is hired to look after animals; he is on the tree enjoying the breeze; the sheep are on the ground exposed and whatever happens to them is not his or her business. That is a hireling... You want to lead change and sustain the vision? You must become a shepherd. And the shepherd takes many things for the sake of the sheep. They run, they fall down, they get up; they run, they fall, they get up again – all for the sake of the wellbeing of the flock. That's a shepherd!

… Somebody has to lead the change. But unless you have the heart of a shepherd you cannot lead *sustainably*. Even if you do some spectacular activities, they are momentary; there is no sustainability in it. You do something today you create a change quick-quick and then tomorrow you have forgotten about the change. The people around have forgotten about change. That is not the heart of a shepherd.

We are called to lead and to do so with integrity of our hearts and the skillfulness of our hands… It is a [morally sound] problem-solving calling. .. Moving from a given state to a desired state; that is problem solving. .. It takes active role of leading - to move from where we are to where we ought to be. It requires a quality-focused mindset to improve situations. It requires a goal-directed activity. [*I linked sustaining the vision to the issue of 'significance' which is a higher level of accomplishment than success in leadership literature*].

… *Leading change sustainably* is about moving from success to significance. Success is when I value add to myself. Thirty-one years ago I was an ordinary undergraduate student. Today I am by the grace of God looking after an institution similar to where I was - similar in the sense of the status as *a University that would produce graduates*. See how successful I am; well, can anybody deny that? No! I have succeeded. Does that define my significance? No! It doesn't define my significance. It defines my success. What I am doing now – capacity-building others; value adding to others is what defines my significance. *It is a way to lead change and sustain the vision that makes the change imperative…*

Called to be a change agent[54]

Murren (1997, p200) was right when he said: "You would be hard pressed to argue convincingly that a person can be a leader without being a change agent".

For us, it was not enough to establish that change is inevitable; nor was it sufficient to argue that the type of change required involved shifts in mindsets or mentalities. A major component of the mission mandate for Salem University (in the context of its transformational academic revolution) was to 'raise global leaders with royalty and prestige who are simply change agents'.

So, it was a constant refrain in all my interactions with the University community that they must become change agents to qualify as leaders. My strategy was first to get members of the community to understand, and then become dissatisfied with, the status quo. As Arnold Michael, a social psychologist from Stanford University concluded from an extensive research project, "change comes from dissatisfaction" (see Murren 1997, p204). Thereafter, I charged everyone of us to take action at whatever level we occupied. I have reproduced below one of such interactions, on this occasion with the Student Leaders Forum.

> … First of all I want to acknowledge all of you for this sacrifice to be here when your fellow global leaders are rushing to meet their parents or sponsors and to have a well-deserved break from a very long year of study. But you are here for a purpose and the purpose for which you are here cannot be over emphasised. We have about 258 global leaders in total, and there are about 40 of you here. … I want you to cast your mind back to the day that we set you apart; the day we commissioned your responsibilities… *[To underline how serious their call to leadership was, I provided some contextual information about Nigeria as follows:]*

> Ok. Let me give us some basic statistics about our country. Nigeria is about 924,000 square meters in land mass. That is about the 32nd largest country in the world - just by land mass. But I want to tell you that within the land mass, we have almost all the types of vegetation you can find in the world: rain forest, grass land, sahel, riverine, salt and fresh water swamps, etc, with annual rainfall between 20 and 80 inches. There are few countries in the world that have a better combination of climatic conditions.

> With our population of about 150 million, Nigeria is the largest concentration of black people in the world. The population of

Nigeria alone is more than 25 per cent of the population of Africa put together; so at least one in every four African is a Nigerian.

Given the land mass that we have and the nature of the vegetation and the soil composition, Nigeria can actually feed Africa - the entire Africa for [many] years uninterrupted. In other words, tell the rest of the African countries about 53 of them: don't farm, just depend on Nigeria alone and for the next [many] years, Africa will feed fully and there will be no problem whatsoever.

Nigeria has one of the finest oil deposits in the world. Nigeria is the eight largest oil exporting country in the world. In terms of our other mineral resources, we have: coal, gold, limestone, iron ore, bauxite, over five trillion cubic meters of natural gas resources, etc.

The question is this: with all these endowments, how come that when it comes to human development measurement out of 192 countries in the United Nations, Nigeria comes 152 - very close to the bottom? Why the poor rating? Three factors (in my judgement) are responsible: **leadership, leadership, and leadership**. When other countries are using what is between their two ears for the development of their national interest, some of our own so-called leaders spend so much of their 24 hours in a day, 365 days in a year thinking of how to diminish the nation by sharing the resources for their personal use. So it seems!

The educational system in the country has collapsed, we all know that. There are about 21 million young people that are within the age of secondary schools and do you know how many people attend secondary schools in Nigeria? Five million! What happens to the remaining 16 million? There are 11 million people within the primary school age and how many attend primary school? One million! What happens to the remaining 10 million? Yet our leaders go to bed at night. Let me correct myself, they don't go to bed at night. That is when they do their skimming. *Take the federal level, for instance.* I am told Abuja is a city of the night; that is when they meet, that is when they skim: how much to take, how much not to take (*talking in generalities, there are exceptions*).

The international community knows Nigeria very well that we are so corrupt. That is why *(I'm told)* any company wishing to come and do business in Nigeria, must set aside certain amount of money for bribery. They call it facilitation money. So our reputation goes ahead of us in many *non-complimentary* directions.

What has happened in the last 15 to 20 years in this country is that there seems to have been a deliberate design to destroy education as the backbone of the country. An educated population is *in all probability a patriotic and* development-oriented population. So if you want to attack development what do you do? Attack education! And our so-called leaders successfully did that. So *because* education has been destroyed, we now have nonentities *and the unemployables*; we now have the uneducated *or unpatriotic* mind taking over the leadership of the nation. And you wonder why our country is going round in a spin - going nowhere?

... Which area in our country can you point to and say we have rest from iniquity? Which area? When it comes to vocational education the developed world ensures that at least 29 per cent of their population must be engaged in technical and vocational education - to sustain their level of development. You know what we have in Nigeria? 1.8 per cent and you think we seriously want to develop?

Time will not permit us to go over a number of other areas particularly the criminal justice which is my field *of academic specialisation*. But I can tell you now that when in Criminology we talk about the prisonisation syndrome, Nigeria ranks very high among the countries of the world. When people are sent to prison and they come out worse than they go in you get the prisonisation syndrome... The rate of recidivism - that is the going into prison and coming out and going in again - is among the highest in the world.

Let me say a few things about the policing system... I can tell you now that Nigeria is also one of the countries that least takes care or looks after their police officers. I have travelled across the world, I never came across anywhere where some of the police officers are actually living/sleeping in dilapidated buildings; uncompleted buildings or buildings that the roofs are just caving in and they are still there with their wives and children. Even in South Africa under apartheid, black police officers apparently lived in better shanties than the ones Nigerian police personnel are made to live in...; and you expect them to do a good job, be professional, and have the respect that they need to project the authority of the uniform?

It is in Nigeria that you will find judges that can be bribed openly. In other countries there are bribery and corruption taking place but probably not as blatant, not as open, not as defiant as we have in our own country. In Nigeria you find prison officers colluding with criminals that are put in their care to do more crime. And you wonder, what is wrong with us? Why are we behaving the way we are behaving? A different species? And yet Nigeria is one of the most blessed countries in the world. [*After impressing on the participants the seriousness of the Nigerian situation, I rounded up with a story about being a change agent*].

I went to this meeting in Abuja… called by the "Foundation for Better Nigeria". I was invited to come and speak. Nobody told me what type of underlying politics was going on, but *soon after I accepted the invitation* I did further research and found out what they were about – party political promotion. It is one nature of mine never to run away from challenges; so I said I will go there anyway, *knowing fully well I don't play partisan politics*.

I got there and I was seated on the high table with Senators *and other dignitaries*. In fact, sitting next to me was the ex-Deputy Governor of a State in the South-South zone. Speeches were being delivered; there was oath taking for the newly appointed officers of the organisation, etc. All of a sudden there was commotion among the people. Then I noticed food was being served.

You know what happened? The entire attention of the participants went away from this important event. They started scrambling for food so much so that nobody could hear anything going on in the hall anymore except "give me, give me, give me, give me"; and they were fighting and rushing. It was the Nigerian scarcity mentality on display!

Now, the interesting part was this. I was the next person to speak; so the ex- Deputy Governor said, "my VC, what do you think?" I said "we have lost the audience; we don't have them with us anymore". So he said, "What are you going to do?" I said watch. *Meanwhile I was angry in my soul and praying silently.* "Lord just give me an insight into what is going on here and show me what to do". Then, I heard: "it is now our pleasure to invite the Vice Chancellor of Salem University to address us".

It looked like nobody else heard what the announcer said because previously the audience clapped at such introductions. Now, nobody clapped. I took the microphone, got to the podium… Immediately I said, "if you are here for a better Nigeria [quipping on the name of their organisation] please rise up with me". Some of the people were shocked - wondering: "what did he say"? I said it again: "if you are here for a better Nigeria and not for your stomach please rise up with me".

They sort of looked at each other and… stood to their feet but there was still some noise from the food scramble. I said it for the third time: "if you are here for a better Nigeria keep your mouth shut now and listen to what I have to say". Suddenly, there was utter silence. *If you dropped a pin in the hall you will hear the sound. Finally, I got the attention of all the participants* and I kept them standing until I delivered my speech completely.

In the speech, I highlighted the state of the nation, where Nigeria was heading if we did nothing extraordinarily different, and how producing a better Nigeria was everybody's business. By this time it was clear to me that the whole arrangement was to support Dr Goodluck Jonathan in his presidential campaign. So, I ended my speech with: "Good luck to Nigeria!".

When I finished, the ovation was more than a standing ovation. One of the Senators ran to me and embraced me, saying: "thank you, thank you, you have saved us"... And *many participants rushed to collect my contact details.* The ex-Deputy Governor held my hand and said, "I thought I was a good politician; you are a better politician than me". I said: "no, I'm not a politician; I'm an agent of change. That's who I am". I can tell you that for the rest of the time everyone was focused until the meeting was over. The ex-Deputy Governor was the second person after me to speak; he had the audience. When he finished his speech and came to sit down, he said, "thank you for getting the audience to listen to me".

Two things I want to underline here: (1) the Nigerian psychology; and (2) the fact that if God has made you a change agent, even in the midst of the most chaotic situation, you can still make a difference.

Free the leader in you[55]

In many instances, people do not pursue change. The reason is not because they do not understand the issue of change or conceptually what needs to be done. More often than not, the challenge is that they have yet to discover that the 'leader' locked inside of them needed to be freed. I used the occasion of one of our internal Global Leadership Conferences to address this matter:

What a privilege to be able to go through this session on leadership. The Conference has been very informative and transformative particularly for those who indeed were not only present in body but present in spirit.

If you have your Bible please turn with me to John 11: 11-14: "These things He said, and after that He said to them, our friend Lazarus sleeps; but I go, that I may awake him out of sleep. Then

122

His disciples said, Lord, if he sleeps, he will get well. However, Jesus spoke of his death but they thought he had spoken of taking of rest in sleep. Then said Jesus to them plainly, Lazarus is dead."

The topic I'm going to talk about this morning is "Free the Leader Within You". For the whole of this week we have had the privilege of being treated to a number of topics in the Conference around the theme of "Awaken the Leader in You". [*I did a "week in review" to summarise the salient lessons presented during the week and to test the extent to which leadership had been awoken in the lives of the participants.*]

We read from John 11 a story of Lazarus who fell sick. The news came to Jesus and He spoke to His disciples "our friend Lazarus is asleep". Let me announce to all of us here this morning that *any* potential in you is a friend. Some people hate themselves so much that the good things God had deposited inside of them are construed as enemies. *On the contrary*, I see those potentials - particularly the leadership potentials that God has deposited in you, as friends. It is not all the time that the friends that you have or the friends within you make you laugh and be happy. There are times when those friends make you to be disquieted.

The disciples did not know what Jesus was saying. The disciples were thinking that, well, Lazarus is resting, sleeping beautifully so let's let him rest. I've come across so many people who allow the leadership potentials in them to sleep beautifully. But they did not know (like the disciples of Jesus) that their potentials were actually dead. They thought: "I'm just taking it cool, I'm just drifting through life...". I tell you this morning, chances are that those friends inside you are dead but you do not know.

I thank God for the Conference because one of the cardinal reasons for the Conference is to do exactly what Jesus did to the disciples. Verse 14: Jesus now spoke to them plainly, "Lazarus is dead." The people God used during this week have one way or the other announced to us that as a matter of fact, the friend in you is dead. Jesus said, "let us go that I may wake him up". Based on the testimonies and stories we have heard *now*... our guest speakers did awaken some dead friends inside us. ...In other words they have made us to become aware of the dimensions of the leadership that are inside of us that we need to activate...

Our topic this morning will take us to another level at which to be awake is not enough. Turn to the Scriptures with me to John 11: 39-44. Those of you who are familiar with the story would know the drama between Jesus, Martha and Mary. I'm not going to go into those details now. But when Jesus said I go that I may awaken my own friend, He had something more in mind:

> "Jesus said, take away the stone. Martha, the sister of him who was dead, said to Him, Lord, by this time there is a stench: for he has been dead four days. Jesus said to her, did I not say to you that if you would believe, you would see the glory of God? Then they took away the stone from the place where the dead man was laying... [Jesus] cried with a loud voice, 'Lazarus, come forth'...".

Today there is a proclamation upon the potential that is lying dead in you; it will have no choice but to come forth in the name of Jesus. Now listen very carefully; let's read verse 44 together: "And he who had died came forth". Ah but there is a problem: the leader within you – asleep or dead - has been awoken. Lazarus could not have come forth unless he had been awoken. However, as he stepped out of the grave... and everybody saw him, "**he was bound**".

In the Middle East there is a way they handle dead bodies: they wrap around them twirling graveyard cloths... Lazarus came out with *such* cloths around him. You have been awoken but you may still be bound. So there is the need for the next level; there is a need for the declaration and commanding of all the forces holding you bound, that you be freed. Jesus said unto them, "loose him and let him go"!

Freeing the leader within is to loose and let go. In the course of the ministration for the days that I was here, I saw the exuberance, the excitement of those that were being woken up. Be reminded that some of us woke up alright, but may still be bound. And until there is a loosening and letting go - until there is freeing of the leader within you, you are not any better than a fighting dog on a leash (the rope that you tie on the neck of the dog to control its moving around). A dog on a leash is like a leader who has had the leader within him or her awoken but is yet to be freed...

At Salem University we are moving beyond just cleaning up our global leaders and our global staff. Because you can be cleaned up on the outside but you still are dead on the inside nonetheless. We are working hard to awaken you (your potentials) and to remove grave cloths around you... There may be a miracle to wake you up; however, unless the graveyard cloths are removed, you will not be effective. **Effectiveness is not the product of being awakened; effectiveness is a product of freedom. You must be freed to be effective.**

… Free the damn thing; let the leaders go and serve God as they were originally intended. Jesus commanded them, loose him and let him go. What was Jesus saying? This is not what God intended for Lazarus; he was not made for this kind of graveyard clothing that we are seeing on him now. He was made for something better, something more glorious; he was made to go, to be on the go. Loose him and let him go; let him be on the go. Be on the go *for Godly service to humanity*! That is your destiny.

… I want to reflect fairly quickly on some of the fundamentals of freeing the leader within us.

1. Get the right perspective on leadership… I commend two books for you to read as part of this process: Dr. Myles Munroe's "Becoming a Leader" and Dr. Sam Amaga's "The Leader God will be Proud of". Look at those two texts. They will assist you... The Greek philosophers according to Munroe "gave the world some philosophies about leadership and that led to the world moving from one stage to the other groping in darkness and sometimes without leadership.

   What did they say? Leaders are born and they are very few: so the rest of us the masses are meant to be followers. So what happens? Some of us would not bother: "well, why should I even try – even the awakening of the leader within me that they are talking about? What if I was not born to be a leader; why do I bother?" In this conference it has been demonstrated to all of us that everyone is born *with leadership potentials*. Everyone is called to be a leader; *all may not respond to the call but* everyone *has the capacity to respond and* thereby be announced as a leader.

   You have no excuse whatsoever. The theory of the Greek philosophers has been debunked, particularly in the 20th century which was one of the worst centuries the world has ever known. All the major world wars have happened in the 20th century. The most dangerous weapon ever manufactured by humanity was manufactured in the 20th century. The bitterest rivalry between nations that we have ever dreamt of took place in the 20th century. And the world has not fully recovered yet. All of them can be traced to this lopsided and warped philosophy that some people are born to lead, while others are born to follow.

Go all the way back to Hitler who believed that only a certain race is born to rule while all other races are born to follow. So any trace of leadership in anybody other than the 'born-leader' race was discarded with alacrity; that was until God punctured his swollen theory in the 1930s when an African American won a race to pick the gold medal in the full glare of Hitler....

Better get the right perspective on leadership. That is why I have being working hard to let even the cleaners know… that they are leaders. I think that message is getting across. Can any of the global leaders testify to what our cleaners are doing? *Big chorus* - "Oh yes!" I have been to several institutions and organisations and I can tell you now that I'll give "A" grade to my cleaners here any day. Are they doing the ideal we are looking for? Not yet! But they are leaders putting in their best. It doesn't matter where God has placed you now, you are a leader; get the right perspective.

2. Discover the foundation, which is your purpose. If there is anything that we must grasp to be able to find our freedom it is discovering our purpose. There is a leader in everyone waiting to serve their generation. Underline the word "waiting" and the word "serve". When you go to hotels you find waiters; what are they doing? They are there waiting to serve you. In everyone, God has designed somebody that would wait and serve their generation. Recognise that, and actualize it; history is replete with the names of *such persons*.

For instance, when Mother Teresa left Macedonia and went to Calcuta India, she didn't set out saying: "I am going to be the famous queen of these downtrodden Indians. No! She was a leader that was prepared and found her purpose by taking her preparation to meet opportunity in India; and today her name has gone down in the annals of history that she is the woman the world cannot ignore. It doesn't matter what your challenges are, *you can be a Mother Theresa in your own area of calling.*

Munroe made reference to Helen Keller. At the age of one, Helen Keller was a bobbly child everybody was happy with, in her family. All of a sudden she was struck with some illness and lost her eyes at the age of two. I'm sure the parents would have said, "Oh this is the end of our wonderful daughter". Somehow, the leader within her was awoken and was freed - loosened and let go. She became one of the most powerful motivational authors the world has known today. If you haven't read any of her books; go and read and you would wonder whether it was written by someone who was blind from the age two.

It is important you note that leaders are not those who watch things happen around them; you better know that very well. You sit down and the world is just twirling around you and you say, "This one looks so good today oh"; tomorrow, "Hum, this one looks so bad today oh"; and you are sitting there like a zombie. That's not a leader. Leaders *who have found their purpose* don't let things happen to them; such leaders don't ask what has just happened? What do they do? They make things happen!

The quickest way to distinguish between a leader and a follower is to just apply this framework: Who is watching things happen? Who is letting things happen around them? Who is asking, hey, something just happen here - what happened and where was I? These are followers. The leaders are those who ask: *"What next?" "What can I make happen in this circumstance?" When you hear that,* you don't need an angel to come down and proclaim to you, "here is your leader follow ye her". No! The leader manifests by making things happen.

Read the life of Jesus Christ and you will notice that He never ever watched things happen. *The moment Jesus stepped into any situation, He started turning things around for good. He knew His foundation - His purpose, and He went about doing good.* You want to be freed? You want the graveyard clothing around you to go off? Discover the foundation - your purpose. You are created to do good works (Ephesians

2:10). So, any time you do anything that is a bad work, know fully well that you have moved away from your purpose... Paul says, "We are His workmanship, created in Christ Jesus unto good works"... So if you move away from good works, you may be awake but you are bound...

Jesus knew His purpose. He read in Luke 4: 18-19 "The Spirit of the Lord is upon me, because he hath anointed me to preach the gospel to the poor; he hath sent me to proclaim freedom to the captive and recovering of sight to the blind, to set free the oppressed; to preach the acceptable year of the Lord." No wonder, He could say boldly in John 18: 37 "For this cause I was born. For this cause I came to the world..."

Have you discovered your own cause? Do you know why you came to Salem University? Do you know why you were born in the first place? If you don't, we may succeed in our efforts to awaken the leader within you but you may not respond to our efforts to have you freed. Who am I? Why am I here? *Where am I going?* These are fundamental questions every leader must answer to be free and effective.

I emphasise this point because as I follow up on all aspects of the University, I get to know that there are some global leaders who are doing their pre-degree here that have no idea what their purpose is. They don't turn up for classes; I'm told that some of them because they had taken this exam again and again without success, they have given up on themselves. They are here because Papa said they must go; they are here because Mama said "if you don't go, I go die oh". Oh that you may find out, what it is that God has purposed for you from the beginning (before you were conceived in your mother's womb); then you can be freed to be the leader God wants you to be.

3. Press forward. Philippians 3: 13-14, states: "... this one thing I do, forgetting those things which are behind and reaching forth to those things which are [in the front]". I forget my past; I'm not going to be bound by whatever experience I have gone through. Forgetting what is behind; reaching forward to what is ahead, that's pressing forward.

I went to Abuja the other time for a book launch by the Vice President of the Federal Republic of Nigeria. I got to the venue and sat down on row number three from the high table. After a while, I needed to dash out to make some phone calls; so I stepped out and made the phone calls. By the time I got back to the entrance door, the VP had entered and the door was locked; there were two hefty security men now at the door.

Listen to what some foolish Nigerians did; thinking they were "pressing forward": one hit the security with his hand, "now let me go in, I'm supposed to be in there". The security said, "do you have ID?" "I don't have ID but I was invited, I need to be in there", he said. Others joined (about 15 of them) and were pushing each other against the security men. I was wondering what was going on. When I saw what was happening right before my eyes, I lifted my voice, "Nigerians, that would not get you inside". I was going to say foolish Nigerians that would not get you inside. I held back the "foolish", I just gave them "Nigerians".

Here was my own predicament. I left Lokoja 5am but in the course of getting ready to leave on time, I picked a wrong wear which did not have my identity card. So when I got to the door, the security man said "Sir, I heard you speak responsibly, where is your ID?" I had none except the voter's registration card. He said "Sir, this one, we no go accept this one oh". I said "this is produced by the money we (*our Government*) spent to buy DCM (data capturing machines)". He said "Sir, so many people fake it oh, how do I know that you are the owner? This ID is not acceptable".

I stepped back. You would have thought, that was the end. I stood there thinking: I woke up 5 o'clock at Lokoja, drove through all the dangers to get to Abuja to be inside there (in fact I had already gone in there, my things were already inside) and I am going to be stopped at the door here? No way. So I was pacing up and down. The security looked at me - because of the way I had behaved, he didn't know who

I was. He said "Sir, have you found your ID? I said "don't worry since you said Mr. VP is in now and your protocol is never to open the door even with my voter's card, I'm not going to force you against your protocol...

So while this security man was still fighting and pushing a number of people away, I looked at my wallet again and lo there was my driver's licence from Australia. So I quietly went to him and said, "Mr Man would you accept *overseas* driver's licence as evidence of my ID? ... He looked at it and said, "Oga Sir thank you very much, please go, go in". I was pressing forward *in the right way* until I got in *legitimately*! You cannot stop a leader. Press forward towards your mark.

4. Stand fast in the "liberty wherewith Christ has made us free and be not entangled again with the yoke of bondage". The graveyard clothing is part of the yoke of bondage: anger, lies, envy, sin, etc. These are all elements of the yoke of bondage. You better stand fast in the liberty Christ has already given you. The liberty of the light of God. The liberty of peace. The liberty of joy. The liberty of justice. The liberty of a leader.

    Let me paraphrase James 1: 25. But he who looks into the perfect law of liberty and continues in it, and is not a forgetful hearer but a doer of the work; this one would be blessed in all what he does – he would be a freed leader. You have been awoken; but you may be bound. It took Jesus to declare with the voice of an Archangel to bring liberty to free Lazarus... Jesus cried out with a loud voice and said, "Lazarus come forth". Even the dead man recognised the voice of an Archangel... "Loose him and let him go". The leader in all of us must not only be awoken; it needs to be freed so that we can be effective in our callings.

Livewire: "My soul had a birthday"[56]

Leaders who have been freed, and have started to take their place as 'change agents', become transformers in their generations. Anyone that touches them or that they touch undergoes a qualitative change. I tried to convey this point to the University community, using several fora and means. At one of such fora (a staff orientation week), I challenged all of us to become livewires whom people would touch and receive lasting positive impact in their lives.

"The day I touched teacher, that day my soul had a birthday", said Ann Silver a blind girl who had lost all hope to be somebody in life until she touched a transformational teacher. So much was the impact of that touch that now teacher is dead but Ann tells us the teacher lives on. Where does the teacher live now? In her life!

Query: If any global leader touches you would he/she be transformed, regardless of what your role in the University here is? If any global leader touches you, can they bear for you the testimony that this blind girl is bearing for her teacher? *In other words, are you a livewire? We say Salem University is a godly instrument for change. Well, you are the University, but are you a godly instrument for change?* ...

The power of touch is beyond description. A woman with haemorrhage for twelve years touched the edge of the garment of Jesus, she was never the same again[57]... *Here are some stories to make my point.*

2.00 am on a particular day in Australia, there was a phone call when I was already asleep. I woke up, felt my way through the dark and grabbed the phone. "Y-e-s who is on the line please?" And there was like an excited voice at the other end. "Sir! Sir! It's me! Sir! It's me!". Then, he said, "Sir I just got your phone number. All this years I have been looking for your phone number. I just got it now. And I am ringing to tell you Sir, that you changed my life."

The person was ringing from Abuja. He said, "Sir you remember me? I was in your class at Ahmadu Bello University in Zaria (ABU)... Jurisprudence! You came to teach us Jurisprudence. I was a law student. I have since graduated. I practised law for a while but now am in the Ministry of Health. You changed my life". *I had no recollection of doing anything in particular for the caller; however, that was his experience from an encounter with me.*

Another similar story. I was at Kaduna airport going to Lagos to attend a conference - a poor lecturer at ABU at the time. I was sitting at a corner in the airport, waiting for the plane to board. Then, I saw this motorcade that drove in. A big vehicle came to a stop surrounded by several others. And I said to myself, "what is going on here?" I just sat there, peeping through the window to see what was happening.

Somebody ran and opened the door to the big car; and this man came out in a flowing gown, immaculate white. He was walking as if he was on top of the world. So, he came into the airport and looked around. All of a sudden, this man began to walk towards me. And you know how your mind would be racing ten million kilometres per hour: "This man is coming towards me. What has he got in mind?" I checked my spirit immediately and the spirit said, "Paul, you have not done anything wrong. Be at peace". The aide-de-camp ran after him wondering where his master was going.

This man came to where I was sitting; and in the glare of many in the airport he said to me: "Good afternoon, Sir." I felt like the ground would open for me to disappear. I said: "Good afternoon. Am sorry, I don't know you". He smiled and said "Sir, you won't. You were my lecturer in part one *(i.e. first year)* at ABU". In those days, we *could several* hundreds of students in the lecture theatre. "Sir, you touched my life. You changed me. I am who I am today because of what you did to us in part one". Then I said, "thank you, thank you very much. What are you doing now?" I was looking for words, I was stammering. He said "Sir, after my graduation I joined the army. I am a military officer; this is where God has placed me. I never knew I will be so-so, but am grateful". I said: "am very delighted for you".

I was 1.72 metres tall in height. You know what, by the time he left, I felt like I had become 10 metres tall. I got up from my seat; I was now walking around the airport. And those that did not take notice of me before, were now saying "thank you sir". That very testimony of the man in a flowing gown changed my status in the eyes of the whole world at the airport.

Who has touched you and has been transformed? Who will touch you in Salem University and be changed *positively* for ever?

The spirit of excellence[58]

One of the traits of leaders whose contacts with people transform noticeably, is the pursuit of excellence. As a personal philosophy, I pursue perfection so that should I fail to reach it (almost invariably so), I can land on excellence. Taking the cue also from the vision of the University "to be a center of excellence…", I sensed the need to explore with, and get commitment from, the University community on the importance of seeking excellence in all our 'building' endeavours.

Thus, at every point in our mental re-engineering efforts, we taught what excellence meant; showed how we were pursuing it; and the exemplary results that were accruing to our efforts. When the time came for the first set of our global leaders to go out and mix with the wider world on the platform of industrial work placements, I seized the occasion to drill more deeply into how 'excellence' must attest to whatever leadership potentials we had awakened and freed within ourselves up to that moment. Below is an excerpt of the address I gave on that occasion.

… This is the last TLTC session we are holding for some time - for those who will be proceeding to their Students Industrial Work Experience Scheme (SIWES). After today, we will see you in *three months time*. It is our joy to bring you to a point where you can step out to check out the *wider* world and then come back *to finish up your studies*. For most of you our joy is boundless. For a very few, we have some trepidations concerning what you will do *and*, what you will be, out there.

For the past few days, I have been trying to overcome flu; my body has been telling me to take it easy. So I wasn't going to come today. But I said to myself if I don't come, I may not see these global leaders again until sometime. So that's why am here. I have two tasks: (1) to introduce the next theme for our TLTC and (2) to then *lead general discussion* in our leaders' assembly. But let me start with the theme.

…This year we've looked at wisdom to handle challenges. I do know that unless somebody is here without some brains, there is no way you wouldn't have caught something useful for your life from the teachings. We've also covered wisdom for supernatural harvest. It is clear from all the presentations that before there is any harvest, there must be sowing. You don't sow any seed, you harvest nothing.

The next theme we shall be handling is, "developing the spirit of excellence." Before I touch this particular theme which by the way will only be introductory, I want to on behalf of the rest of the University community- global staff and students alike- express our joy and gratitude to the young couple that God has used to anchor our TLTC programs in the Chaplaincy. If you can join your hands with me, let's celebrate Osiri Wisdom and Favour Wisdom. *Turning to them, I said*: "We celebrate you". Even though in the presentation to night I will not mention the Osiris by name, some of the elements or concepts I will be bringing out, you will find them in this couple *because they embody* the spirit of excellence.

I remember telling some members of the Board of Trustees who visited not long ago, including the Chairman of our Governing Council, that the Lord who gave this vision of Salem University prepared this young man and his wife for the task of raising global leaders. And I can bear witness anywhere I go - whether it is in this country or outside this country - that I have met a couple that desire, thirst after, and pursue excellence in their area of calling. I can testify about them in those lights. [*Turning to the Osiris again*] "So, well done my able foot soldiers!"

Ok, developing the spirit of excellence. Why focus on **excellence** at this point in our journey in raising global leaders? I reflected on that question and the thought that came to me is very simple. *After harping on leadership all these years, it would be useful to find another concept that brings out the same resonance with the vision of the University. Excellence is it.* For me, leadership and excellence are like Siamese twins. They are conjoined and inseparable. Also, excellence is a mirror image of leadership; if you like, they are two sides of the same coin. In your generation we don't have coins anymore - it is now paper currencies... [*This may make the metaphor a bit inaccessible*]

So, there is no way we can complete our task of raising global leaders in this University without focusing on excellence. As a matter of fact in my judgement, excellence announces the presence of leadership. Anyone who tells you "I am a leader", and you do not see excellence in that person's life, is telling you untruth. You cannot be a leader without exhibiting excellence.

In my view, also, excellence is more visible, more recognisable than leadership. Those of you who are close to me, on a number of occasions when I see you doing something that I believe is indeed very commendable, what do you hear me say? Excellent! Excellent! You hardly hear me say, Leadership! Leadership! No, leadership doesn't come easily as an adjectival commendation but 'excellent' does. When you were writing your examinations last time, I entered the examination halls as I had done on previous occasions. And do you know what I saw? Excellence! Global leaders excellently dressed. I said: "Yes. These are my global leaders".

And as I was there walking around, you might not have noticed but I was doing this silent prayer. I said: "Lord, may this excellence on their bodies reflect the excellence in their brains. Amen". It's because you cannot be a leader without exhibiting excellence... *first in your mind, then outwardly*. Interestingly though, while excellence is more recognisable than leadership, you cannot easily find people referring to themselves as, "I am excellent". It is very difficult. But people say easily, "I am a leader. Don't you know? Don't you see me? I am a leader". Very few people are bold enough to say, "I am excellent! Don't you know? Haven't you seen me?" Your excellence manifests in your actions for others to acknowledge.

Excellence announces leadership. As you go into the world - those of you who are leaving very soon for SIWES and will not be back until October - ask yourself this question: would the world around me see *my leadership through* my excellence? And I note as part of my reflection that excellence is linked to elevation as well. Wherever there is excellence, you can never stay on the ground. Impossible! ... the spirit of excellence in a person is like the air trapped in a balloon. Take that balloon and try to push it even under water, can it remain there? No! That is what excellence does to a person. You cannot stay on the ground.

Even if you trip and fall, you cannot stay down. There are global leaders that we have had to discipline: we sent them away on suspension. Some came back and, believe you me, we have never seen them in our 'bad' records anymore. Their backs never touched the ground again. But there are a few we have disciplined and brought back to the University under a most painful pleading you can expect from parents. And the very moment they stepped back on the Campus, their backs still went on the ground. Why? There was no spirit (air) of excellence in them. Rather, they had chosen to live a life of low existence. Of course, they had to go.

... At times when you look at the characteristics of excellence as we shall consider later, you may think: "No!; it is impossible for any human being to exhibit excellence". Well, sorry to disappoint you. Excellence is not an attribute of God only; it is also an attribute of the saints of God here on earth. God said in Psalms 16: 3 "But to the saints that are on the earth, they are the excellent ones in whom is all my delight". Thus, one of the reasons for giving attention to excellence in our journey of raising global leaders is this: *the excellent ones are* the kind of people in whom God has all (not some but all) of His delight. It's like God deposits the entirety of Himself in those who are excellent. This is enough of incentive, if nothing else, to pursue excellence.

As you go through the Scriptures, there is one individual at least that you can see who epitomises excellence. And that is Daniel.

... In Daniel 6:1-3, we read:

> It pleased Darius to set over the kingdom one hundred and twenty princes, which should be over the whole kingdom; And over these, three presidents; of whom Daniel was first... Then this Daniel distinguished himself above the governors and satraps, because an <u>excellent</u>

spirit was in him; and the king gave thought to setting him over the whole realm (emphasis, added).

One hundred and twenty princes; out of them the King chose three to make them presidents; and who was the first among the three? Daniel! If it were in Nigeria, you can guess *how that could have come about*: because of political connections, bribery and corruption, 'man pass man', 'my papa know your papa', boot leaking, deception, and various other ways that some of us (Nigerians) use in order to get to the top.

That is why in Salem University we say, "smartness can take you to the top but only integrity can keep you there". One hundred and twenty provincial leaders selected to cover the whole realm. Three selected to supervise the 120 and of the three somebody was the number one. Daniel!

…So the princes are going to give account to the three, and the king should fear no harm. People who have excellent spirit in them when they are overseeing areas, their king shall have no fear of coming to harm. … Because an excellent spirit was in Daniel, what happened after that? The king thought to set him over! You can be above without being over. Above means you are at the top *or higher position*. But when you are above and over, there are people underneath you that you lead. We have many "leaders" in this country who are above but they are not over. Because they don't lead anybody except themselves, *and invariably do a bad job at that*. They are above but they are not over any *group of people. They lead for themselves*.

Where did the king think of setting Daniel? …Over the whole realm. Give me a man, give me a woman with an excellent spirit and I can tell you where that person will be located. Global leaders from Salem University, where will you be located? Above and over! Meet your peers anywhere. Meet other students from other Universities. In every circumstance, where will you be? Above and over! God help us! When we see what many of you do, we rejoice. It is just a few who have not understood this yet, but we continue to work towards all of you understanding this *'excellence'* project.

Now quickly let's go through what excellence represents… Some people think that excellence is being the best. It is not the case for us. I came across this story about Michael Angelo who painted the ceiling of the Sistine Chapel *in Italy, a large and renowned chapel in the Apostolic Palace, the official residence of the Pope in the Vatican City*. He painted and cleaned, repainted and cleaned again. After doing that many times, he was lying on his back looking at the painting. One man walked pass, saw what Angelo was doing and said: "Michael

Angelo, why are you worrying yourself like this? It is only a ceiling. How many people would see it? And even if they see it, how many will know whether it has fault or not? Who will know that there is fault?" Michael Angelo looked at him and said "I will know". Listen very carefully. In the journey to excellence, you will know yourself. Those who behave otherwise are just deceiving themselves. If you do not know, you are a deceiver; you are in self-conceit.

Excellence is not being the best but being your best. What does that mean? That ultimately, everything said and done, you are the architect and surveyor of your own excellence. At Salem University, what we try to do is to provide for you an environment where you can architecturally design and implement your own excellence. We are not looking for the best. We are looking for your best. So when we talk about meeting other students from other universities, this is not about foolish competition or foolish comparison. The Bible says, comparing themselves with themselves, they became fools[59]. Don't compare yourselves with anybody. But set the standard for your own excellence... Excellence for us is: doing things well, doing things thoroughly, and doing things completely.

... The manifestation of excellence in terms of doing things 'well', 'thoroughly' and 'completeness' is illustrated in Daniel... *Ultimately, though, being your best is the key to exercising the spirit of excellence*, as you will see from the following remarkable story told by the United States of America ex-President, Jimmy Carter. Before he became the President, he applied to join the Navy Seal (nuclear submarine) which was under Admiral Hyman Rickover at the time. This is the highest group you can find in the US Navy (others being Conventional Navy, Maritime Navy, Mercantile Navy, and Medical Navy) and it is not everybody that can gain access there...

Every officer on aboard the nuclear sub-marine at that time was personally interviewed and approved by this Admiral. We did some analysis not long ago and we discovered that we had interviewed at least 1,900 candidates for work since I assumed duty in this University. And I think I have participated in at least 70 per cent of those interviews, especially for middle to senior levels. Personally involved!

Look at the experience of those who went for the interview

with this man – Rickover. Usually, those people came out shaking in fear, anger or total intimidation. Rickover must be a very terrible man? No! Rickover was looking for excellence. He was looking for people in whom there was an excellent spirit. *Let's see how he did it with* Jimmy Carter.

Carter said when he entered the interview room, he thought there were going to be many people on the panel. He found Rickover alone in the room (*a sizeable room*). Rickover welcomed him and questions began. Rickover said: "Tell me the subjects you like". Jimmy Carter rolled out so many subjects including music and food etc. He wanted to impress this man. *I would imagine.* After listening to him, Rickover said: "how did you stand in your class at the Naval Academy". Jimmy Carter replied, "Sir, I stood number 59th in the class of 820". He was expecting... "Wow! Congratulations, that was a good performance". After all, that placed Jimmy Carter among the first seven per cent.

Rickover asked him, "Did you do your best?" Without thinking, Jimmy Carter answered, "Yes sir, I did my best". Then he realised that it was possible this man had checked his records, made some investigation about him, or knew something about him that he - Jimmy - might not have picked up. Immediately he said, "Sir, No sir. I didn't always do my best".

Now, wait for this. Admiral Rickover turned on his swivel chair and had his back to Jimmy Carter. [*Pardon if I am a little dramatic here*] For some minutes that seemed very long to Jimmy Carter (ten minutes, twenty minutes, thirty minutes, forty minutes), Rickover said nothing. Then suddenly he turned back to Jimmy Carter and asked only one question of two words, "Why not?" Jimmy Carter sat there dumfounded, never had any answer. He left that room shaking[60].

What about you? Are you doing your best? Global leaders leaving us very soon, are you doing your best? … If no. Why not? *The spirit of excellence requires that you seek to do your best in all situations you find yourself. Salem University wishes to cultivate that spirit in you.*

Time as resource

Considering the change we must have, the calling on us to be freed change agents or livewires, and the excellence we must pursue in order to deliver on the vision mandate of the University, it looked as though we were running against time. As if that was not challenging enough, there was all around us a general disregard for time as a resource – totally oblivious to the fact that we do not control this resource. The entire environment with few exceptions was careless about, worse still averse to, timelines and timeliness when I assumed duty in 2008.

No person can become an effective leader without having regard to time as a resource and a high sense of *timing* in what the person does. Further, our task was to raise global (not local) leaders who would operate by global time standards. Therefore, we had no choice but to tackle this issue head on. We led the consciousness about time and timeliness from the front and by example. Hardly any occasion passed that we did not drum on the issue.

We were sensitive about the timing of anything we needed to do, having bound ourselves to the mantra that effective leadership entails doing the right thing, the right way, **at the right time**, and for the right reasons. And, we made sure we attended meetings or programmes with staff and students alike on time or ring ahead of time to let others know if for reasons beyond our control we were going to be late.

At one of our orientation sessions, I addressed the issue of timing – anchoring my presentation to the line in the University Anthem that says: "It is time to rise and lead for change". We then drilled into the universal truth that there is time for everything: vision, purpose, and down to even the mundane things like gathering and casting away of stones[61].

Timeliness

Having a *sense of time as a resource* and not acting in *a timely way* can only defeat the purpose and produce frustration. For this reason, we worked hard to establish a University-wide consciousness about timeliness – for members of the University community and other stakeholders alike. Here is a classical illustration.

For the maiden matriculation ceremony of the University, we invited the Governor of the State as the special guest. Two weeks to the day, I went to his office and intimated his protocol team about our consciousness with timeliness. "At Salem University, our 10 o'clock is 10 o'clock; no African time", I informed the protocol. They said the Governor was comfortable with that. A few days to the ceremony, we were informed that the Governor would be away and that he had asked his Deputy to stand in for him. Immediately, I went to the Deputy Governor's Office and intimated him and his protocol team about our attention to timeliness.

On the day of the matriculation, we were all ready to start the procession at 10 o'clock in the morning. The Deputy Governor had not arrived. I advised the Chancellor for us to start - consistent with our scheduled time. A few people around were apprehensive, wondering how the Deputy Governor might take it. My counsel prevailed and we started. I had promised that whenever he arrived, we would stop the proceedings and honour him with the National Anthem, etc. I was in the middle of my matriculation address when the Deputy Governor arrived at about 11 o'clock. Promptly, I stopped, welcomed him; we had the National Anthem, he sat down, and I continued with my address. A few minutes to 12noon, we were marching out of the hall, having completed the ceremony within the time we scheduled for it.

All those in attendance (the matriculating students, their parents, staff and other invitees) were deeply touched by our sticking to our scheduled time. This was a radical departure from the norm, especially when the programmes involved highly placed individuals. It helped to cement our resolve to enthrone timeliness in all that we did at the University.

Against this backdrop, I was particularly livid on one occasion when the University community played carelessly with time. I arrived at the venue of a programme and very few members of the community were actually seated as at the time the programme started. In the address I delivered that day, I made them know how I felt in no uncertain terms.

How do you treat time? [62]

... [*to the Press men who were present that day*] I would like you to witness what *I am going to do now* because it is the custom of Salem University... What I want to do is house-keeping. Right now in the University community, we have over four hundred and fifty (450) members- staff and global leaders together. When I came in at exactly 10 o'clock this morning, there were fifteen (15) members of the University community in the hall. *We were all expected to be in attendance.* I want to believe that all of us know, that was not Salem University standard.

I attended a convocation ceremony very recently. Some officers of that University told me: "Sir, our vision is to produce change agents." And I said, "that sounds like Salem University". They had organised a banquet that night which was to start at 5 o'clock in the evening. Six minutes to 5:00, I was there. As I entered the hall, I met the Vice Chancellor, the President of the University and one other officer. And there were only four (4) of the celebrants (convocated students) in the room *out of* 224 persons they were expecting.

The program that was to start at 5pm, started at 7:30 pm. The President had already left, probably out of disgust. I wanted to leave but something said, stay back and see how this whole thing pans out, *and in deference to my fellow Principal Officers.* Every minute that passed, I kept telling myself, "this will not be Salem University. This will not be Salem University".

As I said before, it was 7:30pm before the program started. I turned to one of the Principal Officers by my left, and I said, "these are change agents that are going to affect their community for good"? He looked at me and said "Sir, we are so disgusted about what is happening"…

What I saw this morning not just with global leaders, but also with global staff, made me to squirm. It was like a déja vu. Heavenly Lord, is this what our global staff and global leaders would become? Is this how they would treat time? … As I was driving here I saw some of you coming into the hall and you were just walking indifferently even though you were going to arrive late. *This ought not to be so, as far as our attitude to timeliness is concerned!*

The Founder of the University we are celebrating today, on this very day the 6th of August, 2002 received the vision from God. What time? 4:30 am. And, as he had informed me, that was consistent with his practice over the years. At that very time he was up and having conversation with God. Have you ever sat down to think that, if on that faithful day, *he woke up late or* as he woke up to go to his chambers, his body was telling him "no don't do it, just stay back and rest" and he obeyed. Have you imagined that this vision we are celebrating today would not have been here? If he allowed lateness or the failure/weakness of the flesh to keep him away from his God at that very time on that day, you and I would not be here today.

We emphasis in this University, that cleanliness is next to God. Imagine God sitting on the throne with cleanliness on one side. What is on the other side? Timeliness! All the developed countries in the world today have appreciated the principle of timeliness. I have been in meetings where Prime Ministers were billed to be present. I have been in meetings, where the Secretary General of the United Nations was billed to be present. Never one day did I see any of them come late. Never one day. And you want to operate globally? Nigerian time is a destiny killer. African time is a destiny killer. You can find one hundred excuses why you came here late today. None of them will sustain your destiny.

When somebody knows he should be somewhere at a given time and he is not able to be there, when you see such a person's body language, you will know that this person appreciates time. *He or she* will be restless. If you came in late this morning and you are filling comfortable inside you, then you have not got the principle of timeliness in your system yet. I pray that God will help all of us as we continue to work on ourselves until the transformation *with regard to timeliness* is complete. Amen.

Performance Management[63]

Leadership is not about position. It is about performance, whether it is in terms of 'being' or in terms of 'doing'. All our efforts at challenging the mindset about 'change', 'change agents', 'excellence', 'time as resource', etc., were geared towards how members of the University community would perform inside and, more so, outside the University.

One critical way to encourage performance is to appraise it via objectively designed and implemented systems. So, along the way, we embarked upon specific teachings on what performance is and how to encourage it with appropriate management strategies. Excerpts from one of such teachings are reproduced below.

...Everything we have said from yesterday till now will converge in this issue of performance. After everything we have heard, if we go away and do nothing then we have failed, we have wasted our time. So everything we've heard is geared towards getting us to do something; something that we have probably not done before or do what we have done before but in a different way. My Chaplain use to hammer on this leadership aphorism that if you keep doing the same thing the same way and expect different results that is the definition for insanity or madness. So having gone through all of these over the last few years, we expect that (better) performance must follow.

In today's address, I am going to *talk about*: what <u>objective performance appraisal</u> (OPA) means; the various principles involved in OPA; the stages and practice of OPA; and then, OPA and Salem University vision.

Performance is about work. It is not about getting a job or a position. I'm amazed when I look at some of you now and compare you with when you came for the job interview. I recall some of you waited from morning until evening; no one complained. Now you are in the University and when we have a meeting for two hours or the meeting is extending beyond your normal comfort zone, you are no longer the person we saw at the interview. It may well be that your emphasis (at that time) was on getting a job, not on performance.

Performance is all about doing the work... *regardless of* the position you occupy. It is not, "well I am the Vice Chancellor...; that is enough and everybody should be clapping hands for me".

That is not performance. Or "because I am a cleaner everyone should be clapping hands for me"; that is not performance. Performance lies in what Monday Ochedi (one of the cleaners) shared with us earlier in the morning, when the guest speaker asked people to stand up and tell us what task they undertake.

Monday stood up and declared proudly, "Sir, this place we are in, this is my territory and I look after it". To me that is *thinking* about performance. He didn't stand up to say "I am a cleaner", period. I was reminding the Senior Management at the lunch break; I said "I told you that I am very proud of my cleaners here, very proud of them... With all their frailties... and all their faults, I just value them. They keep our Campus uncommonly clean". *Yes, it has taken a bit of chastising from me, but they are flowing in that spirit now and the result is great!*

Being a cleaner (positionally) is not work; it is what you do as a cleaner that is performance-related. It is what you do in the position that defines whether you actually belong to this place or you don't belong to this place. Some of you may remember a Nigerian Professor we employed from *overseas*. The very first week he arrived I spent one and a half hours with him in my office – welcoming him personally and outlining for him our expectations; letting him know the situations on ground and promising him every support he needed to do his job well. One week, two weeks, three weeks, I was watching. In the fourth week, I wanted to see what he was doing, so I checked on him casually to make sure he had struck no impediments. His performance was below expectation, *but he voiced no challenges that could explain the situation.*

At the end of the eighth week, I called him and said, "shall we do some basic review (which is part of performance appraisal) quickly of what you have done to date"? And he sat in my office and said, "Sir, you didn't look after me..." something to that effect. I said "Oh, tell me...". He continued "you know I am from [he called the country] and you didn't give me air-conditioned room... This place is too hot and I can't function properly under such conditions".

During my earlier checking, he made no such complaint. *Further*, if I had seen in him previously a reasonable measure of effort in the direction of his responsibilities, I would have been sympathetic and gone out all the way to wrap around him additional support systems. But he showed no such efforts. So, I looked at him and I said, "Wow! How long have you being here?" He said eight weeks. I said "congratulations! You are from *overseas*. How long have you been away...? 16 years? ...

You may not know, but I can tell you with all sense of humility, I've been away from this country for 21 years living in Australia. *The country you came from* is not any colder than Australia. When I arrived here, for nine months - in fact more than nine months, I had no AC in my office. I do remember how many works I had to destroy because my hand was sweaty and as I was writing it was just smudging. And you want me to believe and accept that because there was no AC in your office you couldn't operate? Could that be the main reason *or there was something else?*"

Well, the long and short of the story is that he is no longer with us here. I can tell you honestly: that very same day, I demanded for his resignation – to give him a soft landing; and if he was not going to resign I was going to relieve him of his post on the spot and pay him out with all his entitlements in accordance with our law and conditions of service. It was not just the lack of performance; it was the whole attitude with which he was "justifying" his non-performance. Such attitude cannot build the University (certainly not at the pioneering stage) nor can it raise the caliber of global leadership that was the vision/mission/mandate of the University.

Let me say it again, performance is about work. Even God worked: "And on the seventh day God ended His work and He rested..."[64]. In Isaiah 43:13 the Lord God says, "I work..." One thing that we must also know about performance is that it deals with work that is time bound. The opportunity to work will never be there forever. John 9:4 says, "work while it is still day for night comes when no one can work". And if you want to know what that night means, read Ecclesiastics 9:10, "there is no work in the grave". So the time you have to work is now that you are alive.

I make bold to also say that work is living. If you don't work, you are dead. A very simple allusion to that can be found in 2 Thessalonians 3:10, "if anyone does not work let him not eat". And if you don't eat, you know what the outcome is likely to be... Fellow global staff, performance is about work which has its origin in divinity, which is time-bound and which determines whether you live or die. It is night when you are dead, *at which time you can no longer work*.

Now, what is Objective Performance Appraisal? Very simple! It is assessing the work done against agreed tasks with no considerations for non-related matters or sentiments, and focusing on achievements, areas for improvement, development needs and the reward or incentive level for work done.

If any of these elements is missing, your performance appraisal is not complete. I said before that, God worked; and is still working. In Genesis 1:31, God actually assessed His own work. He looked at what He had done and He found that it was "very good" ... When you are assessing your work, you look for achievements; you look for areas that can be improved upon, you see where there are developmental needs to be met. In other words, if you did not achieve up to the level that you wanted to achieve, what could you have done - by way of training, capacity building, connections and all other areas that you could have explored to ensure you preformed according to expectation? After that assessment, you look at the reward or incentive regime *which must be commensurate with achievement.*

Revelations 2 and 3 are all about performance appraisal. At every point in those two chapters, God said, "I know your works", you did that which I value, and this I hold against you and then He goes on to say, this you must do and then finally He says, "He who has ears, let him hear". That is performance appraisal per-excellence.

Let me outline some principles that underpin Objective Performance Appraisal:

1. It should be guided by the desire to foster shared understanding between the staff and his or her supervisor. We all need to know that we are on the same page so that when one is heading to the north, the other person should not be heading south because the two may never meet... My point here is this, for you to be able to lead change, for you to be able to do something about everything we've touched upon so far, you and your supervisor must share the same understanding.

    One of the reasons we continually cast vision, talk about the mandate, etc., is because we want everyone to have the same understanding so that we can travel in the same direction... So when you sit down to prepare and plan and do whatever you need to do for the appraisal and for you to be objective, foster shared understanding.

2. Make integrity the watchword. I think the Chaplain did a good job on this yesterday; I don't need to belabour it. For Christ sake, if your staff is a lazy person, I don't want to see an assessment paper that says, "performance - satisfactory". There is no integrity in that statement. And I believe that this is one of the areas that we fall down as a nation.

One time I visited Abuja and went to an office of a highly placed person at the Director level, I don't want to name the organisation. In my presence, the Director called a messenger. There was something urgent she wanted the messenger to do and the messenger just answered "eh hum". I watched the messenger coming into the room – in a space of maybe three or four meters, it took him almost four minutes to get to the Director: one meter per minute!

The Director was apparently so embarrassed. I was watching and saying to myself, this cannot happen in Salem University. "I am very sorry my VC", said the Director. "They handed him over to me; he has been in the public service for thirty-two years. He is still a messenger. Instead of telling him the right to do, they were just pushing him from one office to another".

I bet you that when the previous supervisors of that Messenger were writing an appraisal report on him (if at all), chances are that they all wrote, "performance - satisfactory". If they acted that way, "so they could have peace", it has turned out to be a pyrrhic peace, i.e. a phantom peace – not real. It was a fake peace and while you are enjoying your fake peace, you are actually destroying many people's destinies because I believe if that man had been told the truth about his attitude/performance or ultimately sent out of that place thirty years before that time, maybe by that time, he would have been somebody completely *and positively* different by now.

Revelations 2 and 3: God never did such a thing to the seven churches, not one. He did not say to any of them:

"Oh wonderful" in all areas. In fact the church in Thyatira happened to receive the best assessment; even then, God still found something to tell them that they needed to improve. That is God's own way: being truthful, being honest, and positively stretching in expectation. If somebody is performing well, tell them they are performing well. If they are not performing tell them "you need to work on *such and such* areas". There is no amount of inspiration and aspiration that you have derived from these two days and you go away and you don't want to be told the truth about your work. That will not get you anywhere.

3.   Concentrate on value-based results - the ethics of the outputs and outcomes against the expectations. You do this with an eye on the character and competence of the person that is being appraised. ... Outputs are specific results that come from an activity. Outcomes are the impact of what you have achieved. Both of them must be examined when you are doing performance appraisal. Look at the knowledge and the skills that the person has brought on board and the behaviours that produced those results.

My point here is that, as a matter of principle, when you are doing performance appraisal please don't just focus on the results. Look at the behaviours that supported those results. If you go and steal to balance an account for me, you have failed. If you add ten marks to a student so that you can reduce the level of failure and then come to the Senate expecting Senate to say, "Wonderful, this is a great work you have done, all your students passed", it is a bad job. It does not reflect reality and it does not help the global leaders. It is important that character must accompany competence.

4.   Be developmental. The outcome of your appraisal must develop, build, or construct, and not destroy. I made it a principle in my life that there is no staff of mine that would come for appraisal and go away from me feeling

that he or she might as well go and die now. You don't understand what I'm saying. No staff would come to me to be appraised and, at the end of the appraisal, as he or she is moving out of my room, (s)he says "hum, this one is so hopeless, I *better go and* die now". That doesn't mean it wouldn't be tough, because I hold people to agreed *expectations*. If there is performance below expectation, I am forthright in letting the staff know – but with an eye on capacity building for correction or improvement.

And I can tell you, I have appraised so many high level staff: Heads of Schools, Directors, Registrars, etc. Our own global Registrar can testify. We did his appraisal last year. Registrar, was I patting you on the back and saying "oh wonderful global Registrar, you have done everything perfect"? (Registrar answered: "No!"). Here was my approach: "in one, two, three, four or five areas – wonderful; the other one, two, or three, hum, you need to do something about them seriously; and this is how I suggest you can go about doing it".

[Drawing on my previous experiences, I showed real-life examples going back to 2003 when I was assessing Heads of Schools in Australia and from 2004 to 2007 when I assessed Directors (Executive Level 2) in the Australian Government Public Service.]

5.   There must be no surprises. My principle is: no surprises. The Chaplain can testify to that. When we come to the end of the year and we are going over what you have done, there will be no occasion that we are going to spring something new on you. Given the way we had interacted all along, you would know where you stand before you sit before me at the final stage to address your claims. That's the principle I subscribe to very powerfully.

Let's look at the Stages of OPA
1.   Planning: this is where you define and agree on expectations (tasks, competencies and values). Let me take, for example, Dr. Mrs Okoli as the person that I am doing performance appraisal on. The work will be

defined so she knows what she is expected to do and she will agree that this is what she has to do. I underline the word "agree". Until you have got your staff to understand what the job is and the person accepts that "yes, this is my area and I'm going to do them", you have not started objective performance appraisal yet. Agree.

Does that mean that, in the Nigerian context where everything *seems to be* by command and control ("the lord has spoken and no body questions" mentality of leadership), this approach will upset most of the appraisal practices? Yes! It will, and it will do that for good. When you get a staff to agree on expectations, you have got the heart of that staff; the rest will now be he or she working hard to deliver the results to you. So, we define and agree what the staff is expected to do or achieve in relation to the job content or the key result areas. This can be derived from the schedule of work or job description a staff receives on assuming duty.

You must translate those areas into more measurable targets. Let me give you an example. Let's say one of my Secretary's (Peter's) job contents from his job description is to receive correspondence and process them to my office in a timely manner; that is a result area. In terms of what I expect him to achieve, I would now say, "process every correspondence that lands on your desk to my office within two hours of receiving it". That is an appraisable task: it is now measurable and can be assessed.

So when Peter sits in front of me at the time we are *reviewing his performance*, I will ask him about how many hours correspondences stayed on his desk. Since the times of in and out of each correspondence are recorded, we have an objective evidence. Let's say some correspondence took four hours, already he knows where his performance lies on that measure.

Then you ask about what Peter needs to know to be able to do the tasks effectively (this is about competencies). And finally, how he is expected to behave while carrying out the tasks; this is specifying the value content. All these elements must be clarified at the beginning - at the planning stage.

2. Preparation for review: this is where the staff who is to be assessed will now go back to the agreement; look at what key tasks or targets, competencies, and values had been agreed upon. The staff now completes the appraisal form *outlining* what they have done about those things with concrete evidences which can show that they have indeed achieved those things.

    If one of the result areas was for the lecturer to role model timeliness, then one performance task can be to "get to the class within five minutes of the starting time always". So at the end when you sit down to do the evaluation or assessment, the staff will present to you his claims (i.e. the documentation of what he has done) about his going to class on time. The lecturer can supply the evidence from the students, and/or you can verify from the students about how many times this lecturer went late (if at all) to the class...

3. Appraisal meeting: this is now where you and the staff being appraised will sit down at the end the cycle and you discuss the claims against the expectations that were agreed at the beginning. You identify the good performance, address performance challenges, and develop a forward looking plan for improvement. The focus is on why things had gone right or gone wrong. And what needs to be done either to improve the things that went right or to correct those things that went wrong. Then finally you do the rating and the reward/incentive assessment.

    Drawing on some practical examples of the performance appraisals I had conducted in Australia, I further illustrated these stage with some lessons on how to frame appraisal questions, keep accurate records of the appraisal, etc.

Now let's highlight the significance of the Objective Performance Appraisal for Salem University vision directly. Performance management is key to sustaining the vision: it has to be systematic; it must aim at involving the individual or team in the management system. You must be able to measure what you are appraising. If you cannot measure it, you cannot appraise it. The measurement encourages accomplishment. What gets measured, gets done. If it can be measured, it can be improved. And if you can't measure, you can't manage.

I believe that all I have said this afternoon in relation to performance management calls for participatory leadership; that is the strategy that I believe would support and sustain the vision of Salem University. People perform well when they know and understand what is expected of them and participate in defining these expectations.

Let us perform to live; appraise to improve; lead to sustain and all of them fit into Salem University vision. Thank you very much.

Journey to the high table: the pain and thrill of leading right[65]

One day, I was teaching to get further 'buy-ins' for the vision among the University community. In the course of enumerating the various challenges, a Global Leader raised her hand and asked: "Sir, given all these, how can we survive out there in the world with our new mindset and the passion to change our world in a godly way?".

This question brought home for me a significant reality-check for all our travailing to create 'vision-ownership' among the entire University community. Thankfully, we had been careful not to give any impression that carrying out the task set before us or living the life of Godly global leadership would be easy. In fact, our emphasis on raising awareness about 'change'; and challenging all of us to become 'change agents', free the leader within, become 'livewires', pursue 'excellence', respect the resource of time, and manage performance, was aimed at highlighting the fact that there would be pains we must endure if we were to stand our ground and accomplish well.

I captured such realities in an address, titled: "Journey to the high table: the pain and thrill of leading right". Here are excerpts from that address.

Read with me Hebrews 12:2: "Looking unto Jesus the author

and finisher of our faith; who for the joy that was set before him endured the cross, despising the shame, and is sat down at the right hand of the throne of God."

My view about all of you here today is that you are destined for the high table. From where you are now to that high table there is a journey to be undertaken. Taking Jesus as an example, the joy of sitting down at the right hand of the throne of God was set before him; but the cross and the shame of it stood between him and that throne. Nevertheless, He determined to make that journey. After Jesus went through the things that led him to the cross – *the plotting, the arrest*, the spiting, the beating, the shame, and everything else that was done to him, he went and sat down among the *ordinary folk?* No! He went and sat down on the high table (*the right hand of the throne of God*).

It is the responsibility and the vision of Salem University to prepare people for the high table. This nation needs people of integrity on the high table. In case you will be overwhelmed by the price you are paying right now, I want to let you know that the price you are paying is the price for the high table. The high table of this nation needs to be replaced completely. Some of us may not be there anymore because we have done our own bit, but you have no excuse. You have no reason to not be among those that would displace the inept, the incompetent, and the corrupt heads we have now. There is a price, though. Jesus paid that price and He got the high table.

For everything that we say and do with you today, it is with this vision right before our eyes: that these people (you) are for the high table... The only person who can stop you from getting to that high table is you - yourself: by your mind set, by your attitude, by the way you think, the way you act. You can stop yourself from getting to the high table.

Is God desperately looking for somebody? Yes! "Whom shall I send? Who will go for us?" Those were the questions Isaiah heard. And he said, "I will". You have to determine to say: "Heavenly Father, getting to the high table for your name's sake, getting to the high table for the sake of the people you love in this country,… I will".

…Look at the history of the world. The only time God has ever punished an entire nation whether it is the nation of Israel or the Gentile world was when people began to practice wickedness with confidence. Let me tell you something that is a bit frightening. Nigeria is getting very, very close to that point - practicing wickedness with confidence *or iniquity with impunity*. There is a disposition towards glamourising their wickedness and is like saying: "I'm defying anything that is against my wicked ways. I am doing *my wickedness*, nothing can happen to me. I defy even the God of righteousness".

...The task for us is for the Management to do whatever is necessary so that the world will see the Salem University vision in you... The journey to the high table requires you to become a protégée of the one who called you. There would be challenges, pain, shame, etc. However, a protégée would surmount all these and sit down at the right hand side of the high table.

Concluding remarks

So we travailed, taking every opportunity (staff meetings, orientation seminars, Total Leadership Training Concept programs, addresses to visitors, recruitment interviews, media commentaries, etc.) to create ownership by all for the unique University vision. We did this by loading, reloading, and burning the software of leading right into to the souls of the University community and the outside communities that came in contact with us. There was much travail.

In the end, the entire University community and the community of contacts came a very long way in behaving consistently with the values and principles that we took on or constructed. Of course, there were daily reminders in the conducts of staff, students and guests or visitors that kept the leadership of the University under pressure to continually drive this unique approach. As it is said in leadership literature, 'in times of great change, leaders must over-communicate' in word and deed! We practised this saying and it is part of our notable story today.

---

44 Adapted from Lee and Roberts (2010).

45 This was precisely the 'task' that was revealed to me using the book of Jeremiah in the Holy Bible, before I left Australia for Nigeria to assume the leadership responsibility.

46 John 16: 21, Holy Bible, King James Version.

47 Galatians 4: 19, Holy Bible, King James Version.

48 In my definition, a business ideology consists of an entity's philosophy, vision, mission, and core values.

49 Proverbs 23: 7, Holy Bible, New King James Version.

50 As a social scientist, I am very much aware of the debate between the

materialist and the idealist views of the world. The former, led by Marxism, held that it is the material condition that determines one's reality; whereas the later, led by the Hegelian thought, holds that ideas determine one's world. I am more inclined to hold the view that both material conditions and ideas are in a dialectical relationship in which ideas have primacy.

[51]   "In the first year of [Darius'] reign I, Daniel, ... set my face toward the Lord God to make request by prayer and supplications,... and made confession, and said O Lord, great and awesome God... we have sinned and committed iniquity, we have done wickedly and rebelled... O Lord, hear! O Lord, forgive" , Daniel 9: 1-19, Holy Bible, New King James Version.

[52]   Formulated from a statement by Arnold Glasow, quoted in Newman (1997, p92).

[53]   A newspaper headline captioned it this way: "INEC in a grave yard of reputations".

[54]   An address to student leaders on 21 Feb 2010.

[55]   A closing address for our Global Leadership Conference, 22 May, 2011.

[56]   Address to Staff Orientation on 3 June, 2010.

[57]   Matthew 9:20-22. "And suddenly, a woman who had a flow of blood for twelve years came from behind and touched the hem of His [Jesus'] garment... and the woman was made well from that hour".

[58]   Address to a TLTC session, 29 February, 2012.

[59]   2 Corinthians 10: 12. "For we dare not... compare ourselves with some that commend themselves: but they measuring themselves by themselves, and comparing themselves among themselves, are not wise".

[60] President Carter referred to this experience in his early authobiography, titled *Why Not the Best?* (1975), drawing from Admiral Rickover's powerful question.

[61]   Ecclesiastes 3: 1-8, Holy Bible.

[62]   Address on the Founder's Day, 6 August, 2010

[63]   Address on Objective Performance Appraisal, during one of our staff orientation weeks, 8 April, 2011.

[64]   Genesis 2: 2, Holy Bible. New King James Version.

[65]   An address to the Student Leaders Forum, 21 February, 2010.

6 Edifice: turning vision into reality

For a mature, effective leader... there is one thing even more exciting than clarifying and casting a God-honouring vision: achieving the vision. Forgive me if that sounds elementary, but I run across an alarming number of leaders who would rather cast vision than roll up their sleeves and attempt, with the Spirit's power, to achieve it! (Hybels 2002, p51)

The most immediate evidence of *leading right* is this: turning a vision into reality or, as Hybels put it in the above-quoted statement, 'achieving the vision'. In our formulation in this book, this is about giving concrete expression to what is in the mind's eye (the right thing) in the right way, at the right time, and for the right reasons. Rightly or wrongly, leaders are often times judged mainly by how the decisions and actions they take have moved the vision from the mind or pages of a document into the real world.

The reason for this is not far-fetched. It is this reality (the first part of which I call the edifice) that attests to the genuineness and/or efficacy of the calling, clarifying, softwaring, travailing, and those other attributes that undergird your claim to leadership *qua* leadership. It is also the 'litmus' by which the satisfaction of the project specifications is tested.

These specifications include the 'engineering specification' where the product measures against the design work; the 'client requirements' where the product hits the technical points that make the reality of the vision adorable; the 'functional requirements' where the product matches the technical goal of the approval authorities; and, above all, the 'verification specification' where the product matches the business ideology of the organization. Although not so crystal clear at the time we commenced our work at Salem University, these specifications were very much in our contemplation to deliver accordingly.

Decision at 'ground-zero'

The first time I physically entered the grounds of Salem University, I said to myself, "Man, you are on ground zero, virtually. Brace up"! This was about a week or so after I had arrived Abuja from Australia and had held some sessions with the Board of Trustees and the Chancellor.

Some four buildings or so were completed and scattered over a portion of this vast land of 272 hectares that had been acquired for the University. The generality of the physical works showed that the grounds were a distant shot from being ready for the proposed take-off within the time stipulated. The systems infrastructure was even farther from reality. It was virtually non-existent.

However, with the task well defined, the moral dimension (software) generally conceived, and the strategies to get buy-in reasonably articulated, it was time to get down to action. Although work had to be commenced on several fronts at a time, we were guided by a sense of priority in establishing the various physical and systems infrastructures with which the University finally took off in January 2009.

One of the things that would have helped us to decide easily where to start from was a stand-alone strategic plan document, but there was nothing like that. However, there was a set of documents from which we had to draw the direction and conceptual roadmap for our action. This included the:

- *University Law 2006* – which defined the statutory framework for operations;
- Academic Brief Volume 1 which outlined what I call the University "business ideology" (i.e. vision, mandate and values), organisational system (structures and processes), official requirements for programme implementation, support services, pattern of growth, and a ten-year budgeting guide (human and physical resource needs and cost estimates);
- Academic Brief Volume 2 which outlined the semester structure, configuration of courses by level and semester, and the description of each of the courses; and

- Master Plan which provided the topographical map of the terrain and the location for the building of all approved facilities.

In strategic planning sense, this set provided the ingredients with which we had to figure out the first-order or high-level "imagining" of the purpose of the University, where the University was, and where it was to go. Thus, we derived the focus and direction, and a firm understanding of the goals and objects of the University from these documents.

We were set to run. Together with the one person, Osiri Wisdom, who was assigned to the University business before I arrived, we began to map out all broad areas of our responsibilities, to define specific actions with timelines and to figure out the resources required to get the works done. In a sense, we started by putting together a mini-action plan. Because we badly needed more hands, we pursued recruitment aggressively, sorting out the applications that had been received prior to my coming and organizing/conducting interviews for various positions.

Corporate administration

The area to which we gave attention early was the governance system. Many a leadership effort and/or several visions had been frustrated or killed by faulty governance systems. We were careful to avoid such an outcome in this new journey.

Prior to my assumption of duty in March 2008, the Board of Trustees had been established under the *University Law 2006*. Subsequently, we constituted two other statutory administrative organs – Governing Council and Senate - with substantially full membership within twelve months of the University commencing full academic operations in January 2009. We also constituted the Committees of both organs as provided for in the *University Law*.

To assist us with day-to-day administration of the University, we established a Senior Management Committee, comprising all the campus-based Principal Officers and the Directors of various Units (Academic Planning, Centre for Continuous Education and Entrepreneurial Studies, and Centre for Foundation and Pre-Degree Programmes. Later, the Centre for Entrepreneurial and General Studies was brought on board). This Committee met fortnightly to review and decide on management issues, and there were ad hoc meetings convened to address urgent and important matters that occurred in between the regular meetings.

It was with this governance structure that we built the University through all necessary tertiary institution "rites of passage". The exception was convocation, which was held a few months after my disengagement to confer degree awards on the first set of the Global Leaders who had completed their studies in July 2012 shortly before I disengaged.

Vice Chancellery

As part of our efforts to establish the University on a proper footing, we constituted various offices, units and departments to run the central administration. The arrowhead for the entire project[66] was the Vice Chancellery, which had overall responsibility for the University administrative and academic development. Within that set up, we established the Vice Chancellor's Office, supported by a Deputy Vice Chancellor, the Chaplaincy, the Information and Communication Technology Unit, the Public Relations Unit, the Security Unit and Internal Audit. The Heads of these support units reported directly to me and I, in turn, supervised their activities along with other areas within my broader responsibility and accountability to the Governance system.

Despite the constraint of staff limitations (in terms of number and orientation), we ran an open-door policy to give all staff, Global leaders, and other stakeholders unfettered access and a sense of belonging. Conventionally, the Vice Chancellery, particularly the Vice Chancellor's Office was a highly restricted area in most Nigerian Universities. Our own approach was different. We extended access to all the members of the University and our external stakeholders, not just to 'demystify' the Office but more significantly to improve efficiency and effectiveness of doing the University business. We made a judgment call that unnecessary bureaucracy was not compatible with the pace of work required in a pioneering situation such as we were in and the type of leadership we were determined to deploy.

Although, initially we took the micro-management approach to the University affairs (made unavoidable by the funding and personnel realities), we began early to capacity-build other departments of the University to handle issues in a manner that advanced the vision delivered to us. Most of the time, it was necessary to, and we did, 'jump into the trenches with the troop' to establish the urgency, show the way, and assure quality in all areas of work.

In our oversight responsibility, my Office gave particular attention to the general academic development matters. This focused mainly on managing the Deans of Colleges, coordinating curriculum development, ensuring quality programmes (including lecture delivery and examination practices), supervising quality documentation for external presentation or assessment (such as the NUC monitoring visit reports, annual review meeting reports, and accreditation papers) and, with limited success due to pioneering exigencies, promoting vibrant academic life on the Campus (through seminars, conferences, research consultancies, publications, etc).

Alongside the academic area, we directly supervised the spiritual life and character development as a major pillar of the vision mandate of the University. This responsibility was anchored by the Chaplaincy which Rev Osiri Wisdom and his family led dynamically and excellently. We actively guided the work of this Unit and also regularly participated in its leadership development sessions. This earned me the unenviable title of "the Chief Priest" of the University. Principally, we took to this level of involvement to fulfill our commitment to "leadership by example" and to impart in a hands-on manner key leadership skills from a global perspective.

Another area we focused upon directly for strategic reasons was the Information and Communication Technology platform. We were determined to actualize our dream of making the whole of the University ICT-driven with a view to ultimately making the University operations paperless. Within a relatively short period, we were able to establish a C-Band 2.4 reflector dish-based internet connectivity (then, the state of the art), with most of the buildings within the academic precinct (including staff offices and classrooms) wired.

We ran into difficulty with the development of the intranet (integrated management portal). Had we succeeded there, we would have achieved our paperless regime goal for the management of personnel, admissions, e-payment, payroll, final accounts, library, hostel, clinic, communication, security surveillance, etc. The challenges on ground were enormous. The external ICT service provider was limited on product deployment and change management. The University staff were generally quite averse to ICT platform at that time and would not even enter their basic biodata into the template designed by the provider. Then, funds became a constraint and this limited our choices particularly with regard to the providers we could engage.

This is one area of the entire University project in which we struggled to make a headway. The temptation to engage in some behavioural patterns of the defiant leadership paradigm was high. Indeed, we had to act decisively in a 'defiant' way as one day I directed the University gate to be locked and we held most of the middle level and senior level officers of the University until mid-night to show them how to enter their data into the template of the intranet portal. By the time we closed that night, most had become relaxed and conversant with the system. We had lost too much precious time, to overcome the other constraints.

Security also got our attention early on in the building of the University. Armed robberies and other vices were rampant in our neighbourhood. The University perimeter fence was far from being completed. Internal law, order, and safety were an irreducible minimum for learning and development to take place. So, we tried several systems in our efforts to find the best fit for our pioneering circumstances, including a wholly University-run outfit, fully outsourced services, and a hybrid.

With an eye on the requirements of the unique University vision and our commitment to excellence, starting from the security post at the entrance gate, we needed to set up a befitting security. In the end, the results we got were remarkable. Throughout my tenure, we were able to maintain a commendable law and order regime in the University community. We did this, not through reactive measures but through a proactive and partnership approach.

We 'preached' that security was everybody's business in the University community and thus mobilized all members for alertness and response. We responded promptly to all actual or potential breaches to the safety of life and property on the campus, and this had reasonable deterrent effects. Also, we directly engaged our host community and the law enforcement agencies in preventative relationships. There were no notable or irretrievable breaches even with the expansive land on which the University is situated.

Behaviourally, our security personnel were reasonably proficient. A telling comment was the submission Dr Olorunfemi, a member of the Governing Council, made at one of the Council's meetings. He said the behavior of the security he saw at the gate when he was coming for the meeting was exemplary. The operatives were courteous, thorough and helpful. While the meeting was still going on, I secretly sent for the Chief Security Officer and announced the testimony to him in the public glare of the Council. I congratulated him for a job well done and tasked him to convey the view of the Council to his team. The following day, he came to my office highly elated, and pledged to sustain excellence in the performance of his team. That was Salem University of our travails.

Registry

The Registry we set up comprised the Registrar's Office, Establishment Office, Academic Office, and Housing & Passages Unit. It was the central repository of all administrative actions, coordinating the inflow and outflow of correspondences for the University, providing secretariat services to key governance meetings, organising recruitment and welfare of staff, conducting student admissions, registrations and discipline, etc.

As the senior administrative officer, the Registrar was statutorily the Secretary to the Governing Council, the Senate and, by assignment, the Management Committee. My Registrar (Mr Dan Itodo) served the University well. For the three and half years that he was in that position, he showed a tremendous heart as Registrar for the unique vision of the University. Taking the cue from the Vice Chancellor's Office, he endeavored to enthrone Godliness, accountability and integrity among other core values in the Registry operations which he directly supervised.

In the area of staffing, we ensured integrity in our processes by devising a plan that assisted us with orderliness, transparency, and consistency in shortlisting and judging applicants. Along with this plan, we developed facilitative instruments, including the "Guide for conducting interview sessions", "Generic Interview Questions", "Interview Performance Rating Scale", and the overall "Assessment Format" to standardize judgments, enforce quality control, and minimise bias in selection.

With these instruments, we conducted over 2000 staff interviews resulting in over 400 appointments as at the time of I disengaged - duly processed to the Governing Council, considered and ratified. As mentioned in one of my addresses narrated in the previous Chapter, I personally participated in at least 70 per cent of these interviews. In this, we were driven by the convictions that people were our most important asset and that, in the execution phase of any human entity, no leader should delegate "having the right people in the right place" (Bassidy and Charan, 2002, p109).

Those who entered the employ of the University were provided with a clear framework in the *Conditions of Service* for staff welfare, confirmation, promotion, discipline and disengagement. To ensure that the staff pursed their ultimate best for the interest of the University as a whole, this framework was implemented according to our policies of enthroning meritocracy, mutual accountability, and diligence among other values. Although the prevailing (inhibiting) mindset among most staff made them struggle vis-à-vis our drive of the vision, we consciously avoided using fear, morbid respect, or any other alienating technique of the defiant leadership approach to gain their commitment.

Student admissions, registrations and records were another area we took a stand for the vision of the University. We were mindful that the corruption that was ravaging the university system in Nigeria at that time usually found notable expression or was rife in the Academic Office that handled these matters. Consequently, as part of our anti-corruption battle at Salem University generally, we paid particular attention to ensuring that the

Academic Office of the University gave no room for this malaise. Hence the principles on student admissions I outlined earlier in Chapter Four.

In addition to diligently complying with the admissions requirements as outlined in the Academic Brief that the NUC had approved for the University, we faithfully applied the JAMB cut-off point every year. Also, we conducted post-UTME University internal screening with carefully designed instruments which resulted in about 2,600 admission offers made to suitable candidates[67].

Managing the Student Affairs came up high in our priority in the process of building the University. The specific Unit we created for this role, ensured that there was guidance and counseling on personal, academic and career matters. Further, the Unit (together with the Chaplaincy) guided the establishment of the Student Leaders Forum to provide a context for Global leaders both to experience leadership responsibilities and to have representation or voice in the running of the University.

To ensure serious mindedness, only those Global leaders who scored a Cumulative Grade Point Average of at least 3.0 (out of 5.0) and were of proven sound character were allowed to serve on the Forum. We also encouraged the setting up of Programme-based Associations by Global leaders under the supervision of interested lecturers who acted as their Patrons. Both platforms served the University well as they became additional outlets for our students leadership development programme to be nurtured.

My tenure enjoyed a very peaceful students' governance. Given that we were in the pioneer phase, several amenities presented challenges that ordinarily would have generated some serious disquiet among students. Only once did the students become agitated over some not so well handled changes in fees to the extent of showing a collective disquiet. They marched to my office to register their concerns. Even in that, they were orderly and respectful. In my address to them, I emphasized how proud I was of their behavior which pleasantly exhibited a high level of leadership.

Bursary

We set up the Bursary Department as the central hub for the financial management in the University. It comprised the Bursar's Office, Payroll or Salaries/Wages Unit, Final Accounts Unit, Cash Office, and Stores & Asset Management. The Bursar, as the senior financial officer, was charged with the day-to-day administration and control of the financial affairs of the University. For this Office, we set a very high bar of unqualified integrity and accountability. And, we set the pace by being the first to make ourselves accountable.

Not only did we resolve <u>not</u> to take money out of the University without following the normal accounting principles and procedures that we had established[68]; officers (including myself) who received funds (colloquially called 'imprests') for the day to day running of their units had to, as a general rule, retire with receipts or (where no receipts are obtainable) certificates of honor any money received before a replenishment could be released. Only in rare cases of verifiable urgency did we allow flexibility to this rule. Even then, we did it sustainably i.e. without breaching the accountability value in the process.

While we drove fidelity to the vision, mission, and the core values in every area of the University, the focus on the Bursary to ensure that this culture of fidelity pervaded our financial management was unparalleled. Stories abounded as to how financial mismanagement was rife before my arrival. We were, therefore, extra sensitive in delivering on our commitment to bring the cardinal virtues of probity, transparency, and prudence to bear on our financial operations.

All the Units of the Bursary were sensitized to this commitment and many embraced it with gusto, following our own example. Part of the vigilance demanded of the Bursary was that on no account should the University be made to pay again on an item for which full payment had been made. Here is an example of where such vigilance served the University well. One of the banks with which the University had relationship, lent money on a five-year term to an investment outfit set up by the Chancellor for the building of a structure on the Campus. Under 24 months, the Bank requested that the loan be paid up because the Central Bank of Nigeria (CBN) was coming around to audit their accounts.

How the CBN's coming would be a problem for an entity that was effectively servicing its loan, was not disclosed. In any event, the loan was paid up as demanded and the University was informed accordingly. Indeed, the Bank wrote to acknowledge the payment, advising that the loan had been fully discharged. We kept a copy of this letter on our file in the University in accordance with our corporate documentation policy.

About one year after, the same Bank wrote demanding payment of "outstanding balance on the loan", amounting to about 50 per cent of the original loan. After checking our records in the Bursary, we advised the Chancellor that the demand letter was spurious, and probably calculated to defraud or double-dip. He then contacted the Managing Director of the Bank who promptly apologized and promised to get the Bank to write to withdraw their demand letter. Our vigilance paid off well.

Our resolve to turn around the University's financial records into a comprehensive, organised, defensible and 'available at call' system from the very messy and mutilated financial records we met on assumption of duty in 2008, became a master stroke. Among other benefits, it helped us to deliver an untarnished budget performance which we achieved with realism and prudence as watchwords for how we acquired and expended the resources of the University. And, at the time of my disengagement, we were able to present to the Chancellor, via the Governing Council Chairman, a year by year account of all the monies (receipts/revenues) that came in and all the outgoings (payments/expenditures) that we handled in the University as part of my handover notes, covering the 2008-2012 years.

The challenge of running in a tight financial environment a vision which embodied quite expensive corrective and standard-setting goals, as Salem University did, proved enormous. And this was compounded by the prevailing mindsets of 'impossibility', 'scarcity', 'selfishness', 'mendacity', 'mediocrity', etc. in the University community. However, with appropriate motivation (distinguishing right from wrong, teaching and living the ethics of *leading right* from the front, empowering staff for self-development, etc), we achieved to a notable extent the much needed radical re-orientation towards professionalism, integrity and accountability.

An example of the tangible outcomes of our leadership in this area is with regard to Asset Management. To carry out the work of the University, pursuant to its objects as spelt out in s.7(2)(i) of the *University Law 2006*, we needed to acquire appropriate level of buildings, libraries, laboratories, premises, furniture, apparatuses, and other relevant equipment. We achieved this goal without falling prey to the corrupting influences that usually dominate infrastructural development in this part of the world. On our instruction, the Bursary assiduously maintained a comprehensive register of all assets and receipts that the University acquired. In the account I rendered at the time of my disengagement, these assets tallied well with our expenditure profile in this area.

Another example was with regard to the Cafeteria Services which we started with a private provider. There were transparency, accountability, and differential interpretation issues with the catering arrangement verbally concluded before my arrival. So, we needed to move quickly to replace it with a formal arrangement, guided by a written contract which we designed to ensure that proper contractual obligations were clear to, and performed by, all parties. Our goal was to ensure, among other things, that benefits could start to flow to the University from its own facility.

Despite some baseless personal maligning and vicious attacks that ensued against us in the process, we followed through and repositioned the Cafeteria into a revenue generating service for the University before I disengaged. Some stakeholders struggled with our palpable rejection of gratification, nepotism, favoritism, or any underhandedness whatsoever in managing this sector; but they came around to respect our integrity even if grudgingly.

Infrastructural development and maintenance

As at March 2008 when we assumed duty, infrastructural development in the University was at a stage that required further major work before we could get the University ready for the academic take-off. There were a few completed but unfurnished physical structures in the Campus (about five in total). So, we undertook further development which, together with what was on ground, attracted commendations from various stakeholders – especially the NUC teams that came on monitoring and evaluation, licence renewal, and programme accreditation visits.

Considering the near "ground zero" situation we met on my assumption, we needed to engage the services of a strongly experienced professional to take carriage. This did not happen because such professionals were not easy to find; and when we did find some, resources were too constrained to allow us bring them on board.

Nevertheless, we started work with the few staff (three in number) that I met on my assumption. They were relatively junior in their fields of architecture, electrical engineering, and building tradesmanship, respectively. With them, we began the task of constituting the Physical Planning and Works Department. Since I met them in the "middle" of some few building constructions, the immediate task was to understand the designs to which they were building.

Having not done anything remotely close before – by study or in practice, I shuddered at what I was getting myself to do. Yet, with no professionals at hand other than the young staff with me, it was imperative that I understood the work and the plans they were using to build. Two matters were at stake. One, I needed to be able to assess the 'correctness' and 'quality' of the work done; and two, it fell to me to provide effective guidance for measurements, modifications, work modulations, etc. With courage and some capacity-building for myself, I stepped into the gap and kept the work going.

By and large, we recruited a few qualified professionals in architecture, engineering (mechanical and civil) and building, albeit at middle manpower level, who continued to form the nucleus of the Department that we used to accomplish most of the additional buildings we completed in my time. Along the way, we brought some contractors to handle more technical jobs such as buildings with decking, iron trusses roofs, roads, water boreholes, laboratory furnishing/equipping and some sport facilities. The support of the proprietor in this process was solid.

Physical Planning and Works

The state of physical infrastructure and works in the University at the time of my departure showed that with determination, dedication, and discipline a lot can be achieved even with the most unlikely team. Yes, the demand on my personal supervisory involvement was extremely high. Several times, I would go to construction sites at night to count the number of blocks laid that day by many masons we had engaged in those times and to assess the overall quality of work done. This was to checkmate the practice of many masons delivering less than contracted services – in quantity and quality.

Although the cost on my personal time and health was high, the outcome was highly rewarding. The efficiency gains and quality assurance we brought to bear in the process, showed up handsomely in the volume and 'finishing' of most of the projects we handled. In the span of about four years, we had infrastructures for all areas that made for the smooth running of a well-established University. These included:

- about 23 buildings (including the Senate – housing the core administrative Offies of the Vice Chancellor, Registrar and Bursar) – furnished and functional;
- roads (some compacted and tarred) linking to all the functional areas of the Campus;
- 20 well-furnished classrooms distributed among the three Colleges;
- 12 fully furnished and equipped laboratories for courses in natural & applied sciences and information & communication technology. The equipment in our science laboratories put those laboratories (particularly the biochemistry and microbiology labs) among the best 10 in the country at that time;
- a University Health Services Centre managed by a fully qualified medical doctor in a new standalone property built, furnished and equipped to a mini-hospital standard: admission beds in the male and female wards, and an in-house laboratory where basic medical tests were carried out; and
- utilities for power (five generators of 7, 12, 60, 150, and 450 kvas to complement the energy supply from the national grid) and water (6 boreholes)

Maintenance remains a bane of infrastructural integrity in developing countries, Nigeria inclusive. Assets run down rapidly where attention is not paid to maintenance. Our commitment to providing adequate instructional facilities to guarantee effective teaching and learning in the University would have been defeated (even in the short run) if we did not work hard to ensure that such facilities were properly maintained to ensure durability and efficient use by staff and students of the University.

Thus we focused our minds on the issue of maintenance from the time we assumed duty. Beside the resource constraint, which was not peculiar, the critical factor was the mindset. We constantly had to remind members of the University community to be vigilant, to address any maintenance issues they came across on the campus, and/or report to the Works Department those cases they could not handle. Even the way we used items could hasten their disrepair. Thus, it was a constant refrain to treat University items with respect. In the end, we recorded a large measure of success in this regard, although a lot was left to be desired.

Library

The University Library stood as an empty shell, albeit the most imposing building in the Campus, on my assumption. With the help of the then President of the Nigerian Library Association, Ms Victoria Okojie, we set up the Library and commenced recruitment to fill the relevant staffing positions. The search for the University Librarian with the flare for academic work as evidenced by solid publications and effective computer literacy to drive the installation of the electronic library management system and the establishment of an ICT-driven library, proved particularly difficult.

By and large, we brought up the Library to a remarkable status as one of the very few contemporary university libraries in Nigeria with strong ICT credentials. In addition to the KOHA Integrated Library Management System that we installed, about 50 Public Access Computers were connected to the internet in the E-Library Unit. The printed materials collection had about 7000 volumes, most of which were quite current. And three Resource Centres (with 10 internet connected laptops each) were established for the three Colleges. At the time of my disengagement, the University was running library electronic services Workshops for library staff from other tertiary educational institutions in Nigeria.

Academic management system

At the core of any university system is the academic delivery. We gave particular focus to the academic pattern and phases of development along with the types and durations of degrees to be awarded, the research policy and its implementation, the academic support units, the pattern of growth, and performance indicators that would facilitate quality programme delivery commensurate with the standard of excellence that the vision demanded (Academic Brief Vol. 1, Chapters 4 -10).

After we had analysed the first set of admissions, we noticed that about 15 out of the 29 Programmes were selected by the admitted candidates. One immediate use of this analysis was that we streamlined our staff recruitment to those selected Programmes, thus avoiding haphazard and redundant appointments. The management of this recruitment process helped to significantly keep our recurrent expenditure down. Over the period of my tenure the staffing profile was generally stable, with annual turnover levels (around 5 per cent) remaining well within the normal range[69].

At the commencement of my tenure, the situation with academic staffing in Nigerian universities was already quite dire. It was disquieting to hear at the first meeting we had with the Minister for Education in 2008, along with other Vice Chancellors and stakeholders, that Nigeria could meet only 60 per cent of its university system staffing needs. New Universities such as ours were particularly vulnerable in the search for senior level lecturers.

Nevertheless, we took a stand against some lecturers (across all cadres) from other Universities who were unscrupulously exploiting the tight academic staffing situation in Nigeria. They would secure full time appointments as ongoing or on sabbatical arrangements in several universities at the same time. We took some steps to discourage such lecturers from adding Salem University to their condemnable practices. At interviews we told them that we would not tolerate such conducts. We then gave them the chance to disclose, and we rejected those who already had multiple appointments even on visiting arrangement elsewhere. These steps were no full-proof; however, they minimized the extent to which the University could have fallen victim.

Accreditation

The NUC's policy was that new Programmes that had run or been offered for <u>three</u> (academic) years should be presented for accreditation assessment. All the 11 Programmes we started with in the 2008/2009 session became ripe for such assessment in 2011.

We knew of stories that several Universities devised several means – some not too wholesome - to succeed in accreditation. At Salem University, we took a stand. No unwholesome means would be part of our strategy. Resource constraints at the time increased the pressure on us to flow with the current. But like one of the US Presidents (Thomas Jefferson) once said: "In matters of style, swim with the current; in matters of principles, stand like a rock". We determined to face accreditation in ways wholly consistent with our values and principles.

In due course, the NUC Panels came and assessed our 11 Programmes in tranches at two different times (November 2011 and April 2012). Remarkably all our Programmes passed at the first go (some at full and others at interim levels) - generally unheard of even among established Universities at that time.

As part of the University's commitment to positioning our graduates for professional excellence, we commenced subjecting our relevant Programmes to professional accreditation as well. In April 2012, we presented the Accounting Programme for accreditation to the Institute of Chartered Accountants of Nigeria (ICAN). Again, without engaging in any unwholesome practices, the Programme passed and was granted full accreditation for four years, with effect from April 2012.

One incident in our accreditation experiences stands as a classic demonstration of our audacity to lead right. About six weeks to the coming of the NUC Panel for the accreditation of our Social Sciences Programmes, the only Professor we had in Economics left and returned to his home university – the University of Calabar. We started negotiating a 'visiting Professor' arrangement with him, but this would not be sufficient to meet the NUC staff-mix requirement. Understandably, there was a heightened anxiety in the College housing the Programme as to how to address this situation with Economics.

I called an emergency meeting of the relevant stakeholders, including the Deans, academics, and the University Management Team to review and resolve the situation. The College submitted that since it wasn't long that the Professor left our services, we could and should include his name as a full-time faculty in the documentation that we were preparing for the accreditation Panel. There was overwhelming support around the table for this submission, understandably so.

However, there was an immediate disquiet within me about this submission. Being the Chair, I endeavoured to sensitise the meeting to the integrity implication of that course of action. Most participants were fixated on the need to pass the accreditation. The main argument was that time was terribly against us. This was indeed quite striking because the chances of getting a full-time Professor within that short period were virtually nil. And, the College was strident in pushing it.

I asked: "what if a member of the Panel knows the Professor in question and that he had returned to his own home University. What happens to our claim to integrity, not just for Economics but for all other areas that the Panel was to assess?" There was a voluminous response: "it's only one in a million chance for that to happen"! Still unsettled about it all, I told them that, even for that one in a million chance, I was not prepared to support the submission – because it went against the principle of integrity in all things that we had labored to establish.

Among other things, I was also concerned that we may get the accreditation by such a smart move, but that in the end it would foist a deception on the global leaders and the soul of the University. So, I ruled against the majority drift and promised all necessary support for the Dean to go to the 'highways' and 'byways' to get a number of 'visiting Professors' that would equal that of a full-time Professor in the short time that we got.

Finally, the Panel arrived. Lo and behold, their Chairman was a Professor from the University of Calabar! He knew the Professor who had left us as a close friend and that his friend was back full-time to Calabar from his sabbatical leave elsewhere. You can say, this was serendipity. For us, at least two critical points in the audacity of leading right were on display: (1) in matters of style a conscientious leader can flow with the currents, but in matters of principle that leader must stand like a rock; and (2) an agile leader gets to the future before the future arrives – through the combination of insight[70] and foresight[71].

Leading right takes courage and conviction. As one writer puts it, "it means doing the right thing, even when the right thing isn't popular or easy. But when you make decisions based on your core values [and principles], then you tell the world that you can't be bought – and you lead your team by example".

Needless to say, my staff grew to appreciate more than ever before, my stand on values and principles. It gave them another one (indeed one in a million) opportunity to see that our stand was not about being rigid but being sensitively consistent and constantly focused on the bigger picture. A true leader cannot do otherwise without compromising the destiny of his or her human entity.

Teaching and student academic performance

In the three reports we presented since 2009 to the University System

Annual Review Meetings organised yearly by the NUC, we outlined the performances of Salem University in teaching, among other areas. Key highlights over the period of my tenure included:

- Uninterrupted teaching calendar
- Lecturers not selling handouts or seeking other forms of inducement from Global leaders
- Achievement of generally good student attendance at lectures, helped by our strict implementation of the 85 per cent attendance before any student can sit examinations
- Negligible number of examination malpractices, which were promptly handled in accordance with the rules resulting in suspensions and, in a few blatant cases of disregard, expulsion

As part of our quality assurance and standardization processes, consistent with the university education tradition, we secured the services of senior academics from other universities to assess the quality/standard of our examination questions, the answer scripts, and the final year research projects that were produced in all the Programmes.

It was gratifying to note from the reports we received from these external examiners that, in most of the cases, our students rated very highly in their academic performances. Some Examiners actually increased the marks that the internal staff had given, arguing that the quality of the works merited such higher recognition.

Stakeholders Management

The future of any human entity is tied to the disposition of its stakeholders as much as it is tied to its leadership. Owners, governance organs, government regulatory bodies, professional bodies, sister institutions, investors, customers, etc., are key stakeholders that can make or mar a university administration. We outline below our own experiences in relation to managing some of these stakeholders, in terms of the inherent challenges and opportunities.

Discipline: Staff and Students

"Thy rod and thy staff, they comfort me"[72]. In view of fact that the vision of the University was corrective and standard-setting, together with the deliberate and determined focus on character transformation, we considered it imperative that discipline was cultivated and maintained. The law (including the code of conduct rules) was our "rod" and the welfare policies were our "staff".

Where, despite the application of the "staff", the members of the University community ran short of the standard, we did respond promptly, if necessary with the rod – albeit as the last resort. Although the zeal of the vision might have made some of the responses to appear <u>ruthless</u>, we were careful never to be <u>reckless</u> or to overstep the boundaries willy nilly. That meant that we strove to act accountably at all times and ensured that such actions could stand the test of any scrutiny, including in the law courts.

In spite of our travails, there were discipline cases that could have shaken the foundation of the vision we were building. All such cases were processed through appropriate Committees where the offending staff or students were given fair hearing. And, where sanctioned persons appealed for review of sanctions, the Management Committee and/or Senate considered such appeals. In some cases, the appeals were considered favorably; in others the original sanctions were sustained. On the whole this is one area we particularly abhorred the negligent and manipulative features of compliant leadership. Staff and students alike were in no doubt as to our convictions regarding discipline and mutual accountability.

Litigation

As at the time of my disengagement, the University had taken no one to court. On a few occasions, mainly involving threat to life, criminal conversion, theft, or use of hard drugs by staff or students, the University complained to the Police who decided to take some of the matters to court. In such cases, the University provided all the needed support, including appearing in the courts as a <u>witness</u>.

Mindful of our calling to lead right, we were careful to organise all University matters in line with the core values and principles. By the same token, we did not hesitate to bring such matters to an end where we adjudged the conduct of the other parties to be detrimental to the vision of the University. A good example is with regard to contracts. We indeed terminated some contracts in which the contractors vitiated the terms of the agreements and hoped that the University would take no action as was usual in the wider society. But we had no qualms doing that, because we did not soil our hands in the process of awarding those contracts in the first place.

On two of such occasions, the affected contractors took the University to court on alleged breaches of contract. In one of those cases (RAAD Engineering), the court ruled in favor of the University and cleared the University of any liability whatsoever. The second case (Franko Basic Construction Ltd) had lost steam by the time I disengaged from the University, as the complainant was no longer keen to test the strength of his case. All through, the University was very confident that it would be vindicated and cleared as well, bearing in mind that we acted appropriately and legally. On this ground, and considering the disingenuousness (negative audacity) of the complainant, the University decided to counter-claim and we were quite hopeful of a favourable judgment.

In addition to making sure that the agreements were put on very sound and proper footing, our success was actually enhanced because we maintained comprehensive and clear records of transactions – payments, variations, warnings, termination letters, etc. So that, even without a legal unit in the University, we were able to prepare the briefs capturing all relevant matters that were used by a registered law firm for originating claims (if that became necessary), defence against claims, and/or counter-claims.

Further, one of our efforts from the outset that helped our litigation processes was about capacity-building the staff to pay particular attention to details, especially in all official correspondence – whether with staff, students or external contacts. We emphasized that they never knew where such correspondences might show up. The rule of thumb for us, therefore, was: should any document carrying our signature be read on the national or international media outlets (print or electronic including, CNN, BBC, or www), the University should not be brought into disrepute and we would neither be embarrassed nor be found wanting.

Government Agencies

We enjoyed unalloyed good relationship with key government regulatory bodies, especially the NUC and JAMB. One reason was that we acted as a responsible corporate citizen that complied with legitimate policy instructions from these bodies. In fact, NUC and JAMB held the University in very high regard and did acknowledge the University in terms of exemplar of good practice.

From the beginning of our relationship, we continually sought their guidance in handling matters within their respective jurisdictions and they obliged us generously. They organised meetings from time to time, in which we participated promptly and actively within our limits. For instance, every year, after the release of JAMB results, both agencies jointly called a Policy Committee meeting involving all Vice Chancellors, Rectors of Polytechnics and Provosts of Colleges of Education, presided by the Minister for Education. At this meeting, the JAMB Registrar presented status report on the performances in the examinations and the pattern of applications into various tertiary education institutions in Nigeria. Most critically, the meeting then decided on the cut off JAMB score to be used for admissions for the next academic year, and to this we adhered.

Also, the NUC organized University System Annual Review Meetings (**USARM**); and at those meetings, all Heads of the tertiary institutions were expected to present reports on the performance of their institutions from the preceding academic year. The focus was on (1) teaching, research and community service, (2) success factors and challenges to the achievement of goals and objectives, (3) internal and external efficiencies of the institution, (4) experience of NUC's support towards quality education, (5) budget performance, and (6) other matters of concern.

We presented reports on Salem University for 2009, 2010, and 2011 in three formats: Recurrent/Capital Budget; Statistical report on staff and students; and the full Vice Chancellor's Report (which was delivered in narratives using a powerpoint version). In all the years that we presented our reports, we received voluble commendations – with enthusiastic encouragement to continue with the good work.

State Government: courtesy calls, partnership, consultancy

In my time at Salem University, we witnessed two democratic Kogi State Governments, both of the Peoples Democratic Party extraction. We paid courtesy calls on both, and intimated them in writing of our readiness to partner with them in the development of the State. We also notified them of the fact that the University was hosting students and staff from at least 25 States of the Federation – making it a mini-Nigeria with strategic and sensitive possibilities.

We worked in partnership with one of the Governments to train and certificate about 300 "restive" youth in a three-month customized 11 vocational fields. Apart from this, the interactions of both Governments with the University – a product of a private endeavor and, invariably, a catalyst for economic development in the capital city of their State – was minimal. One of the Governors stepped into the campus only once during my time, and this came after much pleadings.

Global Parents Forum

A major group of stakeholders for the University were the parents of the Global leaders. From the time of the first matriculation, we commenced a Tripartite Partnership Agreement process in which all parties – the Global leaders, their Parents, and the University – committed themselves to producing a quality Global leader at the end of his or her study at the University.

Recognising the potential of such a forum as a platform for effective development for the University, we established a solid relationship with the parents and cultivated in them the desire to do everything necessary to sustain the unique attention that their wards were receiving in the University. They responded very commendably during our time.

In fact, we used that platform to address some discipline matters that arose involving some Global leaders to the satisfaction of all parties. By 2011, we had lifted this platform into an organised outfit, called Global Parents Forum. We drafted its constitution which was ratified and adopted at a general meeting of the Forum. The secretariat of the Forum was based in the University and the Executive Council included the Vice Chancellor as Chair, Registrar as Secretary, Bursar as member, and three other members were elected from the parents to serve in other portfolios.

A development levy per child payable annually was agreed to by the Forum; and shortly before I disengaged, the Development Committee of the Forum was established and began identifying projects to which the paid levies could be applied. Critical as the Forum was, it was necessary to manage the sometimes divergent views/interests of individual parents vis-à-vis matters that pertain to operations of the University. At one time of a particularly challenging security situation in the country, different parents were calling on the University to reopen at different times. The University management had to take a position that was in the overall best interest of the University immediate stakeholders, and that meant going against some of the parents' preferred options.

Inter-faith relations

The University had a policy objective to "encourage the advancement of learning and to hold out to all persons without distinction of race, creed, sex or political or religious conviction the opportunity of acquiring higher technological and liberal education… (Academic Brief Vol 1, p3). Consistent with this objective, we actually admitted candidates from non-Christian religious backgrounds. Consequently, we had Muslim Global leaders who showed generally great potentials to become persons of influence and be worthy in learning and character that was central to the vision of the University.

It was also University policy, indeed identity, that:

> As a church sponsored University, we intend to model our students on the teachings of Jesus that demands love for God which must translate in love for the fellow man; peace at heart which makes the man unruffled by circumstances, for a leader must not waver in the face of challenges… to help raise leaders that will promote peace in our world. They therefore, must be spiritually alive, mentally alert and physically developed to change our world for good (Academic Brief Vol 1, p6).

It was on this philosophical conviction that we based the designing the TLTC programs which aimed to deliver effective character transformation as equal to intellectual development in the vision of the University. We charged the Chaplaincy to anchor these programs (held on Wednesdays and Sundays); and we stated clearly in the Students Handbook that attendance at these programs was compulsory, similar to the requirement of at least 85 per cent lecture attendance before any Global leader could be allowed to sit examinations.

In the first session (2009), some Muslim Global leaders requested to be exempted from the TLTC programs on grounds of their religion and to be allowed to go to town for Friday (Jumaat) prayers. Drawing on the Tripartite Partnership Agreement, we invited the parents of these Global leaders to discuss their request. In the end, the parents fully supported the policy of the University of compulsory attendance at TLTC programs, and of no exit for prayers or any other activity during the session. No further issue came from these Global leaders during my time.

Late 2011, the University received letters from the Federal Minister for Education, the NUC, the Kogi State Commissioner of Education, and the Chief of Staff to the State Governor, all conveying that they had received a petition against the University that we were forcing Muslim students to attend chapel on Sundays. We responded to these letters, stating that irrespective of the days the Programmes were held, they were built upon three pillars of our leadership development program: (1) Developing the leader in you, (2) Developing the leaders around you, and (3) Applying the leadership you have developed. Further, that it was imperative for all Global leaders (regardless of religious affiliation) to imbibe the essence of these pillars if they were to be complete graduates of the University.

We had to meet the NUC on this matter where it was resolved that the University Management should further sensitize the parents about these programmes, especially at the point of admissions, and to explore a day other than Sunday to hold the programs. The Sunday issue was put to the Global Parents Forum at a meeting in 2012 and it was resolved (led overwhelmingly by Muslim parents) to retain Sunday as one of the days for the programmes. Subsequently, text and/or voice messages came from unknown sources threatening to kill, main and destroy me and some of my Principal Officers (together with the Chief Security Officer), with a spurious allegation that "[we] refused to build a mosque on our Campus for muslim students".

In all of this, we were resolute in upholding the policy of the University. Refreshingly, we received incredible support from our muslim students, their parents or sponsors, and the security agencies in the land (Police, Civil Defence, State Secret Services, and Army).

Concluding remarks

Like Bill Hybels said in the passage I quoted at the beginning of this Chapter, we did roll up our sleeves to turn the vision of Salem University into reality insofar as the physical and systems infrastructures were concerned.

We carried out, simultaneously, the establishment of the governance bodies, recruitment for staffing, infrastructural development, framework for and actual practices of student admissions, curriculum development, stakeholders management etc. We did all this, consistent with the vision together with its underpinning values as we understood them.

The edifice satisfied the 'engineering specification' as we built the University in line with the design work we found and interpreted. The main clients (parents and sponsors of the global leaders) found the reality we turned the vision into adorable. With 100 per cent accreditation by the NUC, we could believe that the edifice met the 'functional requirements'. Over and above all these, the story of the 'trophies' in the next Chapter attest to the fact that the University remarkably satisfied the 'verification specification' as we could derive from its core philosophy, mission and values.

Considering the extent we went to raise the edifice with the available funds, it would be an understatement to say the whole thing was stressful. I look back with some giggling to see how someone like me (all modesty aside, a 'thoroughbred' in the social sciences and law) became an 'expert' in buildings and constructions overnight. I learnt ('by force by force', they say) to interpret building/road/furniture construction drawings. I was constantly at the building and construction sites – many of those times late into the night (8-10pm) to ensure the various infrastructures were built according to approved drawings, quantity, and quality.

If blocks can blink, 75 per cent of the building blocks in the University at the time of my disengagement would blink at the mention of our name. Similarly, if systems can sing, 99.5 per cent of them would do so. Pew! We built the University of this unique vision. "Look, the vision was a dream before you came, but now we have a University. No one can ask more from you!" (emphasis added). That was a comment by a member of the University Governing Council (also a highly regarded member of the Board of Trustees) after the meeting of the Council on 4-5 August 2012. Incidentally, it was at that meeting that the Council, among other matters, approved my request to disengage from the University as Vice Chancellor with effect from September 2012.

Vince Lombardi, a venerable management guru once said, "when all is said and done, more is said than done". This was one syndrome in the nation's life that we dreaded at the University because of its disempowering, underdeveloping and corrupting influence.

To counteract that syndrome, we actually modeled and promoted 'leading and managing for results' as one of the mantras that defined our performance across the University community – from the cleaners, through security, departments/units, colleges, to the VC's office. Of course, we stepped on toes, big and small, to get the job done with our mantra of 'doing the right thing, the right way, at the right time and for the right reasons' – in a wider context where mere 'activities' were mistaken or dubiously equated to performance.

---

[66]   For me, the whole business of building the University was a project. This meant that in addition to the leadership dimension, we approached it with the 'project management' discipline of goal setting, resource allocation, timelines, accountability, etc. The staff I managed in the Australian Commonwealth Public Service shortly before I returned to Nigeria became so used to my incessant call for us to 'projectify' our work that they nicknamed this approach "Omajism".

[67]   However, for various reasons mostly external to the University, less numbers took up these offers.

[68]   These procedures demanded, among other things, that any proposal to access the University money must state in writing the official University business being pursued, demonstrate 'value for money' by providing competitive quotes (as appropriate), and get approval of the various levels

of delegation.

[69]   "Any rate below 15 percent annually is considered healthy and no cause for alarm. This means that a company of 200 workers can lose 30 individuals within a calendar year without it becoming a problem" (Bernadette Kenny's report in *Forbes* magazine. http://smallbusiness.chron.com/healthy-employee-turnover-rate-12145.html

[70]   A vision of reality before you act.

[71]   A vision of reality after you have acted.

[72]   Psalms 23: 4, Holy Bible, New King James version.

7 Trophy: leaving footprints in hearts

"No man is a leader until his appointment is ratified in the minds and hearts of his men" (Anonymous)

Over time, I have come to appreciate that nothing speaks more audibly about the ratification of one's leadership than the *footprints (better still, visionprints)* that the leader leaves not merely 'in the sands of time' – momentous as that may be, but *in the hearts of people*. Considering the enormity of the demands for *leading right*, one would be greatly shortchanged if all those efforts do not result in something more enduring than the sands of time can bear.

In this regard, it is the 'legacy' question that is at stake. It is about you being somewhere and moving the souls of your followers or co-labourers to "dance". They know that even though you may be gone, you have made something beautiful to rise within them and that, invariably, you (embodied in that thing) stay on in their lives, and helping them never ever to be the same again. This is impact stuff; and it makes the travails all worth it.

Remarkable as the physical and systems infrastructures that we established for Salem University may have been, I do not hold them up as the trophies of our travails. Rather, it is the footprints in the hearts of people that I point to as our greatest and priceless 'trophies'.

They are the things that constitute the high point, indeed the crowning factor, in all our efforts at leading right. We went through the audacious travails as we did to produce them. They were the legacies that kept us focused. The transformation we set out to accomplish was such that those whose lives the University touched would never ever be the same again; and they were to become people who in turn would leave behind lasting impact wherever they go.

The reality of our world at the time and the imagined future that engaged our attention throughout our tenure, meant that there was no greater aspiration for us. We needed to go for the ultimate that *leadership qua leadership* could provide: "the best footprints we leave are from when we help people to transform their own lives. Transformed lives are a good set of footprints to leave in this broken world" (Leighton, 2012). In the end, we had 'performance trophies', 'love trophies', and 'lifestyle trophies' to exhibit.

A place of importance!

A little over 2 years after we started building the University, I began to develop some consciousness about the trophies that were unfolding right before our eyes. I recall that on the Founder's Day (6 August) of 2010, I addressed the University community where I recounted the importance of the place we could then call Salem University where these trophies were being developed. Below is an excerpt from that address.

...The title of my presentation this morning is: "Here to make a difference."

In every generation, there are people and institutions set apart to make a noble difference in many lives. The founder of Salem University Lokoja, Archbishop Dr Sam Amaga, and the vision of the University that he received from the Lord, on the 6th of August, 2002, belong to this category of difference makers. We gather here today for the second time, since the University successfully took off in January, 2009, to celebrate both the founder and the vision of this University.

The founder, who is now the Chancellor of our University, had a dream of making many mighty. As we look around us today, we witness that dream being actualised over the years... We remind ourselves today of that famous declaration of the founder when he stood in front of this ground and declared: "today you are a forest, tomorrow you will be a city". All of us here today, are in that 'tomorrow'.

You have heard some of our lecturers testify already. We have had the video-recorded testimonies from parents and from some of our global leaders, all of them testifying to the fact that transformation is taking place. When we watched the drama that our global leaders presented to us, for those who may not be familiar with the history or those who have not been here for long - especially gentlemen of the press, you may think that was just a figment of imagination as dramas *sometimes do portray*. What they demonstrated on the stage this morning is our own reality to the glory of God. I want to declare this morning in the spirit of the founder of the University, that all of you here will go away from this place as change agents that the world cannot withstand in the name of Jesus... *Salem University is a place of importance!*

From that time onwards, we began to deliberately note the impact that our efforts were producing. And, truly we became more appreciative of the song writer that says: "Count your blessings, name them one by one, and it will surprise you what the Lord has done". In the areas of academics, attitude, and lifestyle, members of the University community gave us causes for wonder and warmth. They started showing our footprints (visionprints) in the hearts of people!

Trophies

On 17 November, 2011, the Chancellor was on Campus for one of his strategic visits to the University. I felt the urge to present to him some good news. My mind went to the SIWES, internship, and 'love' reports that we had received a couple of weeks before his arrival. I built those reports into my presentation, an excerpt from which is reproduced below.

Performance trophies

You would recall, Chancellor, that our 300 level global leaders in the Sciences and ICT *completed* their SIWES *recently*. We have received reports from the field. The global leaders were graded on four criteria, namely: "familiarity with company operations", "comprehension of problem(s) at hand", "method(s) of approach (creativity or originality of techniques), and "sense of discipline on the job". On each criterion, they were rated on a Likert scale of Poor, Fair, Good, Very Good, and Excellent.

On the criterion of "familiarity with company operations", our Global leaders scored 97 per cent at 'very good' and 'excellent' levels (combined). These are global leaders that went in for a three-month placement...; and within the period, they became quickly familiar with the operations of the companies where they worked to such a high level.

On the criterion of "comprehension of the problems at hand", their performance was 94 per cent; on "methods or approach to problems and the issue of creativity and originality of techniques", they scored 81 per cent; and on the "sense of discipline on the job", they scored 97 per cent. Chancellor, … we are very proud of these Global leaders.

These reports encapsulate the spirit of the vision that God has delivered into this world through you. Let me run through some comments that came from the organisations where these Global leaders had their placements…:

- "Hard-working and highly involved": *We had trained our* Global leaders not to be spectators wherever there go, but to participate positively.
- "Respectful, hard-working and result oriented". *Our message to them all along has been that* it's not just action or activity for the sake of activity. Your activities are targeted on getting something out. That is the spirit you have breathed upon the University and is beginning to manifest in these very uncommon ways.
- "Excellent performance and team-spirited". In a world *where the existential philosophy is* everyman to himself and God for us all, our global leaders go in there and they manifest team-spiritedness. We taught them so.
- "Committed to learning new technology as well as mastering the company's overall business operations" and "Mastered the job as though on the job for 10 years". *Commitment to learning new things is a strong trait of leadership.* And in doing this, what takes regular employees ten years to master, our global leaders mastered in three months! *That is the Salem University spirit that we connected with and poured into them.*

… Let's look briefly at the internship report. Apart from the sciences and the ICT students that went for SIWES, we believed every programme in the University must have placement for our Global leaders and so we announced that anyone who wanted a letter of introduction to go for internship should come for one.

Quite a number of our Global leaders went for that particular instrument. From the reports that we have received so far, you can notice the following:

A female Global leader went *for work practice* at the Nassarawa Judiciary Upper Area Court in Lafia. The Court wrote a report on her. She was "found to be very punctual, obedient, comprehensive, committed and above all performed excellently; … she [stood] the test of time". *Punctuality, ala timeliness is our signature, so also is excellence both of which we continually hammered into our Global leaders' DNA.*

Another Global leader went to the Ministry of Foreign Affairs, Office of the Permanent Secretary. This is the report that came back about her: "exhibited a high sense of responsibility, a calm and matured comportment and a key sense of commitment to duty". That is worth celebrating. And then another Global leader went to Zenith Bank. This is the report that came her performance there: "exhibited high level of dedication and commitment to duty with commendable integrity and reliability… Salem University builds standard, not only intellectually but also morally in students".

It is not possible for any Global leader to go from here and would not show dedication and commitment, unless Salem University has not gone through that person! And as for integrity, has any global leader or global staff seen "integrity" anywhere on this campus? [the audience chorused "Yes"]. Where? "Among the core values"! Where else have you seen it? "Among our colleagues"! Indeed, many of you have demonstrated integrity and we celebrate you for that. *For this Bank to commend integrity and reliability, and go further to observe that "Salem University builds standards not only intellectually but also morally into the students", it must have come in close contact with us. We are thankful for that impact.*

Love trophies

I call the next category of trophies, the 'love trophies'. In John 13: 34-35, Jesus says: "a new commandment I give unto you, that you love one another… [and], by this all will know that you are my disciples…". I wanted to understand the dimension of this love Jesus was talking about, and John 15: 13 caught my attention: "greater love hath no man than this that a man lay down his life for his friends".

Chancellor, we have had stories of love exhibited by our Global leaders. There were instances where some of them prevailed on their parents to pay the tuition fees for their friends who were unable to do so by themselves. And there are countless examples that I can give. Let me *narrate* this one *because it* has touched my spirit so much.

Two Global leaders returned to the University from holidays not long ago. They came late because one of them lost the person sponsoring her (he died suddenly) and she could not get money to pay her own tuition fees. She felt that the end of her life had come. Her friend - another female Global leader - decided that unless and until her bereaved friend was able to go back to the University she was not going to come back. People pleaded with her to go, but she said "I will stay here; I will prevail upon God until He opens doors for my friend".

The University reopened. The one who had money to pay refused to come back and chose to wait on the God of miracle for her friend. You would recall that one of the TAR Mission Mandates was to raise people who would, among other efforts, "depend on the God of miracles". So, together they kept praying until the bereaved Global leader secured money for her fees. Both returned to the University very late.

I got a note from the mother of the one whose sponsor died, explaining why the Global leaders returned to the University late. By the University policy, they had late registration and therefore they had to pay the penalty. The letter initially went to the Registrar and he minuted it to me for decision; and I said "calculate the penalty". The Registrar said, "VC this one is so touching oh". I still said "calculate the penalty", *having developed a principle* never to allow sentiment to override policy. If you allow that in one situation, you must do it for any other similar situation and before you know it (if care is not taken) you leave the impression of losing consistency. And when your consistency is in doubt, your integrity comes under question also. So, in our determination to ensure that we enforced the University policy, the Registrar compiled for me the payment due.

Both *Global leaders that have incurred this penalty are* right now owing the University fifteen thousand naira (N15,000.00), i.e. seven thousand five hundred naira (N7,500.00) each for coming late. As I was pondering upon it, my mind wandered to what Jesus had said and I said to myself: "for someone who had laid down her own life for a friend, it will touch her spirit badly if you don't do something different on this occasion". The battle for me was what else could I do without violating the policy and the principle? [*At this point, I decided to bring out to the front the Global leaders I was talking about. They came and stood with me in front of the room and the audience celebrated with clapping.*]

I said to the friend of the bereaved Global leader: "We celebrate you for that show of love". It is part and parcel of the vision that has been delivered to Salem University. You cannot be a transformer for good unless you love what you are transforming. Yesterday or the day before yesterday the Chaplain taught, "The Tripod of Leadership". If you remember, one of the legs that he talked about was what? [*Chorus*] "Love"!

Turning to the two Global leaders, I said: I have good news for you. You are not going to pay the penalty; you have already paid enough of penalty. *I will pay the penalty on your behalf.* So, this is a cheque of fifteen thousand naira (of my personal money). You go and pay, being the penalty both of you owed the University. Alright! God bless you. Go! *There was a wild jubilation in the hall for the sacrificial love all around – by the Global leader that waited on the Lord for her friend, and by my modelling Jesus who paid the penalty we owed and could not pay.*

Lifestyle trophies

Preparatory to the 2010 Founder's Day celebration, we had put together a documentary on our progress at Salem University, titled the **Salem University Brand**. In that documentary I said: "Today Salem University can point to strategic examples of transformation that is taking place in several lives. Many of our Global leaders, before our eyes, have turned around dramatically, showing all the qualities of leadership". This was borne out by the many testimonies that the documentary captured from students at their various levels of study, and from their parents alike. Some of these testimonies are reproduced below. They are our 'lifestyle trophies'!

Students

Jacquiline Onuorah (Regional Integration and Diplomacy, 300 Level): Salem University has really helped me to see life differently. I no longer talk the way others talk. I have the ability to change people. Salem University has helped me to develop intellectually ... *and* in several *other* ways. I implore you to come to see the kind of wonders that are happening in Salem University.

Edidiong Daniel Uduotte (Information Technology, 300

Level): I have been transformed in the area of confidence which is one of our core values. [Before coming to SU] I used to cheat to pass my exams. *Not anymore*. I now have confidence in myself to work and pass my own exams.

Princess Moses (Computer Science, 300 Level): I am a global leader who has been transformed here at Salem University. I want others to feel this transformation. Spiritually I have improved; academically I have improved. And I am a global leader going out to make a wonderful impact on the lives of others.

Uduak Udo-Imeh (Economics, 300 Level): … I have now found my purpose and vision for life… I used to be an average student in the past, but now I have seen a reason why I should strive on in life and increase in all that I do… Salem University has increased the ability of servant leadership in me. Indeed you find many universities where most of the students don't know their Vice Chancellors, but in Salem University that is not the case. We have a cordial relationship with our Vice Chancellor. In such teachings that he has given to us, he has increased in us certain abilities and learnt experiences he has had through his life. I have been truly blessed. I do not regret my days at Salem University.

Venessa Akpabio (Regional Integration and Diplomacy, 300 Level): My experience at Salem University has been worth the while… I thought I wasn't that good academically, but I came here, got motivated by lecturers. .. I am something going somewhere to happen.

Chinyere Okoye (Regional Integration and Diplomacy, 300 Level): Values are those things that design the life of a person. The core values of Salem University have actually shaped, designed and repackaged my life for a brighter future. I am talking about confidence, integrity, synergy… and of course godliness. All these things, I must confess, is what has made my life the way it is now. I have a confident spirit; I am not afraid, I am not shy; I am actually bold; confidence has made me to stand up for what I believe in. And I know what my convictions are: without convictions, there is no power… I have power to take my stand and face the consequences that may arise from the decisions I make. Salem University has built in me integrity in all areas: spiritual, academic and even sexual integrity… Godliness has been built into my life through the TLTC programs in form of leadership seminars, workshop etc.

Tamunonimi Harrydan (Regional Integration and Diplomacy, 300 Level): So far, Salem University has made a great impact in my life; so far, I have been groomed to the point of seeing situations as challenges and seeking for ways to proffer solutions to them. In that light, I have come to terms with nature that I am not just groomed to be a graduate as a conventional university does, but as a global leader to be a change agent to my world and many generations to come.

Jennifer Igbeta (Information Technology, 200 Level): So far, I can say that Salem University has been a huge, huge source of transformation in my life because looking back at where I came from and how changed I am right now, the change is really massive… Salem University changes your orientation from a pessimist to an optimist.

Daniel Atebije (Computer Science, 200 Level): Spiritually, I have been drawn closer to God through the Total Leadership Training Concept (TLTC) programmes in the Chapel at Salem University, Lokoja. Academically, I have improved to the level of making "As" in my courses. This was really incredible but it was true. From the social dimension, timidity and shyness have been wiped out of my life as I can now communicate effectively. All these came to be through my experience at Salem University, Lokoja. Surely I will end with a fulfilled destiny rather than a compromised one.

Uwechi Ugochukwu (Telecommunications Management, 200 Level): Time management has been a big challenge in Africa as people believe in "African-man-time." But Salem University with her vision of raising global leaders who will always keep to time has revolutionized me to respect time in order to positively change my world.

Aishat Sule (Business Administration, 100 Level): In my few years on earth and particularly in Nigeria, I have always believed right from my Primary School up to Secondary that bribery is the only way up. With my experience seeking admission into public Universities for some years now, I saw and believed one can only bribe her way through until I came to Salem University and saw that I can succeed beyond my imagination doing the right thing God's own way and God's own time. Admission here in Salem University is strictly by merit and not through bribery or who you know. I thank God for Salem University.

Esther Eleojo Akowe (Accounting, 100 *Level*): Anger has always been a very big challenge to me and has destroyed my relationship with people around me but coming to Salem

University, I learnt to forgive in advance and do away with anger. Also, I had a very poor mentality about myself because of my family background but Salem University impacted me to think positively. Furthermore, my academic has improved because of the lecturers who take their times to lecture us. I bless the God of Salem University.

Anita Damiete Hornby (Accounting, 100 Level): I am over joyous because of the peaceful and serene environment with absolute absence of distraction. So far, I have learnt a lot among which are integrity, godliness, mental empowerment and synergy which are some of our core values. Values give direction; hence I have imbibed these values as necessary tools to the top as well as necessary tools to keep me at the top. Seek for me and meet me a few years from now at the top.

Parents

Bishop Great Eromosele: I have a child at Salem University. Salem University is a vision-bound university. That makes it unique. I have had the privilege to interact with the echelon of the School – from the Vice Chancellor through the Registrar down the ladder. One thing that strikes you is this clear-cut commitment to the vision and you see them working hard to fulfill that vision. It is a missing element in the public universities. Salem University stands out.

I can see that my little boy of yesterday, having been through Salem University for some time now, displays some elements that are akin to behaving far beyond his age. He has a better sense of responsibility; displays initiative; is more confident; is proactive in his approach to issues. He is my first child and I see him now taking better charge, playing that leadership role in the family among his siblings. My wife and I can travel and leave Samuel in charge of the home and we are not afraid. We come back and everything is in place. This was not there before he went to Salem. I think that the vision of Salem to produce global leaders is evident in my child. And I am very happy about that.

Mrs Yvonne Udoh-Imeh: My daughter is at Salem University. We thank God for making that choice because we have seen tremendous positive changes in the life of our daughter... In terms of her spiritual growth, it has been tremendous. Before she went to

Salem University, we would have to wake her up in the morning: urge her, cajole her, trick her into coming to family devotion. But now, long before the family wakes up, she's up praying speaking in other tongues... All our desires, aspirations for this child we are seeing it unfolding right before our eyes without us doing any extra thing...

We as a family have even learnt so much through what she's being taught there. She comes home and she shares with us. [Before going to Salem University] it was very difficult for me to get her to read novels in her secondary school... But the very first holiday she came back from Salem University, she mentioned several goods she has read. She leaves some of those good books for me to read. So I am also, at the distant, benefiting from Salem University.

From what she has been taught there, she is living a purpose-driven life. She has been taught and she knows that education is about the total man – your spirit, soul and body. She has been taught to balance it properly. She has been taught to put God first... So, it's so exciting for me that the children there are being brought up spiritually. And at the same time, they have this vision of global excellence and she is so conscious of it.

Barr Mrs Otonyetarie Okoye: I have two of my children at Salem University... Salem University has impacted them greatly. They are purpose-driven. They have a vision for their lives. Also, they are allowed to exercise their abilities beyond the academic environment. Their skills are put to task. That for me is wonderful.

Bishop CC Charles: My son, Wisdom, has been in Salem University for some time now. I observe that Salem University is a home for leaders. A child that wants to grow into a sound leader in our time or generation must get into a home where he can be molded, trained and equipped. Salem University is one of such places you can think about in the world. *With my child*, I notice, God is my witness in what I am telling you, that this boy each time he came back home is more peaceful; is more organised. He is no longer the 'outgoing' type that I used to know. He now wants to look at books; he wants to work on computer; he wants to help his younger ones.

And, you know one interesting thing? He does not take 'no' for an answer now. If you tell him it can't work; he would tell you it can work. That spirit, that zeal was not there before... Yes, I am a Bishop but it takes time to do whatever. He went to Salem University and the School has affected him. There was a time in the past, you tell him to go to school and he would give you excuses why he must not go to school. But now, he keeps reminding me about when the school is to reopen. That he wants to go back to school, that my house is boring and school is better off! His reading ability has changed. His understanding and his behaviours truly have changed. Me and my wife were saying the other day that truly Salem University is doing something in the lives of these children.

Rev Chris Kanu: I have my daughter in Salem University. At the inception I had my fears of what we got in conventional universities where I have some of my children. But after 3 months of staying at Salem University, she came back home (for holidays) and I saw a great difference in her life to those that are in Federal universities. I saw her exhibiting an authority that the other ones do not have – leadership qualities!

First of all, she came and made us to be kind of inferior – everybody, including myself, both the mother and her elder ones – correcting everybody at any given time, trying to exhibit authority, making us to believe in ourselves. She virtually corrects her mother in every word that she says. In authority, we found out that she has become the Joseph in the family. Every time she would always tell us that global leaders do not do things this way.

One of the things that I have found out in her is this ability to believe even when there is nothing to believe… This is faith in action. So, her staying in Salem University has given her an edge over other of her brothers and sisters in other universities; and that has brought happiness into the family… My daughter came back; has taken over in the choir – there are many others that were in before her; she comes in and exhibits leadership… I tried to find out the secret; and found out that there is something that has been imparted in her that others of my children in the conventional universities do not have.

Bishop Dan Okayi: I am the father to Comfort Okayi, one of the students of Salem University. So much has happened to her since she *went* to Salem University … Her language has changed; anything we do in the house, she says global leaders don't do it this way. She tends to correct my English. We have enjoyed so much of her character. She has been a model. Before now, she did not do much for her herself; but now, she does a lot things for herself; takes care her clothing… a lot of maturity has set in. The impact of Salem University over her cannot be overemphasized… My daughter has highly improved... everything is about global leadership.

Mr. Alabi (a lecturer in Management Sciences at Kogi State University, Anyigba and a PhD student at Nnamdi Azikiwe University, Awka): I am also a member of Council of Nigerian Institute of Management. My daughter has just done a semester at Salem University, Lokoja and she already knows so much about entrepreneurial education and principles of courses that I teach. I was shocked by the radical academic and spiritual transformation in her life. I am witnessing the things that are missing in many of our public Universities and this gives me joy, desire and focus to partner with Salem University, Lokoja.

Engr. Ola Ige: I wanted to send my son to a University abroad but later chose to have him at Salem University, Lokoja, having succeeded in Matriculation examination and the Post UME Screening. He is about ending the 1st semester. He came during a short break and we were surprised by his leadership qualities: he started leading the family prayer meetings. He retreated immediately after such meetings for personal academic engagement. The quality of his communication has become so matured and manifesting global leadership view or orientation. We're glad that we made Salem University our choice for him.

Futures in their wombs

As I reflected on these trophies (of performance, love, and lifestyle), I got the picture that our calling, visioning, softwaring, travailing and the resulting edifice, have indeed left some footprints in the hearts of some people. The testimonies by, and about, the Global leaders show footprints in their three broad meanings as: 'marks on a surface', 'spaces filled by something', and 'areas for receiving communication signals'.

Not only has our work at Salem University made marks on the surfaces of their hearts, it has also created spaces in their lives where virtues can fill. Further, it has also defined areas where communication from 'above' concerning their own assignment among human entities can be received and transmitted to their world, including generations of today and of the future.

I am very excited about the fact that all the relevant footprints we travailed for are translating into enviable futures in the wombs of these Global leaders. The capacity to comprehend 'problems'; to deploy creativity and originality of techniques; and to exercise a high sense of discipline, commitment, integrity and reliability - mirrors the philosophy, values and principles that we continually demonstrated to them in thoughts, words and deeds. What is more, these Global leaders can visualize their own place in the 'tomorrow' that would eventuate by the force of their determination to follow through as change agents. Recall their own words:

- "I have the ability to change people"
- I am "going out to make a wonderful impact on the lives of others"
- I have "increased... ability of servant leadership in me"
- "I am something going somewhere to happen"
- My life is "actually shaped, designed and repackaged... for a brighter future"
- I am groomed "a global leader to be a change agent to my world and my generation to come"
- "Seek for me and meet me a few years from now at the top".

The marks on the surface of their hearts, the space they have for virtues, and their receptivity to destiny-changing communications would distinguish them in their character (thoughts, words and deeds) wherever they are. I am witnessing this already in their lives after Salem University.

Sometime ago, I went to the Nigerian Immigration Services Head Office in Abuja Nigeria to get a replacement for my lost passport, and ran into one of our Global leaders working there. She immediately recognized me and greeted very familiarly. Noticing some hesitation in my own response, she said excitedly: "your Global leader!". I then responded more freely, inquiring about her life generally after Salem University and what she was doing in Immigration.

She told me she was working there and wanted to know my own mission there. As soon as I told her, she collected the file and went to work. I was observing her interactions with her colleagues (senior, peers and subordinates). I didn't hear what she told her co-workers, but suddenly many of them turned and looked at my direction admiringly, better still adoringly.

While she was processing my passport, her supervisor came to me and said: "Sir, I don't know what you did to your students at the University, but they are unique. This one [pointing to this Global leader] came to us for her National Youth Corps Service. At the end, we retained her. She's too good. She's an asset to our organization. I wish many VCs could affect their students as she said you did to them". I thanked him for engaging one of our products and for his compliments. Then I told him that the best in her was yet to come and that they should nurture her to reap more from the asset she was carrying inside of her.

Within minutes, my Global leader turned up with a new passport in her hands for me. I saw confidence in her steps. I saw focus in her approach. She carried herself with dignity. And, determination was written all over her. Indeed, I saw at work a heart and a hand carrying our footprints (nay, visionprints). Of course, I was ecstatic! All of a sudden, my mind surveyed the travailing back at the University and I heard a voice in my heart saying: "It's all worth it, isn't it?" I found myself saying quietly: "Yes, Lord! It's all worth it!"

This reminds me of a story about author Jim Collins. After finishing the manuscript of his bestseller work, *Good to Great*, Jim went for a run up a steep, rocky trail in Eldorado Springs Canyon. When he stopped on top at one of his favorite sitting places with a panoramic view of the high country, an odd question popped into his mind: "How much would someone have to pay me *not* to publish *Good to Great*"?[73] His answer was: no amount of money (even beyond the "hundred-million-dollar threshold") could convince him to abandon the project.

Similarly, having witnessed these trophies (plus many more that we have not captured in this book) now manifesting in their own world, and lots more futures in their wombs, I wondered how much anybody could have paid me that could have stopped me from returning from Australia to take up the leadership responsibility which, jointly with others, produced these trophies. Like Jim, I said: "not in this world"! Let me adapt his words further: I am a leader at heart. As such, it is impossible for me to imagine not accepting the call to provide leadership through which people can be transformed if not transfigured!

Many inferences can be drawn from all this. The one we must mention here is that 'authentic' and 'virtuous' leadership paradigms are in the realm of the possible. We have tried them, to some rewarding end. Where circumstances could have led us to the 'defiant' or 'compliant' approach to the University building project, we chose otherwise. It was choosing "not to use our people to build a great work for selfish ends, but to use our *'leading right'* work to build a great people"[74]. This is the heart of any leadership endeavour focused on transformational and transfigurational outcomes.

Epilogue: freedom - ending well to aim higher and righter

"Don't flutter about like a hen, when you can soar to the heights of an eagle" (Josemaría Escrivá, founder of the *'Opus Dei'*)

There is an insatiable spirit in every leader. No matter how high the rise, whatever the accomplishment, and however decorated, it would always seem 'not yet uhuru' to a leader! This phrase, which means 'not yet <u>free</u>' (and so, not the time to rest), comes from the title of a book written by the first Vice-President of post-independent Kenya, the late Oginga Odinga, who observed that despite his country's declared independence, freedom was still ahead. I was always challenging Salem University community with an adaptation of this phrase, as a way of telling ourselves not to rest on our oars regardless of whatever progress we had made at each point in our global leadership development project.

Yes, the edifice and the trophies of our calling, 'softwaring', and travailing at the University had been widely acknowledged. A lot did happen in our pioneering efforts that brought Salem University to a place of limelight and honour where it was at the time of my disengagement. However, we were too close to the actions or too pre-occupied at our post to have noticed what great things God had done at the University in just a few years through mere mortals like us.

Looking back now, I think God has used some events to jolt us to this reality. For instance, we heard a prominent Governing Council member declaring on the eve of my departure: "we have a University" that was once a dream captured on the pages of documents at the time of my appointment. Then, there was Professor Okebukola's observation during the ICPC Team visit on 6 August, 2012 that ours was an "A" grade take-off and he later reinforced it in his address to the University staff: "I can see Harvard University in the making. You should all congratulate yourselves". Remarkable, but humbling!

Recall that at the time we responded to the call to come and pioneer the take-off of the University, hardly did we know what laid ahead, talk less of how far we would have to go. We arrived in Nigeria to confront a tall order in terms of the demand of the University's vision, the less than robust funding base for its implementation, the valley of Baca we had to cross, and the Goliath we had to silence on the way. So, like Solomon who asked for wisdom for the mammoth task of governing a whole recalcitrant nation given to him, we asked God for help. In particular, having regard to His own instruction to me, we reminded Him to help us lead and manage as David did. God had chosen David from the 'wilderness' to come and shepherd His own people and inheritance. And, as the story goes, "he [David) shepherded [the people] according to the **integrity** of his heart, and guided them by the **skillfulness** of his hands" (emphasis added; see Ps 78: 70-72).

No doubt, God did supply to us His grace in abundance! With that grace, we were able to stay focused on integrity and skillfulness in all we did, and encouraged other members of the University community to do likewise. Also, we were able to act with the resoluteness of a General in a just war[75] guided by the conviction that: "In matters of style, [we can] swim with the current; in matters of principles, [we must] stand like a rock" (Thomas Jefferson).

Reflections on paradigms

In the end, we had a University, a damn unique one at that! The infrastructures and the trophies all attest to this. Even as a child under five years, its name resonated remarkably well in the ears of many, far and wide. And many - in Government and community circles alike - acknowledged our work as an exemplar in upright university leadership and management. For all intents and purposes, the results we got were derived from the paradigms within which we conducted our leadership and management of the University.

Defiant leadership

Quite apart from the fact that this paradigm of leadership was at variance with my personal character, we discerned early on that this paradigm would be so ineffective, and indeed counterproductive, for our pioneer responsibility at Salem University. So, consciously, we avoided it. The 'decisive' element, though, was of high value in our circumstances, which we used but only along with a high sense of 'others-awareness'. In word and deed, I severally and continually reminded the University community that I was not on a 'solo champion' mission, and that took us right out of the defiant leadership brand.

To burn this into their souls, I hammered on the issue of 'dispensability'. In my view of life generally, and of leadership in particular, nobody is indispensible. I frequently put before all of us this test: if you want to know how indispensible you are, dip your hand in a bucket of water, pull it out, and measure the hole it leaves behind. That is the measure of your indispensability! My determination was to galvanise people in all segments of the University community and from our external stakeholders to deliver high performance as per the vision. I expected them to do so without the illusion of indispensability; and that when they were done and taken out, the system would continue to run for those who respected its established logic and spirit.

Compliant leadership

If we had operated this kind of leadership paradigm at Salem University as the dominant philosophy with its manipulative manifestations, the story of our tenure would have been tragically different. For sure, some transactional elements or 'contingent reinforcement' are crucial for selection, promotion and other performance management systems with which to move human entities forward. In fact, considering the background from which we recruited the overwhelming majority of our staff, we had to use some elements of 'contingent reinforcement' at the initial stages of their employment.

Our aim there was to ease them into what we knew was new and quite confronting to these staff. However, if we adopted the paradigm purely or predominantly with a view to manipulating performance towards selfish goals, it could have had demotivating and stressful impact on the University community, and produced the unintended consequences of lower or ineffective performance.

Rather than depending on 'deals', which more often than not involved deceptive manoeuvres to gain personal advantage, we accelerated on 'accountability'. This, for us, involved setting clear and fair organisational expectations and consequences for everyone at all levels; and then applying them firmly and consistently - without fear or favour. For the global leaders, we captured this in the *Students' Handbook*; and for the staff, in the *Conditions of Service* Policy. Both documents outlined not only the expectations – which were carefully calibrated to promote the University vision, but also the consequences (rewards and sanctions) for how those expectations were handled.

Here is a simple illustration of how we operationalized accountability without sentiments. The first staff we ever relieved of his post, after he could not defend his conduct against laid out expectations, was related by marriage to the Chancellor of the University. When I presented the report to the Chancellor, he endorsed our action completely. With accountability, we encouraged bona fide responsibility, commitment, and result-orientation. The University was the better for it!

Authentic leadership

When we were called to go and lead Salem University, we aimed at attaining the authentic leadership height. Most of the testimonies that parents, global leaders and visitors bore about the University management, as we saw in the preceding Chapter, point to the deliberate stance we took to effect transformational changes. We thought at that time that this was the highest level of leadership character and performance. Invariably, it enabled us to pursue accomplishment through integrity and to place bonding (ala integration) over and ahead of utility, differentiation and manipulation in our management of the University stakeholders. In this regard, the positive results we got were not surprising.

Virtuous leadership

As I got to know more about the full ramifications of this paradigm of virtuous leadership, I began to understand why a sense of inadequacy started within me concerning how far we went with the vision after I disengaged from the University. Of course, people said we started and then moved the University community far beyond the expectations of that time. And, no doubt, we created a measure of empathy between management and the rest of the community which gave us all a unified perspective necessary for *leading right*.

Further, we aroused enthusiasm for performance through creating a sense of ownership for a common vision; and we sustained performance by fostering new perspectives on work, awareness of organisational mission, ability to go beyond selfish interests towards those that would benefit all, etc. We did all this with every integrity of the heart and every skillfulness of the hand we could muster, which was quite remarkable.

However, in hindsight, these all seem like a tinge of the cardinal and supernatural virtues as we now know them. Imagine how much farther we could have taken the University if we consciously and deliberately pursued, projected, and propagated these virtues – all of us, the Proprietor and the Management inclusive – in all we said and did! Imagine that we had these virtues boldly placed side by side with the core values of the University, and we tutored the University community into making virtuous living a consistent pattern of behaving that was less and less of an effort, and more and more of comfort and pleasure! (see Annas, 1995).

When I think about what we did at Salem University, and the resonance of that endeavor with the rudiments of virtuous leadership, the reflection of Nijenhuis (2014) on Havard's work strikes me quite uniquely:

True leadership is inextricably tied to a virtuous character. When we have virtue, we have the ability to turn our dream into reality. People will want to join us in bringing our dream to our [world] and we'll be able to empower them to that end… The [world's] culture currently reeks of individualism, immorality and death. Only with virtue can we change the hearts and minds of the [people] around us…, with *magnanimity* **we devote ourselves so generously to a cause that we give our very selves.** We hold nothing back from our work and our *zeal* becomes contagious…

Practicing *humility*, we seek to empower those around us by delegating tasks and training members so that we are not irreplaceable. *Prudence* critically analyzes what is the best way to make the biggest impact on campus. To carry forward these actions, we need *courage*, not just boldness and daring, but endurance in the daily grind. *Self-control* is choosing to do what is necessary… when we'd much prefer a [jolly] trip. We need to be students of human nature to bring *justice* with *love*. We have this duty to everyone around us. Character ingrained with these virtues will make us the leaders our [world] needs.

Leadership is more than being able to stand up and talk to a crowd of people. It takes serious effort to develop ourselves into virtuous and excellent leaders but it's so worth it. We will be able see the leaders growing around us, the hearts being changed, and the message of life blowing away the stench of the death culture [in our world].

There you have it - how virtuous leadership drives towards a higher state of humanity, carrying people along! In keeping faith with the unique vision of Salem University and the core values that underpinned it, and staying true to our own pre-calling self, we had to walk along the path of this drive. To make the vicious stench we met on ground (locally and nationally) to go, we had to levitate above rather than wallow in it and then gain the legitimacy to call on others to join us in fighting the vices that were producing the stench.

This made our striving towards the cardinal and supernatural virtues inevitable because only the power of such virtues could have freed us from the gravitational force (either from the coercive or the manipulative field) that could have pulled us down into the prevailing quagmire. From the least to the highest office (among staff and students) of the University community, our determination to find strength on the wings of virtues - highly fortified by habitually practising our established values and principles, was palpable.

We deliberately placed those values and principles above expediency, partisan loyalty, popularity, short term gain, and personal gain. We did not allow for duplicity or relative morality. We strove to base our operations solely on truth inherent in virtues and discarded anything less. The Salem University that emerged under our watch was the product of these endeavours and those of the proprietor, etc.

It is human nature, we are told, that when you see a person of unblemished moral character you involuntarily adjudge him worthy of your esteem and confidence, even if you'll come to hate that reality on regaining control of your not-so-noble senses. This initial reaction might be because there are "such multitudes in this apostate world who are dishonest, idle, faithless, intemperate, unfriendly, and unkind". So that, when you meet a person who is "honest, industrious, faithful to his promises, and punctual in his engagements, you are attracted towards him just moments before your unregenerated nature kicks in. But then, if such persons add to these laudable qualities a "friendly, humane, generous and amiable spirit and urbane demeanor", now you are highly tempted to believe that such a man is unreal.

As imperfect (relative to or quite distant from virtuous leadership) as our own leadership efforts at Salem University were, several people did find us <u>unreal</u>. Naturally, one would have been highly elated or satisfied in the contemplation of his own 'excellencies' if not of exultation, from such reactions of the multitude around him. Instead, the thought that such 'commendation' would in fact be a reflection of how far 'apostate' our world had become (on the criterion of *leading right*), made us to become quite restless. Ironically, though, it was the reactions of this kind that has made us more determined to press on with the journey towards virtuous leadership, and the proclamation of it.

My point in narrating our experiences at Salem University in some detail, has not been to let everyone know how good or virtuous we were. That would be like the Pharisees in the time of Jesus Christ in the Palestine of the first century *anno domino*. They practised righteousness for show, and Jesus condemned them for that. He called them 'whitewashed tombs' (beautiful outwardly; full of dead bones and all uncleanliness inwardly) and 'hypocrites' (appearing righteous outwardly; full of hypocrisy and lawlessness inwardly)[76].

I am conscious enough to know that "humility, like courage, is not just one of the virtues, it is a meta-virtue, in that it colors the way all the other virtues are practiced. No goodness is attractive or complete without it". Much more pungent in our consciousness is Jesus' warning that "unless [one's] righteousness exceeds the *'righteousness'* of the scribes and Pharisees, [one] will by no means enter the kingdom of heaven"[77].

Thus, the primary essence of the narration of this personal odyssey is not to call attention to ourselves. Rather, it is to point attention towards something far greater than our own journey. That thing is the phenomenon called *virtuous leadership* which we have detailed in Chapter Two and is as needful to turn our world around in all its facets as it is practicable. This is one inference our odyssey can sustain. It is the art of the possible around a brand of leadership seen by many to be too idyllic to attain.

Disengaging

When a particular call in a tasking odyssey to lead right comes to an end, such as the one that took us to Salem University, the leader normally experiences 'freedom' rather than 'loss'. It is a double-edged freedom in which one responsibility finishes well and on a celebratory note. But then, the freedom seems not to last as, suddenly, the leader becomes available again to take up another demanding responsibility that almost invariably pops up.

My disengagement from Salem University as Vice Chancellor and the responsibility we have picked up thereafter, illustrate this 'freedom' situation. In sharing this part of my journey, I emphasise with both events that not only does leading right require sensitivity about the time to end, it also retains the possibility of challenging you to aim higher (be upwardly directed) beyond whatever level of excellence at which you thought you have served. Thus, in the leading right genre, 'getting from here to there'[78] is normally an 'aiming higher and righter' phenomenon.

Three and a half years into my role as pioneer Vice Chancellor of the University, I began to notice some restlessness in myself. Initially, I thought it was the usual weariness that comes to test one's fortitude after carrying a heavy pioneering responsibility for sometimes. Yes, by this time, I had suffered near-death health challenges on two occasions. In the first instance, I had a health breakdown in which I became like a parboiled vegetable. I lost colour and vitality; and my eyes suddenly turned deep yellow.

When the University Doctor came and saw me in that condition, he feared the worst. Although he did not show it, as doctors are trained to conduct themselves, his demeanour showed that he was less hopeful than I was about my pulling through. Nonetheless, he commenced treatment on me: putting me on drips, handling laboratory tests, and prescribing some medication. To cut the long story short, I pulled through, dare I say, with divine intervention. As the Doctor later confessed to me, he had previously lost his own older brother to an illness with similar symptoms and was therefore extremely traumatised with the thought of losing me as well.

On the second occasion, I returned from the University to my residence after one of those many long arduous days and went to take my bath. As soon as I stepped out of the bath, my legs gave way from underneath me and I collapsed, narrowly missing an object that could have hurt me badly. From that day and for the next six weeks, I could not walk; nor could I sleep well because of the excruciating pain. By this time, we had a new Doctor for the University. He came and saw me in that terrible condition and was highly perplexed. On examination, it was discovered that the lower end of my spinal cord and my nervous system were affected.

Coincidently, a fellow Vice Chancellor, Professor David Kerr, was passing by Lokoja and came to the residence to see me. He observed that another Vice Chancellor had a similar challenge and had to be flown to Israel for some time before he was saved from a potentially total paralysis. Inside of me was the agitation about having to leave the University for such a protracted time even if there were funds to support the treatment. In any event, I held unto the belief that my case was going to be different.

All the while, with the exception of the few matters that I could delegate which I did, I was running the core affairs of the University - most of the time lying flat on my back. My recovery on this occasion was equally extraordinary. Other than going for an X-ray once, and taking some tablets that the Doctor prescribed for me, I stayed and recovered in the residence – occasionally sneaking into the University at odd hours (to see things for myself) with my vehicle seat reclined to reduce the pain-inducing pressure in my lower back.

Such was the grip of the vision of the University on our souls, that we thought less of the resulting impact on our personal health. Add to this high cost, the machinations of faceless saboteurs who preferred a leadership with which they could establish unholy alliances for their personal gain – at the expense of the unique vision of the University, it would have been perfectly natural for us to contemplate disengaging sooner rather than the time we did. However, rather paradoxically, we were indeed quite enraptured (filled with great joy) by the building of this unique University that the thought of disengaging before the end of a second tenure (other than the act of God) was far from our mind.

So, it came as a shock when I received a clear instruction as to how much time I had left to lead the building of the University. It happened in this manner. Late July 2011, my wife and I travelled to Australia – mainly for medical check-up and to catch up with our children and grandchildren whom we hadn't seen for a while. In one of the afternoons of early August, 2011, I was sitting on the balcony of an apartment of Reuben our second born, and reading the Bible – more for a lifestyle pleasure than seeking any particular information.

There, I 'chanced' on the story of Apostle Paul in Corinth making tents during the week and debating about Jesus Christ with the Jews by weekends. Then arose opposition and blasphemy against him which upset him greatly and led him to change his focus from his fellow Jews: "Your blood be upon your own heads; I am clean. From now on I will go to the Gentiles"[79].

In his new focus, Apostle Paul started getting some good results: "Then Crispus, the ruler of the synagogue, believed on the Lord with all his household. And many of the Corinthians, hearing, believed and were baptized"[80]. I read further that God spoke to Apostle Paul in the night by a vision: "Do not be afraid, but speak, and do not keep silent. For, I am with you, and no one will attack you to hurt you; for I have many people in this city"[81]. In a rather personal way, I found myself empathizing with Apostle Paul. Then, I came upon the portion that shook me to my leadership foundations: "And he [Apostle Paul] continued *there* a year and six months, teaching the word of God among them"[82].

From nowhere, I heard virtually audibly: "You have one and a half more years at Salem University. And, I will be done with your frontline leading role *there*". This would take me only to a few months after the end of my first tenure. Therefore, there was room for me to argue. However, as far as I was then concerned, my timeline with the University had been drawn up for me! In light of God's dealings with me over time, I had only one fulfilling option: obedience.

My wife and I returned from Australia and continued with our services. The only different thing for me was I now had my eyes on a more clearly defined finishing line, but the integrity and intensity with which I delivered my services did not diminish. Rather, there was a greater sense of urgency in my steps and a renewed drive to finish what needed to be done, but the University community did not know what the driving force was because I had not informed them.

Five months later (December, 2011) the instruction about the time I had left at the University was growing louder rather than fainter in my inner ears. So, I called the Chairman of the University Governing Council and verbally informed him about my plan to disengage from the University as Vice Chancellor after the end of my first tenure. His first reaction sounded like he thought it was a big joke and then I sensed in his voice what seemed like disbelief. This did not surprise me because, academicians would 'kill'[83] to become Vice Chancellors in Nigeria as well as in other countries of the world. So, on the face of it, my verbal advice could not have made sense to the Chairman.

Sensing this disbelief (real or feigned), I followed up by submitting in writing to the Chairman in January 2012 a notice of my intention to disengage as Vice Chancellor. I copied the notice to the Chancellor of the University. I thought this must have put the matter beyond any reasonable doubt or disbelief. Still I did not advise the University community (staff and students) of my impending disengagement – mainly to sustain till the end the high yielding morale we had labored to cultivate for performance.

However, in March 2012, the Chairman led some members of the University Board of Trustees to the Campus and, in the presence of my Management Team, presented me with two letters. One was a letter of commendation for my leadership over the previous four years. The second one was a letter of re-appointment for a second tenure as Vice Chancellor of the University.

The first letter (of commendation) seemed normal to me, and I accepted it – openly declaring that the commendation was not for me as a person but for the entire Management Team with whom I served in building the University. The second one (of reappointment) struck me as bizarre. I was not expecting it; certainly not after I had expressed in writing my intention not to accept a second tenure appointment. The Chairman, who apparently was the only one in the room that was privy to my earlier notice, must have noticed the expression of surprise on my face. So, I merely received the letter with the comment that I appreciated the vote of confidence it conveyed and that we would wait to see what it portended!

The following month (April, 2012), the Chairman led another Board of Trustees delegation to the Campus as a follow up to some of the issues we had highlighted during their earlier visit in March 2012. Since the discussion went on, apparently oblivious to my impending departure, I felt the right thing to do as a leader was to now directly inform the delegation of the Board of Trustees and my Management Team, which I did. Most were shocked at this news from me; and I had to let them into the fact that both the Chairman and Chancellor of the University had known about my plans five months prior.

At that meeting, I decided to give the University additional ten months notice, one of which was to be taken as sick leave and three as accumulated terminal leave. This meant, rather fortuitously, that my complete disengagement as Vice Chancellor would take effect from January, 2013 - exactly one year and six months from the month (August) I received my timeline instruction in 2011. Even after this open declaration of my intention to disengage, we did not slow down our pace of work, nor did we slacken in our adherence to the values and principles with which we had labored to raise up a relatively Godly community of staff and students.

Many people counseled me to reconsider my stand and accept the second tenure. In fact, some of my fellow Vice Chancellors said I was mad to leave at that time when I had labored with my Team to build the University to the point of gaining prominence within an extraordinarily short period of time. Some said, "why not stay and enjoy the second tenure during which you would be doing little but just be reaping the fruits of your labour? Why leave all that for somebody else to come and reap?"

All these were good-intentioned sentiments. However, they missed the mark. I came in obedience to a calling for a specific assignment – to lead the laying of a strong and notable Godly foundation for a University that was envisioned to do something unique in the blighted and troubled educational/moral firmaments in Nigeria. By the same instruction or calling, the endpoint was determined. It would have been foolhardy of me to have disobeyed on this occasion.

Yes, as at the time the endpoint came, I had no other job to go to. The next thing in store for me was still very hazy. So, there was no external allurement for me to leave the University at that time. My good-intentioned advisers were probably concerned about this. However, they did not know that even though nothing was on the horizon, my compass was already pointing beyond the University. For me, it did not matter where I was heading, so long as my purpose in life was in secure hands.

On one of my last 'days' at the University, I was sitting in one of the courtyards in the University when the Chaplain of the University, Rev. Osiri Wisdom, came to me to know what was engaging my thoughts so deeply. I remember telling him that I was reflecting on the whole life of leadership, especially in such a blighted world. Then I stated: 'when all is said and done, I want to find myself in one and only one place – at the centre of God's will'. I knew then, that staying on "to enjoy the fruits of my labour" would not place me *there*.

On a journey towards virtuous leadership, the leader must stay true to his or her calling, and be constantly mindful or sensitive to the timing surrounding that calling. Any contrary conduct on my part in this circumstance would have been out of place and patently self-defeating. Thus, when the Governing Council approved my request to disengage from the University as Vice Chancellor at its meeting on 4-5 August 2012, an indescribable sense of freedom came over me. I felt light; I felt fulfilled.

Because my successor was not appointed before the D-day came for me to leave, I had to prepare a comprehensive handover note (a 137-page document) detailing how we started, what we did, the monies received and spent in the University for the duration of my tenure, the assets we acquired plus the amounts we paid for them and their locations within the University system, and the outstanding matters that required the immediate attention of the incoming leadership. I lodged copies of this report in the Vice Chancellery and the Registry of the University for ease of accessibility. And on my way literally out the University and the country (heading back to Australia) in late September, 2012, I submitted a copy to the Chancellor via the office of the Pro-Chancellor (Chairman of the Governing Council).

It was the concluding remarks in that handover note that came in handy when the feeling of "there was more that we could have done" troubled me relentlessly after my disengagement. It did that by simply reminding me that the mandate of my leadership calling to the University was to lay a solid Godly foundation so that others could come and build upon it. Not only was I referred to the wise words of Apostle Paul in 1 Corinthians 3: 10-13[84]; I actually conveyed my irrepressible desire in a prayer for God to strengthen the hands of the incoming leadership to fight the good fight in lifting the University to a higher level.

This confirmed for me that we finished our job well. And, there are living witnesses to attest to the efforts: the software systems, the edifice of the physical infrastructures, the accreditation by the NUC, the notable footprints in the hearts of people, and the graduation of the first set of global leaders. So also were the various congratulatory messages I received from far and near after I departed. "All is well that begins well and ends well".

"The highest tribute we can pay a person is that we trust him to lead right". I have adapted this saying from what Miss Maude Atkinson said about Atticus Finch, the main character in the classic *To Kill a Mockingbird*. This classic is a gripping, heart-wrenching, and wholly remarkable tale of the coming-of-age in a US South poisoned by virulent prejudice. In this world of 'great beauty and savage inequities', a crusading local white lawyer, risked everything to defend a black man unjustly accused of a terrible crime of raping a white woman in Alabama of 1932. The whole story, narrated through the eyes of a young girl watching her white father do this, speaks loudly about the audacity of *leading right*. The Atticus Finches of this world would deserve the highest tribute of all times in my estimation.

Beginning again

My wife and I went back to Australia at the end of September, 2012. The next three months were particularly difficult, to say the least, as we both ended up in the hospital for stress-related ill-health. Hardly had we recovered before we began to receive some nagging thoughts about the next phase of our lives. As I was increasingly getting nudged to return to Nigeria to further contribute to the journey towards virtuous leadership, I received the congratulatory message that I reproduced in Chapter Two of this book.

Of particular relevance at that juncture was the portion that stated thus (i.e. after felicitating with me on the successful completion of my "glorious and eventful tenure as the pioneer Vice Chancellor" and "the giant strides made by the University within the short period of its existence [which was] quite validating and evidently points to your passion and drive for excellence"): "We hope you will be returning [from Australia] home shortly to Nigeria, noting the enormous task of building a great nation for our God and humanity...".

It is reassuring that people could pick up what I was already contemplating about returning to Nigeria, as this writer might have done. But I bet you, there is no gainsaying how much I was struggling with what that would mean in particular for me and my family. Our children and grandchildren would have preferred that we settled back into our Australian life, and be closer to them. Humanly speaking, that was our own desire too. And, considering the uncertainty that was inherent in going back to Nigeria, and the fact that the vigour of our youth had significantly been used up, the option of settling back into a semi-retired life in Australia was extremely tempting.

However, my conviction that everything rises, stands and falls on leadership, had been fortified during my time at Salem University. Indeed, I had become so concerned about the destiny of Nigeria, Africa and some other parts of the world in light of the debilitating strands of leadership that had taken these human entities to very precarious positions. The disquiet in my bones at the thought of staying back in Australia and leaving these entities (Nigeria in particular) to their own leadership (mis)fortunes became palpable.

The potential of the virtuous leadership brand to make a positive difference generally and in Nigeria particularly, had grabbed my inner soul and would not let go of me. How could anyone (exposed to the realities as I was) live peacefully with himself or herself if they failed to share the liberating features of the virtuous leadership brand, the glimpse of which we have had on our leadership journey up to that time? Such prospect was frightening to contemplate.

I could understand better the experience of prophet Jeremiah who contemplated not talking about God anymore because he found himself in "derision daily" and was mocked by everyone for mentioning the damning word of God over the sinful nations. Even so, Jeremiah exclaimed: "His word was in my heart like a burning fire shut up in my bones; I was weary of holding it back, and I could not"[85].

When the option of returning to Nigeria seemed inevitable, several questions came to the fore. Assuming we returned to Nigeria, how was I to go about propagating the power of this virtuous leadership there? Can this brand of leadership be spread through the normal leadership development programmes or is it peculiarly practiceable only by individuals who naturally possess virtuous personality traits? Assuming it can be taught as part of the normal leadership training programmes, what platform would I use to deploy it? Would Nigerians be receptive to this kind of programme, considering how entrenched the defiant and compliant leadership paradigms had become?

To address these and many more questions, I embarked upon an intensive study of the relevant materials, and contacted some authorities in this area for guidance while I was still in Australia. Subsequently, we returned to Nigeria from Australia in February, 2013, and I began investigations about how to set up the necessary platform. On advice, I registered a management and leadership training outfit, *Omaji Leadership Solutions*, with the Corporate Affairs Commission in Nigeria and secured the Certificate of Registration **No. CRBN 306903**. The business focus is to train for <u>performance</u>, coach for <u>attitude</u>, consult for <u>competence</u> and connect for <u>synergy</u> in all matters of virtuous leadership and management.

Our approach is to open new horizons on management and leadership by exposing participants to a broad range of ideas, models, experiences and fresh perspectives. We are intentionally unconventional in our delivery so as to challenge existing assumptions and beliefs, and encourage participants to think deeply and creatively about leadership paradigms, ultimately guiding them towards virtuous leadership for sustainable greatness.

For the operation of the outfit, we fashioned the vision "to be a Lighthouse in Character-Centred Leadership Business". The mission is to "empower committed persons and organisations to transform themselves into Character-centred Leaders known for elite performance in all facets of life". All our activities would be thoroughly informed by our core values of Integrity, Skillfulness, Accountability, and Professionalism. And, by all legitimate means necessary, we are committed to propagating the core (cardinal and supernatural) virtues of Wisdom, Courage, Justice, Temperance, and Transcendence which form the pillars on which virtuous leadership is built. Our imagined future is a world shaped by virtuous leadership.

Fully determined to deploy continuous learning, improvement, growth and the building of trusting relationship based on the highest virtuous standards, we have organised our solutions along four dimensions of management and leadership:

- Attitude: *We coach, using international coaching frameworks, to cultivate or raise the conscience – values, virtues, and vistas – of leadership*

- Aptitude: *We train, using innovative action learning strategies, to build or improve the competencies – skills and knowledges – of leadership*

- Altitude: *We consult through site visits, leadership character tests, and customised solutions to lift the carriage (personality and performance) of leaders in terms of exemplary actions and attainments.*

- Atlas: *We connect leaders through local and international networking in order to broaden their horizons and enlarge their technical/relational repertoires with which to accomplish desired results.*

In the course of our inquiries, we got to know that we needed to be formally accredited to provide training in management and leadership in the Nigerian context. The Federal Government agency responsible for the necessary accreditation is the Centre for Management Development. From September 2013, we enrolled into the Centre's Basic and Advanced courses to train for accreditations as qualified individual and organisational trainers in management and leadership. By December 2013, we had successfully completed the courses and obtained accreditations (Nos. **0000423** and **0000089**, respectively).

Another segment of our journey towards virtuous leadership has begun. And, we had the freedom to begin again. This time, the task is to confront the decadence of our time predominantly far beyond the student enclave. The territory is wider, seeking to raise, develop and/or strengthen leaders everywhere to lead right – standing on *virtuousness* - perchance humanity may see some light out of its self-inflicted quagmire. Thus, the training plan has been devised to be deployable in all areas and at all levels of the society.

Our experience to date shows that the overwhelming majority of the people struggle with *leading right*. Iniquity with impunity has gotten them highly compromised. The moral dimension of holding responsibilities has been virtually relegated to the background. Deception has been elevated to the state of the art level. As the line between right and wrong gets more and more blurred, so also is the line between public office and private estate. Accountability is virtually non-existent, and so the generality of public office holders treat their official roles as personal business outfits which must answer to their personal profit or deliver services to no one else. In the circumstances, lawlessness is paraded without compunction.

At the same time, we have noticed pockets of upright and conscientious people who are struggling to keep their heads above the suffocating stench of the murky waters of a greed-driven corruption. These people are isolated, scattered and extremely vulnerable to capitulation unless they can be connected to each other quick enough for support lines.

One time, I made a presentation to the Education Summit organised by the House of Representatives Committee on Education. Soon after, a participant ran to me to appreciate the opportunity to know that there were people of integrity that had held the position of Vice Chancellor in Nigeria. She then narrated how the Governing Council of her institution was compelling the Management of the institution to corruptly share the limited resources of the institution, and how she was being victimized for taking a stand against it. I encouraged her to stand at her post, knowing fully well that she would be vindicated in due season.

A few other similar stories have prompted us to find a way of linking the conscientious officers with each other for synergy and mutual reinforcement. For this purpose, we have now registered an outfit, *Virtuous Leaders Development Network* (VLDN), with the Corporate Affairs Commission as a non-governmental organisation (No. **745385**). This outfit has taken the 'atlas' component of the *Omaji Leadership Solutions* mission and expanded it into an independent platform to service this perceived need of connecting people with disposition towards virtuous leadership who might be feeling vulnerable from isolation.

The main objectives of the VLDN are to:
1. cultivate virtues for excellence in personal life, corporate leadership and nation building;
2. connect 'rivulets' of virtuous leaders through local and international networking in order to broaden horizons and enlarge technical/relational repertoires for the lifting and betterment of nations; and

3. educate and train persons from an early age on the need to imbibe right virtues, attitudes and good character in life.

Concluding remarks

It takes audacity to lead right in an apostate world. The price is invariably high. However, from our own experience over time (most recently at Salem University), we are bold to say it is a doable project! It is equally undisputable that the reward can be exceptionally fulfilling.

Our search for epistemological grounding has helped us to locate our effort of leading right within paradigms of leadership, among which we found the defiant, compliant, authentic, and virtuous brands most illuminating. In philosophy, behavioural pattern, and outcomes, these brands show clearly delineated *personalities* with predictable impact on the destinies of human entities. For instance, had we indiscriminately adopted in the Salem University project the defiant and compliant brands with their predominantly coercive and manipulative tendencies respectively, that unique and much needed vision would have been highly compromised in our hands.

On the contrary, the vision moved from being a dream on the pages of documents to patently becoming an academic community of exemplary stature in responsible leadership[86]. This outcome came about because, by conviction and obedience to a calling, we were guided towards the authentic and virtuous brands of leadership. By the appeals and grip of these two brands, we were careful to interpret the vision and clarify its task faithfully. Subsequently, we resorted to so much travailing which resulted in us:

- establishing and deploying the appropriate software (values and principles) that kept us grounded in integrity of heart and skillfulness of hands;
- creating and leading vision-ownership among the University community that magnetized the community to the vision and helped us to deliver commitment and morale beyond our challenging pioneer constraints;
- raising physical and systems infrastructures that came to stand as an admirable edifice of a vision turned reality; and
- producing trophies of Global Leaders in whose lives transformation in thinking and acting has been implanted for the benefit of their immediate human entities and the world at large.

The old axiom is true, though. We get the leaders we deserve. We get the government we vote for. In our judgment, Salem University vision as interpreted by us got the leadership it deserved. It is possible that, were we of a different breed stooped in defiant and compliant leadership paradigms and had we interpreted the vision merely as a commercial or transactional venture, a different leadership would have ensured with alienational and transactional outcomes.

There is also the exceptional situation when God intervenes with His grace, raising a leadership that is patently unmerited either by the nature of the vision or its proprietorship. In such situations, God might be wanting to bring 'salvation with His own arms' to a destitute world. Or, it could simply be that God wanted to show the 'art of the possible' for the kind of leadership that the captains of the world would deny ever possible.

In any event, a great insight from our experiences to date is that if we want to pursue and possess a vision with better leadership or government; if we want to restore our individual liberty; if we want organisational re-engineering; if we want national rebirth with true freedom and not the enslavement of misgovernment; and if we want a world with upward spirals of positive dynamics, then we must first understand the paradigms of leadership, and then change our expectations to aim higher and righter in all our ways.

The classical command and control approach of the defiant leadership paradigm and the 'convictionless', ambivalent, and manipulative streaks of the compliant leadership paradigm are patently deficient in the face of the enormous challenges that are confronting our contemporary world. Therefore, it was gratifying for us to find that such realization gave rise to the clamour for the relatively progressive and empathetic approach of the authentic leadership paradigm with inherent capacities to evoke vitality, collaboration, and creativity for performance and people development.

Nevertheless we wondered why, despite the claims to authentic (transformational) leadership in certain quarters, the "seven deadly leadership sins"[87] – which parallel the seven deadly sins in the Judeo-Christian-Islamic traditions[88] (Kilburg 2012, pp46-49), continue to pound our senses of decency and humanity.

Then we found the significant historical episode in which scholars have in our own lifetime revived interest in the transfigurational capabilities of the virtuous leadership paradigm. For instance, we now see a thesis that "the difference between executive teams that are able to preserve their countries or organisations over the long term and those that are not is based largely on the degree to which those leaders possess and enact the [cardinal and supernatural] virtues of courage, temperance, justice… wisdom [and transcendence]" (Kilburg 2012, p74).

Such scholarship has demonstrated the patent truth that if we want better human entities, we must replace our old leaders with a new breed who would be beholden to a higher and righter standard of governance. On a very micro scale, under the umbrella of the Salem University vision, we have tested this truth by our dogged devotion to raising global leaders who would provide selfless service towards creating a higher humanity.

We had to shake people out of complacency by raising the matter of legacy before their eyes and making them see that they are history makers. And we modeled optimistic engagement with the world (decadent and troubled as that world may be) so that, like salt, leaders could see how they can go in and arrest decay. Ultimately, our focus was on raising not more followers but other leaders; and that called for rare commitment, genuine delegation, and empowerment.

Yes, the task was difficult – akin to raising 'saints in Sodom'. However, we understood that if we dithered and sacrificed our principles for pleasure, as Quinn (1996, p. 158) observed about courage and virtuous leadership, both we and the vision would have invariably taken steps "toward slow death". So, we accepted the necessary risk "because it [was] the right thing to do". Further, we determined to carry out all the necessary components of the vision in the right way, at the right time, and for the right reasons, no matter whose ox was gored.

Virtuous leadership to which our efforts at the University aspired, even if subconsciously, is a 'calling not command', and a 'ministry not management'. Those called in this manner are 'humble laborers not governing monarchs', 'leading servants not slick celebrities' (see MacArthur, n.d). They, above all, exemplify sacrifice, devotion, submission, and lowliness.

Jesus Himself gave us the pattern when He stooped to wash His disciples' feet, a task that was customarily done by the lowest of slaves[89]. Not only did Jesus model it, he began mentoring the disciples in this pattern, with a view to ultimately making them and many more generations to come virtuous leaders (Godly shepherds, visionaries and administrators). If the Lord of the universe would do that, no leader has a right to think of himself or herself as a 'bigwig' in this dire circumstance.

Propagating virtuous leadership is a task that must be done. Our commitment to it is quite strong. Nelson Mandela's life bequeathed an enviable legacy because of the power of commitment which he had espoused so eloquently in his fight against apartheid in the 1960s.

> During my lifetime I have dedicated myself to this struggle of the African people. I have fought against white domination, and I have fought against black domination. I have cherished the ideal of

a democratic and free society in which all persons live together in harmony and with equal opportunities. It is an ideal which I hope to live for and to achieve. But if needs be, it is an ideal for which I am prepared to die (Mandela, speech at his Rivonia Trial, Pretoria Supreme Court, 20 April 1964).

You have heard it said often that 'evil triumphs where good people do nothing'. I say to you that more evil triumphs with impunity where good people propagate no virtuousness. Abraham Lincoln once prayed: "Oh God, may the people of principles become the principal men of this nation". He who knows the right thing to do and fails to do it, to him it is a sin. We have been endowed with so much that we have no business sinning this way. Let it begin with you and me. For a start, join the conversation at www.omajileadershipsolutions.com

---

[73]   Collins (2001, Preface).

[74]   Adapted from Jack Hyles' "Don't use your people to build a great work; use your work to build a great people", quoted in Maxwell (2001, p34).

[75]   Not too dissimilar to "the General who burned the boats upon landing, leaving only one option (succeed or die)". This is how Collins (2001, p20) described Darwin E. Smith, the CEO who never wavered or looked back from a daring decision and "created a stunning transformation, turning Kimberly-Clark into the leading paper-based consumer products company in the world" in his own time.

[76]   Matthew 23: 25-28, Holy Bible. New King James Version.

[77]   Matthew 5: 20, Holy Bible. New King James Version.

[78]   This is a metaphor that Bill Hybels used to define 'Leadership' in his address to the … Global Leadership Summit at Willows Creek.

[79]   Acts 18: 6, Holy Bible. New King James Version.

[80]   Acts 18: 8, Holy Bible. New King James Version.

[81]   Acts 18: 9-10, Holy Bible. New King James Version.

[82]   Acts 18: 11, Holy Bible. New King James Version.

[83]   Stories abound concerning Professors going to extremes lengths to get appointed and/or remain Vice Chancellors. This is not only because of the perceived pecuniary benefits; the position crowns it all for one's academic career. No more heights to conquer after this!

[84]   'According to the grace of God which was given to me, as a wise master builder [in our own case, as a favored amateur builder], I have laid the foundation. It is time for another to build on it...'

[85]   See Jeremiah 20: 7-9, Holy Bible. New King James Version.

[86]   In Cameron (2011, 26) you will find a discussion of this category of leadership as encompassing the art of building and sustaining social and moral relationships between leaders and different stakeholders, in which the leaders deploy a sense of justice, recognition, care, and accountability for a wide range of positive instrumental results and human goodness.

[87]   They are: (1) failure to execute well; (2) failure of integrity; (3) failure of nerves (cowardice and untimeliness); (4) failure of self-control (emotional incontinence); (5) error of domination dynamics (abuses of managerial relationships and supervision); (6) error of immodesty (inflated expectations and egos); and (7) the error of unbridled secrecy (collusions and cover-ups).

[88]   They are pride, covetousness, lust, envy, gluttony/drunkenness, anger, and sloth.

[89]   See the story in John 13, Holy Bible.

References

Alban-Metcalfe, J. and Mead, G. (2010) "Coaching for transactional and transformational leadership", in Passmore, J. (ed. 2010) *Leadership Coaching: working with leaders to develop elite performance.* Kogan Page Ltd, London.

Amaga, S. (   ) *The Leader God will be Proud Of.*

Annas, J. (1993). *The Morality of Happiness.* Oxford University Press, London.

Ayers, R. S. (1994) "Turning your vision into reality", https://www.asis.org/Bulletin/Dec-94/ayers.html

Bacal, R. (2013) "The ONE Thing, And The ONLY Thing We Know For Sure About Leadership Effectiveness". http://leadership.blognotions.com/2013/12/30/the-one-thing-and-the-only-thing-we-know-for-sure-about-leadership-effectiveness/?_m=3l%2e0018%2e33%2esu0akvbtmr%2e2pi.

Bai, B.; Huo, X.; Licona, B.; and Caldwell, C. (2013) " Virtuous Leadership   –   Insights   for   the   21st   Century", http://www.stu.edu/Portals/Business/News/Virtuous%20Leadershi p%20Final%20Paper.pdf

Barker, C. (2007) "Virtuous Leadership", http://blog.aim.com.au/virtuous-leadership/.

Bennis, W.G. and Nanus, B. (1985) *Leaders: The strategies for taking charge.* New York: Harper and Row.

Bossidy, L. and Charan, R. (2002) *Execution: the discipline of getting things done.* Crown Business, New York.

Burns, J. M. (1978) *Leadership.* New York: Harpers.

Cameron, K. (2011) "Responsible Leadership as Virtuous Leadership", *Journal of Business Ethics,* Vol 98, pp25-35.

Clark, T. (2009) *The Leadership Test: Will You Pass?* Oxonian Press, Utah, USA.

Cochrane, B. (n.d) "What is a Virtuous Leader?" http://www.mooreteacitizens.com/what-is-a-virtuous-leader.html

Collins, J. (2001) *Good to Great.* Random House Business Books, London.

Covey, S. (2003) *Principle-Centred Leadership.* Free Press, New York.

Dubrin, A.J.; Daglish, C.; and Miller, P. (2006) *Leadership.* John Wiley & Sons, Milton, QLD Australia.

Evanson, P (2011) *Leadership: the Jesus Model.* www.ctkonline.com

Friedman, E. H. (2007) *A Failure of Nerve: Leadership in the Age of the Quick Fix.* Seabury Books.

Goleman, D.; Boyatzis, R. and McKee, A. (2002) *Primal Leadership: learning to lead with emotional intelligence.* Harvard Business School Press, Boston, Massachusetts.

Hamm, J. (2011) *Unusually Excellent: the necessary nine skills required for the practice of great leadership.* Jossey-Bass, San Francisco, USA.

Havard, A. (2007) *Virtuous Leadership: An Agenda for Personal Excellence.* Scepter Publishers, Inc. USA.

Hooper, A. and Potter, J. (2000) *Intelligent Leadership: Creating a passion for change.* Random House Business Books, London.

Hybels, B. (2002) *Courageous Leadership.* Zondervan, Michigan USA.

Idachaba, F.S. (2013) *No Easy Harvest: An Autobiography.* University Press PLC, Ibadan, Nigeria.

Jacobsen, S. *Towards a Meaningful Life,* cited in Cochrane, B. (n.d) "What is a Virtuous Leader?" http://www.mooreteacitizens.com/what-is-a-virtuous-leader.html

Jinkins, M. and Jinkins, D.B. (1998) *The Character of Leadership: Political Realism and Public Virtue in Nonprofit Organisations.* Jossey-Bass Publishers, San Francisco.

Kaak, P and Weeks, D. (2013) *The Handbook of Virtue Ethics.* Acumen Publishing.

Kilburg, R. R. (2006) *Executive Wisdom: Coaching and the Emergence of Virtuous Leaders.* American Psychological Association, Washington D.C. USA.

Kilburg, R. R. (2012) *Virtuous Leaders: Strategy, Character, and Influence in the 21ˢᵗ Century.* American Psychological Association, Washington D.C. USA.

Lee, G. and Roberts, I. (2010) "Coaching for authentic leadership", in Passmore, J. (ed. 2010) *Leadership Coaching: working with leaders to develop elite performance.* Kogan Page Ltd, London.

Leighton, C. A. (2012) "Leaders leave footprints for transformation", http://www.streetarticles.com/leadership/leaders-leave-footprints-for-transformation.

Liu, L. (2012) "Learn how to turn your vision into reality", http://www.marsdd.com/news-and-insights/learn-how-to-turn-your-vision-into-reality/

Lorenzen, J. (2009) "The Audacity of Leadership", http://onmovements.com/?p=591.

MacArthur, J. (n.a) "A Few Good Shepherds", http://www.gty.org/resources/articles/A104/a-few-good-shepherds.

Maxwell, J. (1993) *Developing the Leader within You.* Thomas Nelson Publishers. Nashville, USA.

Maxwell, J. (2000) *The 21 Most Powerful Minutes in a Leader's Day: Revitalize Your Spirit and Empower Your Leadership.* Thomas Nelson Publishers. Nashville, USA.

Maxwell, J. (2001) *The Power of Influence.* RiverOak Publishing, Tulsa, Oaklahoma.

Maxwell, J. (2011) *5 Levels of Leadership.* Center Street, New York.

Munroe, M. (2005) *The Spirit of Leadership.* Whitaker House, New Kensington, PA).

Munroe, M. (2009) *Becoming a Leader.* Whitaker House, New Kensington, PA.

Murren, D. (1997) "The Leader as Change Agent", in Barna, G. (ed.1997) *Leaders on Leadership.* Regal Books, California, USA. Pp199-212.

Newman, B. (1997) *10 Laws of Leadership: Leading to success in a changing world.* Marvelous Christian Publications, Benin City.

Nijenhuis, M. (2014) "Reflection on Virtuous Leadership"……..

O'Brien, M. D. (2007) "A vitally important book", a review of Havard's *Virtuous Leadership*. http://www.amazon.com/Virtuous-Leadership-Agenda-Personal-Excellence/dp/1594170592.

Oestreich, D. (2009) "Is Leadership a Calling?" http://www.unfoldingleadership.com/blog/?p=585

Okorie, L. (2011) *Footprints: Leading beyond today.* Destiny Image Europe, Italy.

Omaji, P. (2010) "Leadership: An Imperative for Development", Keynote address to Development Think Tank, Lokoja, Kogi State, Nigeria. 14 August 2010.

Omaji, P. (2013) "Raising authentic leaders: a clarion call to Universities". Occasional paper delivered to the Caleb Leadership Academy Lecture Series, Caleb University, Imota, Lagos State. 13 March 2013.

Omaji, P. (2014) "Leadership without ego", Address to the Workshop on Leadership Change Management, Work Ethics, Value Re-orientation and Negotiation for NPA Executives, organised by Ken Nnamani Leadership and Development Centre. 28 August, 2014. Rock View Hotel, Abuja.

Pearce, C. L.; Waldman, D. A.; and Csikszentmihalyi, M. (2006) "Virtuous Leadership: A Theoretical Model and Research Agenda". *Journal of Management, Spirituality & Religion*, 3:1-2 (2006), pp.60–77.

Quinn, R. E., (1996). *Deep change: Discovering the leader within.* San Francisco, CA: Jossey-Bass.

Sashkin, M. and Sashkin, M. (2004) *Leadership that matters: the critical factors for making a difference in people's lives and organisations' success.* Gospel Press, Benin City, Nigeria.

Stallard, Michael Lee (n.d) "John Wooden and the Power of Virtue in Leadership" http://michaelhyatt.com/john-wooden-and-the-power-of-virtue-in-leadership.html.

Tarrant, D. (2007) "Deconstructing Leadership", http://blog.aim.com.au/deconstructing-leadership/

Thayer, Lee 2010, p11: *Leadership Virtuosity.* Xlibris Corporation. USA.

UNNAB Alumni Association (2012) *Testaments of Transformational Leadership: A celebration of Oluwafemi Olaiya Balogun.* Abeokuta, Nigeria.

Usman, U. H. (2012) *Crisis of Leadership in Nigeria: the Realities and Way Forward.* Ahmadu Bello University Press Ltd. Zaria, Nigeria.

Washbush, J.B. (2005) Management Decision, Vol. 43 Issue: 7/8, pp.1078 – 1085

Index

A

absentee landlords, 28

abundance, 103, 106, 187

Academic Brief, 50, 55, 90, 93, 148, 154, 160, 167, 168

academic management system, 95, 212

Academic management system, 160

Academic Programmes, 95

accountability, xvi, 29, 38, 47, 48, 70, 74, 86, 92, 150, 153, 154, 155, 156, 164, 188

Accountability, 50, 63, 86, 199, 200

Accreditation, 160

Admiral Herman Rickover, 130

Admission Data Input Layout, 93

admissions, xiv, 92, 93, 94, 98, 151, 152, 153, 154, 160, 166, 168, 169

Africa, 25, 45, 47, 82, 111, 112, 113, 179, 198

African Command Office, 45

Ahmadu Bello University, 46, 47, 73, 124, 209

Alban-Metcalfe and Mead, 27, 28

alienational, 26, 202

allurement, xii, 196

Altitude, 200

alumni, 82

ambassadors of peace, 58

America, 34, 82, 107, 130

and righter, v, xi, xviii, xix, xx, 22, 23, 41, 192, 203

Anthem, 59, 63, 81, 106, 132

Apostle Paul, 194, 197

Aptitude, 200

Archbishop Sam Amaga, 61

armed robbers, 55, 72

Asia, 25, 82

assimilation, 27

Association of Vice Chancellors of Nigerian Universities, 101

Atlas, 200

Attah House, 46

Attitude, 69, 200

audacity, vi, xx, 33, 52, 53, 161, 162, 165, 197, 201

Audacity, i, ii, xx, 207

Australia, xii, 45, 47, 48, 49, 50, 52, 55, 65, 69, 73, 74, 105, 110, 123, 124, 137, 141, 143, 148, 185, 193, 194, 197, 198, 199, 206

Australian Commonwealth Government Public Service, 48

authentic, xi, xix, 23, 25, 27, 28, 31, 33, 43, 83, 92, 94, 96, 98, 185, 189, 202, 203, 207, 208

Authentic, 27, 189

autobiography, vi

Awaken the Leader, 116

Ayers, xvi, xvii, 206

B

Bascal, ix
Bayo Adewusi, 65
Beginning again, 197
beginning well, xi, xii
Bennis and Nanus, viii
Bible, 46, 49, 71, 78, 104, 109, 115,
   130, 194
Biblical David, 101
Board of Trustees, iv, xvii, 44, 46, 50,
   51, 126, 148, 149, 170, 195
Boko Haram, 81
Bossidy and Charan, xvi
branding, x, xi, 86
bride, 82
bukas, 105
Burns, viii, xix, 28, 206
Bursary, 92, 98, 154, 155, 156
business ideology, 54, 103, 147, 148

C

Cafeteria Services, 156
Caleb University, 23, 208
   Caleb Leadership Academy, 23, 208
Cameron, xx, 24, 29, 32, 36, 206
Canada, 47
Central Bank, 155
Chancellor, 50, 51, 59, 60, 62, 63, 64,
   66, 75, 94, 99, 102, 103, 132, 148,
   150, 155, 156, 172, 173, 174, 175,
   188, 193, 195, 197
Chapel, 47, 71, 76, 77, 78, 79, 85, 129,
   179
Chapel of Peace, 79
Chapel of Redemption, 47
Chaplaincy, 126, 150, 151, 154, 168
character, vi, xiv, xv, 29, 35, 36, 38, 43,
   46, 47, 55, 56, 57, 58, 59, 60, 62, 63,
   65, 67, 69, 75, 84, 85, 89, 94, 96,
   100, 140, 151, 154, 163, 168, 182,

184, 187, 189, 190, 191, 197, 200,
   201
Christian, xxi, 36, 46, 66, 70, 85, 167,
   203, 208
Christmas, 76
CIA report, 80
civility, 62, 64
clarion call, 23, 208
Clark, vi, vii, xx, 38, 206
cleanliness, 134
client requirements, xvii, 147
Cochrane, 39, 41, 206, 207
Coleman, xii, xv
Collins, x, 185, 206
competence, xv, 24, 47, 100, 103, 140,
   199
compliant, xi, 22, 25, 27, 31, 38, 39, 43,
   52, 164, 185, 199, 202, 203
Compliant, 26, 27, 188
Conditions of Service, 153, 188
Confidence, 50, 63, 85
conflict management, 58
confusing, vii, viii, xiii, 22
consequence, 24, 99, 104
consistency, 35, 78, 153, 176
Constitution, 33, 107
container mentality, 67
corruption, 26, 34, 40, 51, 60, 62, 64,
   91, 93, 94, 113, 129, 153, 201
cosmopolitanism, 103, 108
cosmopolitism, 108
courage, iii, xi, 29, 30, 31, 35, 39, 157,
   162, 190, 191, 203, 204
Covenant, 51, 73
Covey, xiv, 88, 97, 206
Craftiness, 78
credibility, xiv, xvi, 24, 34, 85, 103
Criminality, 74
criminogenic, 74
Criminology, 65, 69, 73, 74, 81, 113
crucibles, 78

D

Daniel, iv, 105, 128, 129, 130, 177, 179
Darius, 128
Dave Kraft, xviii
David, 109, 187, 193
decadence, iii, xx, 32, 53, 66, 100, 200
decay, 33, 40, 80, 204
defiant, xi, 22, 25, 26, 27, 31, 32, 38, 39,
    43, 52, 113, 151, 153, 185, 199, 202,
    203
Defiant, 25, 187
destinies, vi, xx, 47, 62, 83, 139, 202
destiny, vi, x, 42, 61, 63, 67, 76, 77, 79,
    83, 106, 118, 134, 162, 179, 184,
    198
developed countries, 66, 134
Diaspora, 73
differentiation, 25, 189
Diligence and Resourcefulness, 50, 86
Disciplinary Committee, 93
Discipline, 163
Disengaging, 192
dominion, 78
Dubrin, et. al, 87

E

Economic and Financial Crimes
    Commission, 97
edifice, xvi, xvii, 84, 147, 169, 183, 186,
    197, 202
Education Summit, 201
EFCC, 82, 97, 98
Embassies, 73
Empowerment, 59, 64, 68
engineering specification, xvii, 147, 169
Enron Company, 25
entrepreneurial skills, 62

entrepreneurship, 64, 69
Europe, 106, 208
excellence, xv, xix, xx, 22, 26, 34, 36, 37,
    52, 55, 56, 59, 61, 63, 65, 89, 94, 96,
    97, 101, 103, 125, 126, 127, 128,
    129, 130, 131, 135, 138, 144, 152,
    160, 161, 175, 181, 192, 198, 201,
    212
exemplary global leader, 83

F

Favour Wisdom, 126
favoured firstborns, 61
FCS, 46
Federal School of Arts and Science, 46
Financial management, 90
flute or harp, xiii
footprints, xvii, xviii, 171, 172, 173,
    183, 184, 197, 207
Foundation, 114, 149
Founder's Day, 64, 65, 172, 177
Free the Leader, 116
freedom, xviii, 35, 90, 117, 119, 121,
    186, 192, 196, 200, 203
Freedom, xviii
Friedman, 33, 206
functional requirements, xvii, 147, 169
Futures, 183

G

Genesis, 78, 138
Ghana, 68
global impact, 55, 56, 57, 94
Global Parents Forum, 166, 167, 168
God, v, 29, 50, 52, 57, 58, 61, 62, 63,
    64, 65, 76, 78, 79, 80, 82, 85, 89,
    103, 105, 106, 109, 110, 115, 116,

117, 118, 119, 121, 123, 125, 126, 128, 129, 134, 137, 138, 140, 145, 147, 168, 173, 174, 176, 177, 179, 180, 181, 186, 187, 193, 194, 196, 197, 198, 202, 204, 206

Godliness, 50, 63, 85, 153, 178

Goliath, xv, 101, 102, 103, 187, 212

Gongola State, 46

goodness, 29, 42, 43, 192

Governing Council, iv, xvii, 44, 51, 54, 126, 149, 152, 153, 156, 170, 186, 194, 196, 197, 201

Governor, 63, 64, 89, 114, 115, 132, 168

Graduate Fellowship, 47

graveyard, 101, 117, 118, 120, 123

Greek, 118

ground-zero, 148

Guest Book, 51

H

Hamm, xiv, 24, 104, 207

Harvard, 51, 72, 186, 207

Havard, xx, 24, 34, 36, 37, 190, 207, 208, 212

Head Boy, 46, 47

hearts, xvii, 22, 110, 171, 173, 183, 184, 190, 197

Helen Keller, 119

heritage, 62, 85

Himmelfarb, 32

history, vi, xii, 32, 34, 40, 41, 43, 52, 61, 62, 63, 88, 101, 119, 145, 172, 203

Holy Bible, 212

Holy Spirit, 58

honesty, 78, 86

Hooper and Potter, xii, xvii, 87

House of Representatives Committee, 201

human entities, vi, x, xv, xx, 28, 29, 37, 39, 42, 43, 183, 188, 198, 202, 203

human entity, x, xiii, xv, xvi, xvii, 43, 53, 153, 162, 163

Humility, 35

Hybels, xvi, xxi, 147, 169, 207, 212

I

ICPC Team, 51, 89, 90, 93, 95, 186

Imagined Future, 80

impossibility, 55, 103, 107, 156

Independent Corrupt Practices and Other Related Offences Commission, 51

Independent National Electoral Commission, 106

Indigenous Australians, 48

Infrastructural development, 157

innovation, 34, 78

insanity, 61, 135

insecurity, 26, 40, 49, 62, 64, 74

integration, 28, 71, 189

integrity, iv, xiv, xvi, 33, 47, 48, 50, 57, 58, 59, 61, 62, 63, 64, 65, 70, 74, 78, 80, 84, 86, 89, 103, 108, 109, 110, 129, 139, 145, 153, 154, 156, 158, 161, 162, 175, 176, 178, 180, 183, 187, 189, 194, 201, 202

Integrity, 50, 63, 78, 86, 199

intellectual, x, xi, 23, 24, 36, 47, 57, 59, 87, 89, 168

intelligence, 57, 61, 62, 64, 65, 78, 80, 89, 94, 207

Inter-faith relations, 167

IPPLE, xiv

J

Jesus Christ, xviii, xxi, 31, 58, 71, 120, 191, 194

Jimmy Carter, 130, 131

Jinkins and Jinkins, xv, xxi, 100

John Adams, 33

Joint Admissions and Matriculation
   Board, 67
Jonathan, 115
journey, vi, vii, xv, xviii, xix, xx, 23, 29,
   31, 37, 39, 42, 43, 45, 49, 53, 61,
   100, 104, 127, 128, 130, 145, 146,
   149, 191, 192, 196, 198, 200
justice, iii, iv, xi, 29, 31, 35, 81, 94, 113,
   123, 190, 203

K

Kaak and Weeks, 34
Kaduna, 124
Ken Lay, 25
Kilburg, ix, 24, 25, 38, 203, 207, 212
Knowledge, 59, 68
Kogi State, 45, 55, 63, 64, 166, 168,
   182, 208
Kogi State University, 55, 182

L

Lazarus, 115, 116, 117, 118, 123
leader within you, 77, 78, 79, 117, 121
leaders around you, xiv, 71, 79, 168
leadership, iv, v, vi, vii, viii, ix, x, xi, xii,
   xiii, xiv, xv, xvii, xviii, xix, xx, xxi, 22,
   23, 24, 25, 26, 27, 28, 29, 30, 31, 32,
   33, 34, 35, 36, 37, 38, 39, 40, 41, 42,
   43, 44, 45, 46, 47, 49, 50, 51, 52, 53,
   54, 55, 56, 57, 60, 61, 62, 66, 69, 70,
   71, 72, 73, 75, 76, 77, 78, 79, 80, 83,
   85, 86, 87, 88, 89, 94, 96, 97, 98, 99,
   100, 103, 106, 110, 111, 112, 113,
   115, 116, 118, 119, 126, 127, 128,
   132, 135, 137, 142, 144, 146, 147,
   149, 150, 151, 153, 154, 156, 163,
   164, 168, 171, 172, 174, 177, 178,
   180, 182,183, 184, 185, 186, 187,
   188, 189, 190, 191, 192, 193, 194,
   195, 196, 197, 198, 199, 200, 201,
   202, 203, 204, 206, 207, 209, 212
Leadership Development, 76
leading right, vi, vii, xi, xii, xiii, xiv, xvi, xvii,
   xix, xx, 37, 38, 39, 40, 41, 43, 52, 54,
   96, 100, 101, 103, 144, 146, 147,
   156, 162, 171, 185, 189, 191, 192,
   197, 200, 202
legacy, vi, xv, xvii, 39, 41, 60, 100, 171,
   203, 204
Leighton, xviii, 172, 207
Library, ii, 98, 159
Library Management System, 159
Lifestyle, 177
Litigation, 164
Livewire, 123
logo, 58
Lokoja, vi, 45, 50, 60, 65, 67, 89, 122,
   172, 179, 183, 193, 208
looters, 55
Lorenzen, 33, 207
Love, 58, 175, 177

M

MacArthur, 204, 207
Machiavelli, 84
Magnanimity, 35
maiden, 60, 62, 132
Maintenance, 158
malpractices, 65, 95, 163
Manz et al, 33
mass penury, 40
Master Plan, 148
matriculation, 62, 83, 132, 167
Maxwell, vii, viii, ix, xi, 103, 208, 212
Meadows, viii

mediocrity, 103, 106, 107, 156
mendacity, 103, 108, 156
Mental Empowerment, 50, 63, 86
meritocracy, 103, 106, 153
Michael Angelo, 129
micro-management, 150
Middle-East, 82
military rule, 26
mindset, xiv, 85, 102, 103, 109, 110, 135, 144, 153, 159
Ministers, 48, 134
Ministry of Foreign Affairs, 175
monies, 91, 92, 156, 196
moral dimension, xiv, 96, 148, 200
Mother Teresa, 119
Mt Everest, vii, xx
Mubi, 46
Munroe, viii, ix, xx, 118, 119, 208
Muslim, 70, 71, 167, 168, 169
Mysterious, viii

N

National Assembly, 106, 107
National Institute for International Affairs, 68
National Pledge, 106
National Universities Commission, 51
National Youth Corps Service, 46, 184
natural sciences, ix
Navy, 130
Nelson Mandela, 27, 204
new 'city', 82
New York, 72, 206, 208
Niger-Delta, 81
Nigeria, vi, xii, 26, 45, 46, 47, 48, 49, 50, 51, 52, 55, 56, 59, 65, 66, 67, 71, 72, 73, 74, 76, 80, 81, 82, 91, 101, 106, 107, 111, 112, 113, 114, 115, 121, 129, 146, 153, 155, 159, 160, 161, 166, 179, 184, 186, 194, 196, 198, 199, 201, 207, 208, 209

Nigerian High Commissioner, 73
Nigerian Television Authority, 65
North East, 81
Northern Territory of Australia, 48

O

O'Brien, 36, 208
O'Connor Uniting Church, 47
Obajana, 67
Obama, 107
Obasanjo, 73
Objective Performance Appraisal, 137, 138, 144
Oestreich, xii, 208
Oginga Odinga, 186
Olorunfemi, 152
Omaji, i, ii, v, xix, 26, 27, 37, 38, 62, 63, 65, 75, 199, 201, 208
One-on-One Program, 65
Osiri Wisdom, iv, 126, 149, 151, 196
Oxford, 51, 206

P

Panel, 161, 162
paradigm, xix, xx, 24, 25, 26, 27, 28, 29, 32, 33, 37, 38, 41, 43, 53, 59, 104, 151, 187, 188, 189, 203
Paradigms, x
patriotism, 60
peace, 35, 58, 71, 97, 107, 123, 125, 139, 168
Pearce, 26, 29, 208
pen robbers, 55, 72
Peoples Democratic Party, 166
performance management, xv, 101, 144, 188
Performance Management, 135
personal odyssey, vi, xi, xviii, 52, 192
Peter, John and James, 31
philosophy, xiv, xvii, xxi, 25, 27, 28, 29,

42, 50, 55, 58, 59, 89, 103, 118, 125, 169, 174, 183, 188, 202

Physical Planning and Works, 157, 158

Pioneer, 62, 212

pioneering, 52, 96, 97, 137, 150, 151, 152, 186, 192

policing system, 113

politicians, 72, 107, 108

polygamous, 75

possibility, xix, 85, 103, 107, 192

potentials, 31, 65, 67, 68, 72, 94, 116, 117, 118, 126, 167

President, 46, 47, 72, 73, 74, 82, 89, 106, 121, 130, 133, 159, 186

Presidential Villa, 72

Principal of the College, 46

Principal Officers, 92, 133, 134, 149, 169

principles, xiii, xiv, xv, xvi, 42, 61, 85, 87, 88, 89, 90, 91, 93, 95, 96, 97, 98, 99, 100, 135, 138, 146, 153, 154, 161, 162, 164, 183, 187, 191, 196, 202, 204

prisonisation, 113

problem-solving, 75, 110

Professionalism, 199

Professor, iv, vi, 51, 62, 63, 65, 73, 74, 75, 76, 81, 101, 136, 161, 162, 186, 193

Professor Peter Okebukola, 51, 101

Proprietor, 89, 90

prosperity, 62, 64, 107

provincialism, 103, 108

Q

Qua Ibo Church, 46

Quinn, 204, 208

R

radicalizing agenda, xi, 37

rapist, 55

recidivism, 113

redeem the time, 76

Registrar, 92, 141, 152, 158, 166, 167, 176, 180

Registry, 152, 153, 197

RESTORE, 63

revenue, 91, 93, 156

rightness, 29, 43

S

saints in Sodom, 55, 84, 103, 204

Salem University, iv, vi, xii, xiii, xiv, xv, xvi, xvii, xviii, xix, xx, xxi, 37, 43, 45, 48, 50, 51, 52, 53, 54, 55, 56, 58, 59, 60, 61, 62, 63, 64, 65, 66, 67, 69, 70, 72, 73, 74, 75, 80, 81, 82, 84, 85, 86, 87, 89, 90, 91, 93, 94, 95, 96, 97, 98, 99, 100, 106, 109, 111, 114, 117, 121, 124, 125, 126, 129, 130, 131, 132, 133, 135, 139, 144, 145, 146, 148, 152, 153, 156, 160, 161, 163, 166, 169, 171, 172, 173, 174, 175, 177, 178, 179, 180, 181, 182, 183, 184, 186, 187, 188, 189, 190, 191, 192, 194, 198, 202, 203

Samson Amaga, 48

sanctification, 29

sands, xvii, 52, 171

Sashkin and Sashkin, xix

savvy, 69, 103, 107

scarcity, 103, 106, 107, 114, 156

scary, vii, viii, ix

Scriptures, 78, 116, 128

searching for its soul, 74

Secretary General, 72, 134

security, 41, 62, 64, 76, 122, 123, 151, 152, 167, 169, 170

selfishness, 103, 106, 107, 156

Self-Reliance, 59

Senators, 114, 115

Senge, viii

Sense of Priority, 50, 63, 86

Shashkin and Shaskin, viii, xiii

shepherd, 42, 109, 110, 187

significance, xviii, 97, 103, 106, 110, 144

Simon Jacobsen, 39

simpleton, 103, 107

skillfulness, 109, 110, 187, 189, 202

Skillfulness, 199

Sodom and Gomorrah, 55

Software, xiv

softwaring, 84, 100, 147, 183, 186

Soria, 37

South-South, 114

spiritual, 57, 61, 71, 85, 151, 178, 180, 183

St Peter's College, 46, 47

Stakeholders Management, 163

Stallard, 33, 34, 209

Student Affairs, 154

Student Leaders Forum, iv, 72, 111, 154

Students Industrial Work Experience Scheme, 126

Synergy, 50, 63, 87

T

Tarrant, 29, 209

Task, 60

temperance, iii, xi, 29, 31, 203

Thayer, viii, ix, 209

The Prince, 84

The Reconcilers Ministry, 46

thieves, 55

Thomas Jefferson, 33, 161, 187

Time as resource, 131

timeliness, xv, 132, 133, 134, 143, 175

Timeliness, 70, 132, 134

Total Leadership Training Concept, 69, 71, 77, 146, 179

transactional, xix, 27, 32, 96, 188, 202, 206

transcendence, iii, xi, 29, 203

transfiguration, 31, 37

transfigurational, 31, 34, 40, 42, 185, 203, 212

transformational, xix, 28, 31, 33, 51, 62, 63, 64, 71, 72, 80, 96, 104, 111, 124, 185, 189, 203, 206, 212

Transformational Academic Revolution, 50, 57, 60

trophies, xvii, xviii, 169, 171, 172, 173, 175, 177, 183, 185, 186, 187, 202, 212

trumpet, xiii, 54

trustworthiness, 78, 86

U

ubiquitous force, x

UK, 47

United Evangelical Church, 46

United Nations Commission on Crime and Justice, 82

United States of America, 107

University Law, 148, 149, 156

University Management, 55, 161, 168

University of Calabar, 161, 162

University of Ilorin, 101

University System Study and Review, 51

Upper Area Court, 174

US, 47, 82, 130, 161, 197

Usman, 26, 209

V

value-based results, 140

values, xi, xiii, xiv, xv, xvi, xvii, 30, 32,

47, 50, 60, 61, 63, 65, 66, 71, 79, 80,
84, 85, 86, 87, 88, 89, 90, 96, 97,
100, 109, 141, 143, 146, 148, 153,
155, 161, 162, 164, 169, 175, 177,
178, 180, 183, 189, 190, 191, 196,
199, 200, 202

verification specification, xvii, 147, 169

Vice Chancellery, 150, 197

Vice Chancellor, vi, xii, xviii, 43, 45, 46,
48, 49, 50, 51, 52, 54, 60, 61, 62, 63,
65, 69, 94, 97, 98, 114, 133, 135,
150, 153, 158, 166, 167, 170, 178,
180, 192, 193, 194, 195, 196, 198,
201, 212

Victimology, 48

Vienna, 72

virtuous, v, xi, xviii, xix, xx, xxi, 23, 24,
25, 28, 29, 31, 33, 34, 37, 38, 39, 40,
41, 42, 43, 53, 185, 189, 190, 191,
192, 196, 198, 199, 200, 201, 202,
203, 204, 206, 207, 212

Virtuous, i, ii, 28, 31, 40, 189, 201, 204,
206, 207, 208

virtuousness, xx, 29, 33, 36, 38, 39, 44,
200, 204

vision, xii, xiii, xiv, xv, xvi, xvii, 25, 28,
29, 34, 38, 43, 48, 50, 51, 52, 54, 55,
56, 57, 59, 60, 62, 64, 65, 66, 72, 74,
79, 80, 83, 86, 87, 89, 90, 96, 97,

100, 101, 104, 106, 109, 110, 125,
126, 127, 131, 132, 133, 134, 135,
137, 138, 144, 145, 146, 147,148,
150, 151, 152, 153, 155, 156, 160,
163, 164, 168, 169, 170, 172, 174,
177, 178, 179, 180, 181, 186, 188,
189, 190, 193, 194, 199, 202, 203,
204, 206, 207

vision ownership, xiv, xv, 100

visioner, 66

visionprints, xvii, 171, 173, 185

W

Washbush, x, 209

Weberian, 43

Whitney Jr, 104

wife, v, 40, 41, 49, 82, 126, 180, 182,
193, 194, 197

wisdom, iii, xi, xii, xvii, 29, 30, 31, 35,
38, 41, 52, 58, 59, 64, 84, 126, 187,
203

Y

yesteryears, 62

Z

Zenith Bank, 175

Author's profile

Paul Omojo Omaji is a Professor of Criminology and Vice Chancellor Emeritus. He trained in Sociology, Criminology, and Law in Nigeria and Australia. He has researched, published and lectured in these fields for about 30 years across Nigeria, Australia, Singapore, India, South Africa, the US, Canada, UK, and Sweden.

Professor Omaji has had over 40 years of community and professional leadership experiences. These include senior executive positions in the Australian Government public service where he provided policy advice at ministerial levels and led his teams to deliver successful implementation of government programmes in local communities and overseas countries, including the US, UK, Sweden, Denmark, Austria, the Czech Republic, Italy, and France.

Professor Omaji has also served as an official at all levels in the university system, culminating in his appointment as a pioneer Vice Chancellor of a private University. He is currently the Chief Executive Officer of *Omaji Leadership Solutions* and the *Virtuous Leaders Development Network*.

www.ingramcontent.com/pod-product-compliance
Lightning Source LLC
Chambersburg PA
CBHW060014210326
41520CB00009B/878